THE OBSOLETE SELF

THE OBSOLETE SELF

PHILOSOPHICAL DIMENSIONS
OF AGING

Joseph L. Esposito

University of California Press
Berkeley · Los Angeles · London

University of California Press
Berkeley and Los Angeles, California

University of California Press, Ltd.
London, England

Library of Congress Cataloging-in-Publication Data
Esposito, Joseph L., 1941–
  The obsolete self.
  Bibliography: p.
  Includes index.
    1. Aging—Psychological aspects. 2. Aged—Psychology.
3. Self-perception. 4. Life cycle, Human. I. Title.
HQ1061.E84 1987   305.2'6   86–16104
ISBN 0–520–05695–7 (alk. paper)

Printed in the United States of America

1 2 3 4 5 6 7 8 9

Contents

Introduction

Although in ancient times to live a long life was almost to qualify as a philosopher, philosophy has not focused much on the subject of aging. Perhaps philosophers have accepted a prejudice that until recently has affected biology: that post-maturational life is a progressive *departure* from normalcy, so that as biology should study ideal or typical biological processes, philosophy should be concerned only with general, ageless conditions of mind and personality. Aging is thought to be a disintegration of human life, a slow devolution of the human form. Even Simone de Beauvoir, in her monumental study *The Coming of Age,* accepts aging as an ultimate biological phenomenon that individuals and civilizations to a greater or lesser degree repress. Yet it is perfectly appropriate for philosophy to question this acceptance.

When we define the phrase *aging person,* we recognize a number of philosophical assumptions, both about the nature of persons and about the relation between physical time and biological processes, as well as certain normative assumptions about the value of different experiences. To see that this is so, imagine a society with no concept of the temporal dimension of living. Such a society would see life, for example, as mechanistic and physical. Growth would be the accumulation of bodily material, maturation the end of that accumulation, and aging the breaking apart or drying up of the body. Such a society would not need a complex concept of growing old but simply one of wearing out or falling apart.

A philosophical treatment of aging must isolate and consider the various assumptions underlying our concept of aging. For example, do *persons* age? Do only their bodies age? What is the relation between the body and the mind of an aging person? But it must also raise other, broader, questions. Once we have a tolerably clear definition of aging, we must ask about its implications for the most desirable course of social life. Although philosophy has traditionally considered persons as moral agents in asking about the course of social life, it has neglected the possible implications when the moral agents are aging persons. Generally, an aging person is thought to be someone who has lived longer than a young person; the aging person, moreover, is thought to be entirely a person until the moment of death, at which point he or she ceases—from a human perspective at least—to exist. Such a view may help protect the social and moral rights of persons, but it also precludes an examination of the ways aging can affect personality and moral perspective.

Aging is a multidimensional concept, as much sociological as biological. Indeed, aging can be understood more clearly as psychosocial than as narrowly biological. Biological aging itself is as mysterious today as it was for Galen and Hippocrates in ancient times. Perhaps it is even fair to say that with the rise of systematic medical investigation we have lost the sense of wonder about the phenomenon of aging, taking for granted that humans age as inevitably as leaves fall or fruit ripens.

Psychological aging, too, is a mystery. That people, in a world with ample signs of aging, discover how growing old affects their very sense of identity and personal worth only after they have lived to maturity suggests that we remain in an embryonic form of mind until that discovery—timeless, ahistorical beings with little concrete sense of bodily alienation. Once we recognize that we are aging, a new identity crisis becomes possible: not the crisis of youthful development in which we ask What will I be like when I am grown up? but a crisis in which we wonder Will I still be myself when I have grown old?

Sociologically, aging is much less a mystery. Generally, it means the beginning of social extinction, the time when an individual becomes obsolete as an active member of bustling society. This résumé of the meaning of growing old is brutal, but unless we confront it squarely, we will not be in a position to consider ways to overcome social obsolescence. Modern societies require that individuals integrate many skills and decisions. It is probably safe to say that the influence of social dynamics on an individual life—the conditions of economic production, population changes, political trends and fads, the introduction of new technologies, and so forth—is already at least as great as the influence of particular individuals in a person's immediate surroundings. More people than ever before live almost exclusively in the public sphere during their waking hours. Growing old thus becomes an increasing psychological burden just when modern medicine is relieving the elderly of some of the physical afflictions of age.

Those in the mainstream of social life too often regard the elderly of all classes and means as ancillary members of the societal family. Rendered obsolete by their very dedication to stable careers, they are like soldiers who return from battle worn in body and mind but are not allowed to take time off for rest and recreation until they are asked to retire to the rear ranks. The sociological analysis of aging questions a number of tenets that are at the heart of modern mores. Because aging prepares an individual for death in a biologically systematic way, it also has systematic ramifications for the way society categorizes, utilizes, and values individuals. Individuals, because they age, acquire a predictable use value that would be impossible to assess if death were purely accidental and aging did not exist.

Artists and writers have often attempted to convey what it is like to find oneself among the aged. Until now their message has been nearly unanimous: aging is symbolically a catastrophic event, no matter how gradually it occurs. It appears almost suddenly in a glimpse in a mirror, in the transformation of a lifelong friend's face, in the reactions of the young to one's very presence. From an etiologic point of view, its emergence is like that of cancer—a small, silent, secretive violation of bodily integrity that eventually consumes and wastes the entire organism, dragging down and crushing the spirit. Twenty-six centuries ago, the Greek lyric poet Mimnermus of Colophon asked:

> What, then, if life, if love the golden is gone? What is
>   pleasure?
>   Better to die when the thought of these is lost from my
>   heart.
> The flattery of surrender, the secret embrace in the
>   darkness.
>   These alone are such charming flowers of youth as befall
> Women and men. But once old age with its sorrows
>   advances
>   Upon us, it makes a man feeble and ugly alike,
> Heart worn thin with the hovering expectation of evil,
>   Lost all joy that comes out of the sight of the sun.[1]

Old is ugly; young is beautiful—so it is commonly thought. But even worse, the old know what they are missing, and the attractiveness of youth is enhanced because young people do not know how fortunate they are. The Mimnermuses of today live in shabby apartments in southern California and watch from their benches on the boardwalk as the latest generation plays in the "sight of the sun." They too may feel the embarrassment of the ancient poet.

The poets, however, convey not only lost pleasure but also something worse—physical degradation. Here is Michelangelo's frightening image:

> My long-drawn-out labours have broken, undermined and dismembered me, and the inn to which I am travelling, the inn at whose common table I shall eat and drink, is death. . . . I cage a buzzing wasp in a leathery bag full of bones and sinews. . . . My face is a scarecrow's. I am like those rags they hang out in times of drought and that frighten away birds. A spider runs about in one of my ears and in the other a cricket chirps all night. Weighed down by my catarrh I can neither sleep nor snore.

Echoing the poets, philosophers—Cicero, Seneca, Plautus, Bacon, Emerson, Camus, and Russell—have also given us

---

1. Quoted in *World Masterpieces*, 3d ed., vol. 1, ed. Maynard Mack (New York: W. W. Norton, 1973), p. 260.

their pessimistic advice about aging. It is nearly always the same: the cancer is growing, face the inevitable with courage, but be stoically prepared for complete humiliation when the time comes. This classic response has only recently been called into question. As long as each aging cohort embraces the pessimistic view of aging as decline, it prepares the next generation of aged—currently in middle age—to embrace similar views.

But it is not enough that the aged themselves acquire a new attitude about the dignity of agedness, as suggested by Simone de Beauvoir, Alex Comfort, and B. F. Skinner. A new attitude about aging must pervade social values as well. Younger cohorts must build a philosophy of aging while they are still young. To do this they must be able to reflect on the important questions of social life: where does its deepest value lie, and to what extent can individual purpose harmonize with it? True dignity for the aged cannot be based only on stoic isolation but must also rest on the view that all the phases of human life have value and integrity. To achieve such a pervasive dignity of life we must change not only aging persons' attitudes about themselves and the prevailing cultural values but also the very mechanics of social life—the rhythms of work and play; of love, sex, and friendship; and of wealth and poverty in all the stages of the life cycle. Toward this end, this book makes a small beginning.

The overriding theme of the chapters that follow is that aging presents a multifaceted series of challenges—biologically to our sense of organic familiarity, psychologically to our sense of personal integrity, and sociologically to our sense of social worth and justice. These challenges are made all the more difficult by the biological mystery of aging, despite our considerable confidence that someday it will itself be rendered obsolete as a human affliction. Today not only are the old made to feel out-of-date, as they have been traditionally, but they must also fear that they can never enjoy the possible benefits of a future world without aging.

This work examines the philosophical components of our various conceptions of aging. Aging should no longer be regarded as merely a phenomenon of nature but should be seen in relation to our distinctly human worldview, as a component that changes or ought to change as other components in that worldview change. Amazingly, medical science, which until recently regarded aging as an uninteresting disintegration of the once marvelous constellation we call the human body, has just begun to wonder about and to study aging.

Not only is the simpleminded notion of biological aging becoming less useful on a scientific level, but also the notions of the aged as psychologically unfocused or socially unproductive are becoming obsolete on the experiential level. This work seeks to uncover the assumptions behind the traditional belief that psychosocial aging is a process of progressive obsolescence.

Traditionally, the structuring of social activities by age and the stereotyping of social roles by age have helped to establish the system of beliefs and values of industrial and postindustrial society. But as habits of thought they are themselves implicated in the justification and rationalization of dominant socioeconomic realities. We must isolate and observe these beliefs and values and hypothesize alternative realities.

The first three chapters will investigate the prevalent assumptions about biological, psychological, and sociological aging. The remainder of the work will challenge and test these assumptions and will suggest alternative approaches for developing individual conceptions of aging and for planning the future role and importance of the elderly in society.

I first became fascinated with aging as a problem in metaphysics and the philosophy of science. But as someone in his middle forties I also began to realize that the pattern of life I had implicitly accepted from our culture was at variance with my own experience as well as with the experiences of many in my generation. We take for granted that Joan Baez and Mick Jagger should be doing now what they were doing more than twenty years ago. But I suspect that other generations have not held such a belief about what is and is not appropriate conduct for their members. And so my interest in the issues of metaphysics expanded to include issues of social identity and obsolescence.

Even if by Roman standards I should now be taking my place among the elders, I stand only in the middle age of life, perhaps for that reason still able to juxtapose the experience of true vigor against a real premonition of future decline. Perhaps this book could be written only out of the hope and maturity of middle age. But I hope not. I want to be continually proved wrong about the experience of aging, as I have been already. I hope that late in life I will be able to confirm the truth of Bernard Baruch's comment on his eighty-fifth birthday that "to me, old age is always fifteen years older than I am."

1

The Aging Body

Aging is generally considered to be a biological process. All that is born must die, and aging is thought to be one of the ways the body prepares for death. Aging has a special status among human characteristics; unlike some biological processes—procreation, for example—that are a matter of choice, aging is beyond our control. It happens against our will. But what precisely is it that ages? The entire body? Only parts of it? The entire person? These questions may be approached from a variety of perspectives. To begin, this chapter will consider aging from a biological point of view, one that focuses on organic change.

THE CONCEPT OF AGING

Is aging a process in its own right or the absence of process? Our answer to this question depends on the assumptions we make. If we believe that we pursue scientific study without making assumptions, then we might reply that the answer depends on our first understanding what aging is. If we assume that aging is a biological process, we will look for specific biological aging mechanisms that account for it. If we think of aging as the absence of any specific process, we must decide whether that absence is of theoretical interest. For much of the history of biological research, aging was seen as merely a degenerative process, and as such of little scientific interest. The human being was thought to be a manufactured entity like a clay pot, and while the activity of the potter was interesting, how the pot disintegrated through use and abuse was not. Surely there were ways to extend the lifetime of the pot by careful handling just as many a wise prescription could be directed toward good health. But the ancient practice of medicine was nonetheless focused more on the urgency of curing the ill than on resisting the aging process itself.

In the nineteenth century, when biological science began to be systematized, scientists thought that organisms were composed of gemmules, or life units, which were continually expended and disassociated from the organism, thereby producing aging and eventually death. In 1908, however, Charles S. Minot published his cytomorphic model of aging, which maintained that aging was an inherent structural requirement of biological organisms. "Natural death is the consequence of cellular differentiation," he argued.[1] In his view, the rate of cell turnover affected the aging process. Each multicellular animal consisted of cells acting both individually and in harmony with one another. Thus it became possible to think of aging as a growing disharmony among interacting cells, each differentiating in a fixed, irreversible direction: "The body begins its development from a single cell, the number of cells rapidly increases, and they go on and on increasing through many years. Their whole succession we may appropriately call a cycle. Each of our bodies represents a cell cycle. When we die, the cycle of cells gives out."[2] Minot's model marked a departure from previous theories of aging to the extent that it took seriously the need to give a detailed and systematic explanation of aging. Because he assumed that aging involved a specific biological mechanism, Minot wanted a theory to explain both the onset of aging and its course of development. He held that this theory should be formulated in terms of cellular biology.

Aldred S. Warthin in 1929 took a different perspective:

We are defending the thesis that senescence is a normal involutionary process, and its underlying laws and phenomena are essentially identical with those of the minor involutions of

1. Charles S. Minot, *The Problem of Age, Growth, and Death* (New York: G. P. Putnam, 1908), p. 250.
2. Ibid., p. 229.

the growth period of the organism. The main differences between the minor and the major involutions are those of degree, purpose and the organ or tissue involved. The minor
involutions affect simple specialized structures that are more
or less temporary in function, and as soon as this temporary
function is fulfilled, are unnecessary to the general economy
of the organism and are disposed of without affecting the
more permanent vital functions. The major involution, senescence, affects all the vital organs and functions, not for any
purpose of further growth and evolution, but for the purpose
of getting rid of the organism, itself, as a whole. This can
mean but one thing: the individual human machine has fulfilled its function, and, now useless, stands in the way of the
progressive evolution of the species.[3]

Like Minot's theory, Warthin's was more a proposal for a
theory than a theory itself. Whereas Minot focused on the
need for a biologically meaningful account of cell and organismic cycles, Warthin looked for a similarly meaningful account of organ and organismic involution and purpose. Both
of these approaches illustrate some of the problems theoretical gerontologists face even today: Do we look to parts of
individual organisms or to species and phyla to explain aging? Should we seek an aging process that contains a programmed temporal dimension or one that simply takes time
to complete? We will attempt to sort out and examine these
and other questions in due course.

In current theoretical gerontology, aging is defined as the
normal, inherent, irreversible, and progressive deterioration
of biological function, terminating in death. Gerontologists
also believe that a number of different aging pathways lead
to the same result. Organisms are complex systems of subsystems, and how these systems can go wrong is related to
the number of ways they normally operate. The more things
a system can do, the more things can happen to it. This
accords with our uncritical commonsense apprehension of
how aging occurs. Yet although we think we understand

3. Aldred Scott Warthin, *Old Age: The Major Involution* (New York: Paul
B. Hoeker, 1929), pp. 76–77.

what aging is, the more we reflect on it, the more obscure the concept becomes. Perhaps realizing this, one gerontologist recently observed that "the biologist has no operational definition of aging. In point of fact, the central problem of the science of aging is: What is aging?"[4] In other words, we cannot be sure about the causes of aging until we have a fairly clear idea what we are trying to explain.

This situation is not unusual in science, where we sometimes cannot be sure we have been studying a genuine problem until it has been solved or nearly solved. Lucretius theorized about "atoms" well before they could be recognized with modern instrumentation. The ancient atomists, it turned out, made a lucky guess—indeed, we really have no reason to use their word *atom* for what we describe today. We cannot really say, "There are Lucretius's atoms," for we adopted the word *atom* to mean simply the smallest particle of matter and have retained it as a convention of scientific communication even though more elementary particles have been discovered. Despite scientists' discoveries, the philosophical meaning of the term—the most elementary particle of matter—has remained the same. Terms such as *atom* are part of the metaphysics of science, whose function is to supply empirical science with ideal conceptual structures to guide the investigation of concrete problems. Without such nomenclature, we would not even know where to begin, let alone how to proceed in our research.

We are in much the same situation with the concept of aging. We are not sure what we seek to explain. We observe certain manifest things about biological organisms that the term *aging* is used to describe. For example, we know that organisms undergo exchanges with their surroundings; we find it inconceivable that a biological organism could function without being dependent on something else. Furthermore, we know that those exchanges seem to fall into patterns we designate as cycles, and these cycles themselves

4. I. W. Richardson, "The Metrical Structure of Aging (Dissipative) Systems," *Journal of Theoretical Biology* 85 (1980): 752.

seem to form larger patterns we call rhythms and life periods. We also know that those exchanges may be terminated at any moment. From this knowledge, we develop folklore about living and dying, using a metaphysics of passing away that we designate as *aging*.

We desire, however, a clearer understanding of the term. Aging is said to be "normal." What does "normal" mean? In wartime a beleaguered soldier may say: "In war it is only normal that men should die young." Perhaps he has been fighting too long to remember a time when men died normally of old age. But is aging itself normal? The ancients thought that aging was not part of the natural order, that it was normal for humans only because they lived in a contaminated world. Aging was an affliction of mortals, the result of sin or rebellion. In saying today that aging is normal, we are not consciously denying the ancient perspective. We mean that if life goes on normally, that is, as it always has, then all men and women who do not die accidentally or by sudden illness will die of old age. Thus aging pertains to a particular way of dying. "Dying of old age" means dying in a gradual, nonaccidental way. If we tie our idea of normalcy to a concept of the accidental in this way, we must go on to ask what an accident is.

An accident is a chance episode, always unexpected, that affects the "normal" state of some object. When a wagging tail knocks a vase off a table, an accident occurs. To be unexpected, accidents must occur suddenly, and their duration must be brief relative to the time scale of the entity that calls an event "accidental" by virtue of its short duration. Besides the scale of time, the scale of size also determines the limits of the accidental. In stormy weather we do not think an accident is happening to the earth, despite sudden and violent local events. But if a giant asteroid streaked toward the earth, we would think of the threatened collision as an accident. The magnitude of the event affects our response: the earth is too big to be significantly affected by storms but might well be destroyed by an asteroid. In human terms, aging might conceivably be accidental on the

microscopic level, while its effect is gradual and unpro-
nounced relative to the entire organism. Normal aging, in
other words, may be a prolonged, expected process that
occurs without the influence of some object of comparable
size on the object that is said to be aging.

Turning next to the notion of aging as inherent deterioration, let us imagine, as some have, that the organism
contains certain irreversible characteristics. The heart, say,
has only so many beats, metabolism only so much calorie-
consuming potential. Similarly, printers may think of their
presses as having only so many hours of usable life before
the rollers and gears wear out. Whether the press runs
nonstop or only several hours a day, it will age at the same
rate during its time of activity. Aging is inherent, at least in
this sense. According to traditional rate-of-living theories,
the less one eats (within limits, of course), the longer one
tends to live. Such theories posit that something within the
organism itself directly produces aging the way friction produces machine wear. We can clarify the notion of inherent
biological aging by speaking of an aging program in the
organism, a series of planned or regulated episodes that
occur in a normal environment.

Still we must ask how aging can occur in a so-called normal environment. After all, it is from the "normal" environment that organisms emerge in the first place. Although the
environment to this extent plays the role of a divinity, creating organisms and allowing them to flourish, in the same
environment one organism grows while another grows old.
Thus the environment is not a neutral background for organisms but appears to play a role in their aging. If organic
life consists of various exchanges between organism and environment, then the older organism has engaged in more of
these exchanges, which may account for its decline. In this
sense, aging is not "inherent."

If we thus posit that our own aging is not inherent, we
might wonder what kind of environment would produce life
only to fail to sustain it. With this question, we begin to
discover the anthropomorphic features in the notion of inher-

ent aging. The recognition of aging as decay may have served as an unrecognized rationale for the belief in a beneficent God. Growth and senescence represent a tug of opposites. The organism generated in another kingdom degenerates when out of its proper environment. But it discovers its degeneration too late and can save itself only through divine intercession. By contrast, if the organism arises from this world in all respects, one must account for evolution and involution, growth and decay, in a unitary conceptual framework. Either aging is inherent in each organism, in which case it is also inherent in the species, or it is inherent in the unavoidable interchange between organism and environment. If we say aging is inherent in the interchange, we do not say much more than that it does not result from a deus ex machina; if aging is inherent in each organism or species, then the environment is at best neutral with respect to aging, and the individual and particular species somehow cause their own aging. It is probably this latter alternative that is usually meant by those who speak of aging as inherent. In either case, however, we are enlightened very little by saying that aging is an inherent biological process in this world.

Aging, as defined above, is also said to be irreversible. Aging systems are often described as dissipative, systems that give up something they require but can never get back. Either the organism loses its ability to retrieve what it has given up or it retains that ability but is thwarted by competitors in its environment. But we must distinguish something possessed only once and lost from something that, having been lost, has also been regained on one or more occasions. This latter possibility raises a problem for our notion of aging as an irreversible process. Because growth is a process of acquiring new structures and abilities, an organism originally acquired any structures and abilities it has now as well as any it has lost. Organisms are not instantaneously created, as was Adam, in mature adult form. Whatever is constructed can be destructed, and whatever is destructed can be reconstructed. If this reconstruction is not possible in organisms that age, certain necessary and sufficient conditions must determine why. It begs the question to say that only young organisms are constructable and only old ones are no longer reconstructable. All organisms are made of indestructible material that is continually undergoing turnover. The young heal faster but the old also heal. How, then, do we begin to demarcate a process that is truly irreversible from one that is not?

We have not been able to answer this question to any satisfactory degree even in the field of physics (thermodynamics), where the variables are fewer. From a mechanistic point of view, all processes are reversible and the second law of thermodynamics is regarded as a "second rate" law of physics. In the mechanistic view there are no irreversible processes because any given configuration of even a gas may be repeatable over a sufficiently long period of time. Such a guarantee of reversibility is theoretical and abstract, based only on the assumption that gaseous constituents randomly, spontaneously interact. In the case of biological organisms, we have a practical guarantee that generation can take place because otherwise we would not have had an organism in the first place. That guarantee places an even greater burden on those who claim that there must be some irreversible situations in organic life, the eventual result of which is aging and death.

When we say that an automobile ages, we mean that through use many of its parts wear out. However, automobiles do not exist in, and have not evolved out of, a universe of their own. They are made by people and need constant attention to operate properly. So when we speak of an automobile aging, we assume something about the conduct of the persons who use it. We appeal to the laws of physics to explain the wear and tear of the motor and chassis and to psychology and economics to explain why at the end of, say, a year, the car is no longer as good as new. Psychologically its novelty has worn off, and economically its value has depreciated more than the owner could recover by replacing each part when the first signs of wear appear in it. Furthermore, people's assessment of the worth of commodities such as automobiles depends on social conventions that are themselves articulated out of the deeply entrenched beliefs of a culture. In the case of aging organisms, however, we cannot distinguish the reversible from the irreversible on purely theoretical grounds. All we can do is formulate heuristic principles to guide research. The maxim here suggested is that, in the absence of specific impediments, whatever is constructed will be reconstructed. It is possible to choose a simpler maxim to guide experimentation: for example, whatever is constructed will eventually destruct. However, in choosing the former we place on the agenda of scientific research the problem of explaining why organisms that age also possess remarkable regenerative capacities. Such a choice is likely to produce more fruitful hypotheses and to advance science further along the road of inquiry than would choice of the alternative maxim.

Closely connected with the notion that aging is irreversible is the notion that it is progressive. Every day we are one day older. But does everybody age just one day each day? We often speak of the accelerated aging of presidents and the pathological aging of children suffering from progeria, our judgment in each case based on a distinction between chronological age and biological age. Everybody ages one day per day, but aging can happen at a faster or slower rate than that of mechanical time. By what standard of time should we measure progressiveness? The laws of mechanics do not vary with the direction of time, and if time in the mechanical world were reversed, everything would just go backward. If some biological processes are irreversible, however, then the old cannot become younger no matter what we say about time. The passive aspect of progression is that regression is not possible. There is no going home again for individual organisms. But an active aspect is also needed, something to push the organism further away from home. In nature such a push requires, it should be observed, an improbable metaphysical condition in which an ordered process not reducible to individual aspects of organic life governs biological organisms. If an organism ages in a progressive fashion, some mechanism is forcing aging to occur much as gravity forces falling bodies to continue falling at an ever greater rate of speed.

But perhaps progressive aging means not that we age ever more rapidly, but that aging is proliferative: first two wrinkles appear, then four more, then eight more, then sixteen more, and so forth. In this case we do not know whether aging is truly progressive until we know it is irreversible, and if it is, we still need to know by what standard of time to measure its progress. When we compare chronological and biological age, we can observe that no biological aging takes place during early development, limited aging takes place during maturation, and finally the rate of biological aging increases steadily as the organism approaches death. To say that biological aging is progressive after maturation is to say that more aging occurs after a certain time has elapsed than occurred before this period. Perhaps during moments or even days in the life of a sixty-year-old person no aging takes place. But those who argue for a progressive notion of aging maintain that by some measure of time sufficiently small relative to a lifetime, aging must continually and increasingly take place. Such an argument shows clearly that progressiveness rests not only on the assumption of irreversibility but also on a hidden assumption of "forced" and directed aging. Otherwise it would merely beg the question at hand. After all, there must be *some* unit of time during which no aging takes place. The existence of such a unit could be established by ascertaining the fastest physical or chemical reaction that occurs in the body; any reaction slower than that would be one in which no aging occurred. Moreover, any interval in which aging is thought to occur must be one in which aging is also thought to be unavoidable. But even if we make that interval as large as we please, we still cannot be certain why aging must take place within it. Thus, to say aging is progressive is to say very little beyond what we all can observe unless we also establish a specific mechanism of irreversibility and of inevitability.

The notions of irreversibility, progressiveness, chronological age, and biological age sharply come to the fore in
the famous paradox of the twins in special relativity theory.
According to this theory, if one twin travels near the speed
of light (approximately 300,000,000 meters per second) on a
journey to a distant planet and returns to earth, he will be
much younger than his earthbound sibling because time
slows down during travel at very high speeds. But surely
one would have to be confused to think that time per se can
affect aging or any physical process whatsoever. Time is a
measure of process, an ordering of ordering. To measure it
requires something close to what we normally mean by
mind. Time is more than mere regularity. Regularity could
exist in a universe with no intelligence; but would there be
time, the marking of sequential regularity?

According to special relativity theory, each twin looking
at his watch measures the sweep of the second hand from
zero to one as taking one second. But if the earthly twin
measured his brother's watch against his own, he would
find that his brother's moved just one second while his own
moved five. (The figures are based on the assumption that
the rocket ship traveled at about 98 percent of the speed of
light.) Nothing seems unusual to either twin. Each thinks
that he is chronologically aging at a rate of one second per
second, and each thinks that he is biologically aging at a rate
of one second per second. But when the twins meet again,
they discover that the astronaut is much younger, perhaps
half his brother's age. For example, if the rocket traveled at
80 percent of the speed of light for eight light-years, the
returning astronaut would be eight years younger than his
brother. Each would perceive the length of the trip differently. The earthbound brother would think it had lasted
twenty years whereas the astronaut would think it had
lasted just twelve years. One brother is "too old," the other
"too young."

The problem posed by the twin paradox is in part how to
characterize the brothers once they meet again. The trip that
results in their differing psychological perceptions of its du-

ration has also changed their physical characteristics. It is easy to understand how we can perceive motion subjectively or relativistically. At the beginning of a journey, we may notice that we are not sure whether we are moving forward in a train or the station is moving backward. But it is much harder to think how our perception of aging can be subjective in the same sense because there is in aging no gestalt switch from young to old and back again. The astronaut in fact remains young and perhaps lives for many years after his brother has died of old age. No psychological reorientation would appear to be able to alter that fact.

Let us imagine that the astronaut is a trained experimental physiologist. When he measures enzymatic reactions, energy transport, and the lifetime of free radicals, will his results conform to the data gathered on earth? If they do, can the physical change be permanent? If they do not, what is affecting the space-borne experiments? Being a well-trained astronaut, versed in special relativity theory as well as in physiology, he soon recognizes that his clock measures temporal intervals according to the time dilation specified in special relativity theory; he also recognizes that his rate of aging is half that of his brother's. To return to earth the same age as his brother, he decides to speed up his bodily processes by subjecting them to catalytic agents that operate very rapidly on earth and fast enough during space travel (about twice as fast) to compensate for the slowdown of bodily function. If we accept this process as physiologically possible, we can see that the twin paradox relies on a rate-of-living theory of aging: if we can slow down bodily functions, aging will take place more slowly. The paradox also helps us distinguish chronological and biological aging, for the astronaut who speeds up his bodily processes will think that he has aged much too much during the time of the trip, whereas his brother will think that he has aged just the right amount (though being versed in special relativity himself, he recognizes the sacrifice his brother has made for him).

The twin paradox suggests that aging is determined by the rate of systematic activity, a rate that depends on the number of interacting parts and the rate at which they interact. A system with ten parts that enters into a reaction every half second has twenty reactions per second. Another system with only five parts requires a faster rate of reaction to have the same number of reactions per second. If in space travel approaching the speed of light age retardation takes place, it must be because the reactions of the body slow down. If they slow down to a state of latent death, no aging would take place at all. In space travel, matter appears to become heavier; reactions slow down, but not to the point of organic dissolution. The fewer reactions per second, the less opportunity for variations to occur, and vice versa. If, for example, a human body engages in one thousand individual reactions per second in a normal state, including those reactions that monitor and correct normal deviations, and if those reactions are suddenly increased to, say one thousand one hundred, then in the one hundred unmonitored reactions there would be opportunity for systemic damage. But how could the organism be made to speed up or slow down its activity when its mechanism is so carefully designed to maintain homeostasis within normal limits? And why would it allow abnormal reactions to occur? In the case of space flight it would have no choice; everything slows down. On earth, in its natural ecological niche, it presumably does have a choice. The environment remains normal, yet its systematic reactions somehow become abnormal.

If the twin paradox suggests a connection between systemic reactivity and biological aging, it does not tell us anything about the precise nature of that connection. We still do not know why aging must be a deleterious process. If the twins aged only chronologically, then retardation would take place, but aging would not. Such an organism would behave like a thermodynamic gas that becomes more disorganized as its temperature rises and that settles down into crystalline order as its temperature approaches absolute zero. This is the image of the body that Bernard L. Strehler suggested:

> The central assumption of our theory [of aging] is that fluc-
> tuations in demand for energy expenditure are due princi-
> pally to more or less random fluctuations in the internal and
> external environment of the organism. These stresses are
> moreover assumed to be distributed exponentially as is a
> Maxwell-Boltzmann distribution of kinetic energy among gas
> molecules. Thus, the frequency of stresses of a certain mag-
> nitude increases exponentially as the rate of energy expendi-
> ture required to offset them decreases linearly.[5]

As long as we postulate deleteriousness, this hypothesis
presents no difficulty. But in a sense we beg the question at
hand—what are the causes of aging?—if we assume that
stress specifically affects aging. We know that trauma has a
deleterious affect on the body. Stab wounds, poisons, and
viruses all can lead to a systematic breakdown of biological
process and even death. Are there similar agents that cause
aging on a microscopic scale? And if so, in what sense can
we speak of microscopic disorder as aging?

We have considered inherence, irreversibility, and progressiveness as components of the concept of aging and
must now consider deterioration. Although ordinary language invariably associates aging with deterioration, we
must ask if such an assessment is merely subjective. When
we say that a work of art ages, we mean that an undesired
chemical process takes place, one that eventually destroys a
work we hope to possess for all time. And when we say that
cheese ages, we mean that a biochemical process takes place
to produce a tasty result. Both processes involve deterioration, a breakdown of organic form. Although the materials
of organisms—atomic and subatomic particles—are themselves ageless, their combination and recombination takes
place over time. Everything in the body takes place in sequence, as organic constituents fit together like pieces of a
puzzle. With deterioration, the pieces fail to fit.

Contemporary scientists describe the body as a hierarchy

5. Bernard L. Strehler, *Time, Cells, and Aging* (New York: Academic
Press, 1962), p. 104.

of feedback loops beginning in the intracellular biochemical world and progressing from the cellular metabolism to organ and then to organism. Accordingly, one does not speak of a liver or lung dying but only an entire organism. Even amoebas die. In Aristotle's time biologists spoke of that "for the sake of which" bodily activities occurred. In ordinary language we say that the heart pumps blood so that we can continue living. When aging takes place, then, at what *level* do we speak of deterioration? We might answer that it happens at the cellular level, for surely the cell, if no longer the unit of life, is at least still the unit of aging. But this reply, in which an aging subsystem represents the deterioration of an entire organism, fails to account for the vast majority of cells that function well enough to maintain life even in an organism of advanced age. This is to say not that an aged organism can be neatly divided into healthy and diseased components but rather that as long as life continues, much more is right with the organism than is wrong if one looks far enough down the microscopic ladder.

Yet if organisms die when so much is still right with them, there must be a threshold below which life cannot be sustained. When trauma occurs, this threshold is easy to describe. Because organic life, for example, requires a certain level of blood pressure, massive bleeding that is not stopped causes death. But when death occurs as a result of incremental changes—the progressive, relatively gradual process of aging—the cause, less easily described, must lie in the small changes that lead to bigger organic changes. An automobile runs well as long as it has some gas in its tank. When the tank is empty, however, the car stops because its engine cannot burn air. The construction of the car determines once and for all how it operates and how it responds to limiting conditions. Organisms are like automobiles that know both when their tanks are running low and how to go about filling them. Unlike machines, they do not just suddenly stop.

Deteriorative aging, in other words, is a systemic process. But how comprehensive is the deterioration? Am I getting old because the organs, skin, and bones that make up my body are getting old? The answer is not as obvious as it seems. Let us imagine a world where no aging takes place, where people, in other words, die only as a result of accident or violence, yet a world where the only external sign of deterioration would be the weathering of the skin. In that world an inhabitant whose skin got wrinkled enough would go for medical treatment to have it smoothed out again. Now let us imagine a world where all the outward signs of aging are possible but where aging does not take place because its outward signs can be erased. In both cases the model for explaining what is going on is a disease model, not an aging model—one that raises a question of dysfunction, not of deterioration.

How does this deterioration in the imaginary world differ from our own situation? The difference cannot be that in the imaginary world doctors say some particular agent has caused the diseased organs whereas in our own world doctors just say the cause is aging or being too old. Our doctors know that specific agents affect the condition of each component of the body, no matter how small or large. Nonetheless, they lapse into other language, saying that someone died of old age because they are really powerless to repair the damage that has been done. Our attitude toward aging is like that of the doctors. Because of its inevitable outcome, we define aging as a deteriorative process. We say we are aging, in other words, because we believe that our organs, skin, and bones will become diseased in a manner that modern medicine cannot reverse. In short, to say that aging involves deterioration is both to espouse a brand of fatalism and to perceive aging as happening to us. *We* deteriorate. Our organs just get diseased along the way.

I suggest, then, that the unit of aging is the organism— not any organism, but only the conscious organism capable of thinking fatalistically. My dog ages because I interpret her deterioration as irreversible; she may simply not feel like her old self. But is aging ultimately a mere state of mind? Do we reduce an empirical phenomenon to a mental one, as philosophers have often done in the past? In saying that the concept of aging relies on value judgments about the process taking place—it is like the aging of works of art, but worse because aging organisms cannot be restored—I am not suggesting that it is merely subjective. We could not wish away aging by rejecting fatalism. I am suggesting, however, both that the empirical conditions from which our concept of aging derives in part are modifiable in principle and that the ideas on which this concept rests may change, modifying our view of aging.

The empirical conditions may change once and for all if, for example, medical research finds the fountain of youth. Now aging is inevitable, and fatalism is the natural attitude toward it. Perhaps soon aging may victimize only those who cannot afford the cure for it. Our concept of aging itself may change if we change our concept of what ages. If it is *I* who ages and if aging is inevitable, then to age means to be someone who is on the road to death. Thus the concept of aging relates to the concept of death. In this respect, it is puzzling why believers in an immortal soul should continue to find bodily deterioration so tragic. If they accept the prospect of a disembodied immortality, then aging, though inevitable, is more like the shedding of a diseased skin than the deterioration of a self. We may have too much egotism and pride, too great a visceral sense of accomplishment in just being an organism that sees the light of day and experiences earthly life, to believe that immortality can overcome the disappointments following the recognition of aging. It is doubtful, in any case, that the religious imagination has had much effect on the concept of aging. People regret getting old no matter what the glories of heaven are supposed to be.

Even though what ages is a question open to psychohistorical analysis, it cannot be separated entirely from our notions of bodily aging. The biologists must decide what ages, just as they must decide what evolves. I suggest that to speak of aging is to speak of wholes that age, not parts. But it still remains to describe those wholes and to decide whether their reality is essential or merely conventional.

From a biological point of view, it is fruitless to say that I age unless the "I" is given some biological specification. Here, however, difficulties rapidly mount, for we need an account of organic life sufficiently complex to allow for the mechanism of progressive decay and sufficiently simple to account for the unity of self-awareness we designate as that "for the sake of which" we live. Because aging is connected with death and death is the cessation of the organism, to the extent that we identify the self and the organism—at least commonsensically—we conceive of aging as having to do with the "goals" or "functions" of the entire organism. Aging is not just a feature of an organism but a process whereby the entire organism systematically ceases to be. It is a holistic phenomenon both because it affects the entire organism and because the entire organism is said to age.

Although theoretical gerontology must ultimately develop a clear idea of the ontology of its subject, in the meantime the field faces less difficult obstacles, including methodological confusions of the sort long since eradicated from most other sciences.

SOME PERSISTENT METHODOLOGICAL DIFFICULTIES

People who live to a ripe old age are often asked their secret of longevity. Very few withhold that secret, yet its revelation seems not to affect the longevity of those who learn it. Indeed, if there really is such a secret, it has not been divulged; otherwise it would have been incorporated into human practices. In fact we do not understand fully the relation between life expectancy and individual ways of life. Does our physiological inheritance determine the way we live, or does the way we live determine the subsequent development of that inheritance? Because the customs and habits of our lives develop over decades, one can easily see that an incomplete picture of aging would result if only people over the age of, say, eighty were the subjects of aging research.

We can obtain a more complete picture of aging by studying a cohort of people from birth to death, keeping extensive records along the way (for some of the researchers are also sure to die). But even such longitudinal studies as are currently underway face a number of difficulties. We cannot be sure that the language we ask the subjects to use describes their lives precisely enough to be relevant to the study of aging. For example, although we feel confident saying that heavy smoking contributes to lung cancer or even causes it, we also know that smoking is a localized phenomenon in which particular organs have direct contact with a carcinogen. If an old person has cancer, we are not sure whether specific mutagens caused the local indications of degeneration—which might not have occurred without them—or whether the degeneration was caused by aging itself.

Further complicating the search for causes is the immense variability of each person's genetic material relative to that of any other person. The number of genetic constituents in the individuals we must study is formidable. Is our conceptual net fine enough to catch these minute fish? Even more formidable, however, is the prospect of tracing all the ways these constituents combine throughout a lifetime. Currently this knowledge is far beyond us. As theorists of aging we are like nineteenth-century chemists before the development of atomic theory: we are not sure what our subject includes and excludes.

Because of these difficulties, theoretical gerontologists often link their accounts of biosenescence with pseudoexplanations and empty descriptions. For example, nearly all clinical discussions of aging attribute patients' conditions to the effects of aging. Sometimes aging is presented as a *result*, a process that occurs because of the passage of time. At other times, it is presented as a *cause* that alters normal physiology and function. Furthermore, aging is sometimes attributed to an aging component of the body: those organisms with such a component must age. This bootstrap ascent to an explanation is familiar enough in science. It is natural to think of material things being composed of smaller material things, elastic gases of elastic molecules. Science profits from this circularity as long as some scientists can approach the circular system from yet another point of view, using some part of it in a way that sheds new light on other parts. In this way, scientists approached the modern theory of the atom in light of electromagnetic theory and quantum theory, changing the way we view the macroscopic objects of common sense. The situation in theoretical gerontology is complicated by the vagueness of the central concept, aging, which denies the field the data of contemporary biological knowledge. Do wrinkles cause aging? Or does aging cause wrinkles? Even elementary propositions are open to doubt. What seems certain, however, is that each species has a characteristic maximum lifespan. Even if we cannot distinguish clearly between pathology and aging, organisms of each species must have *some* features that affect their lifespan and relate to the normal signs we associate with aging.

THEORIES OF AGING

Some theories of aging attempt to isolate specific causal agents at the beginning of each aging pathway. Some attribute aging to systematic interactions or the failure to achieve systematicity. Still others explain aging in terms of the dynamics of the evolutionary process. We shall now survey these theories.

CAUSAL THEORIES

Causal theories rely on a mechanistic view of the body and its parts. Mutation theories, for example, explain aging as the result of chemical mutagens and ionizing radiation that bombard the living organism. The successors of liver cells exposed to radiation are likely to show a higher incidence of abnormal chromosomes than the parent cells. So, it is argued, the body is exposed to a cumulative dose of ultraviolet radiation from the sun that corresponds to the proliferative effects of aging. Some mutation theories (somatic theories) contend that mutation occurs quantitatively throughout the cells of the organism; other theories (genetic theories) emphasize the qualitative deteriorative effect of an "aging hit" on the genetic material of the cell. Radiation experiments, however, do not always support the quantitative view of aging. If radiation dosage correlated well with the degree of aging, we could predict the dose needed to double the normal rate of aging for an organism; in experiments with fruit flies, however, some flies exposed to high levels of radiation actually lived longer than normal. Another problem of somatic theories is that many short-lived species resist the mutational effects of radiation better than many long-lived species.

Somatic mutation theorists admit that aging hits alone do not account for the onset of senescence. The body is a complex system of connected parts—perhaps like the waterworks of a city—so that a poison introduced at any point in the system spreads throughout it by the system's own natural flow of energy. The theorists imagine this process as initially mechanical (hence "aging *hit*") and then biological (hence "*aging* hit"). They see somatic mutation as analogous to a biochemical assault on the body. The aging hits bombard the organism, starting a war. Eventually the continued action of many mutagens has a macroscopic effect, impairing whole subsystems of the body. This metaphor has quasi-theological implications: the organism born in an innocent state is polluted by the worldly environment, which causes first its degeneration and then its death. But such a theological reading is difficult to justify if we remember that all organisms maintain their integrity of structure and function even as they undergo exchanges with their environment. Warfare is persistent, yet organisms survive and flourish, and the question of why organic degeneration takes place at all is not answered by somatic mutation theorists. Although it is easy to think of each organism as a solitary soul wandering around a battleground under cross fire—in only a matter of time a bullet will strike it dead—a more accurate picture of biological activity is that of a war game in which no one goes into battle without sufficient protection to repel mortal wounds. Those who are wounded heal and return to battle.

Ultimately, somatic mutation theorists must postulate a dysfunction between organism and environment. But they cannot explain why organisms that undergo aging are produced in the first place. To save the theory, a subsidiary hypothesis is required to account for the hostility of the environment. The conditions of an industrial polluting society render the subsidiary hypothesis plausible. Perhaps the environment that supported the human animal during eons of its evolution has changed during the past, say, five hundred thousand years, and aging is simply the result of this loss of harmony. Perhaps, as the ancient myths suggest, aging is of relatively recent origin and somatic mutation theorists are correct after all. This question requires at least investigation before somatic mutation theory can become plausible.

Genetic mutation theory, in contrast, postulates a mechanical destruction of the command and control network of the body—its genetic structure. Like a demented general, the genome issues inconsistent orders that its dutiful soldiers carry out. Because of the inconsistency of commands, the body eventually works against itself, using its highly complex and efficient mechanisms to multiply the effect of each aging hit. Accidental destruction of genetic information leads to the breakdown of DNA activity; to errors in the silent, nontranscribable regions of the gene; to the restructuring of amino acids; and to a modification of the proper sequence of DNA repair. Bombing the command center is always a top priority in warfare, but again, does the war metaphor suggest the right way to look at genetic mutation? How has the genome survived all these millions of years under battle conditions if it has not had some means of protecting itself? On an evolutionary scale the life of an individual is but the blink of an eye. Genetic mutation theory is plausible if we believe that the genome is no sooner formed than it is on the road to destruction. But this belief itself is plausible only if we accept another that lies outside the realm of mutation theory: that organic life is a vehicle for selfish genes, and organisms need only live long enough to pass on their genes to the next generation of progeny. The real biological individual is the gene; the organism is only its container. But now, of course, we are far beyond the limited scope of genetic mutation theory proper and into evolutionary theory as well.

Another causal theory based on the metaphors of common sense is the wear-and-tear theory, which proposes that the organism is like a machine that wears out. Aging begins not with aging hits but with aging "scrapes" and "rubs." The internal parts rub against each other and the metabolic process literally cooks the body the way a furnace cooks itself during its operation. During this cooking the fine details of morphology are lost. Follicles fall out, nerve cells lose their dendritic arbor, neurofibrillary tangles increase, morphological degeneration of striated skeletal and heart muscle cells occurs, the structural integrity of extracellular proteins such as collagen and elastin is lost as cross-linking occurs (thus producing rigid forms that hinder organic activity), and, most catastrophic of all, illicit cross-bonding of segments of genetic macromolecules randomly occurs, leading to mutation and a failure of replication.

The wear-and-tear theory proposes that certain physical conditions ultimately determine the onset of aging. If organisms like those produced by nature must be as complex as they are in order to survive, then they must have certain physical specifications. For example, they must be warm-blooded and have a certain minimal material structure at maturity. According to wear-and-tear theory, having these requirements subjects an organism to aging influences. The heavier a body is, the more weight its upper parts exert on its lower parts; the more complicated and calorie-intensive an air-breathing system is, the more it is subject to injury by its intense energy consumption; and so forth.

Attractive as it is, the wear-and-tear hypothesis has a fundamental difficulty. Aging is much like a machine wearing out; feeling "worn out" is in fact a common complaint of the elderly. But even as it appeals by metaphor to common sense, this hypothesis leaves unexplained the acceleration of aging in cases of progeria or the rapid senescence of spawning salmon. Nor does it explain the various manifestations of aging in different phyla: do certain coelenterates, platy-helminths, mollusks, annelids, and reptiles age or physically wear out? Wear-and-tear theory must be able to distinguish between gradual, progressive aging and reversible wear—like the calluses that go away after several work-free days. In the case of nematodes, rotifers, anthropoids, birds, and mammals, the signs of aging are definitely pronounced and are more like what we associate with the aging processes in humans. The wear-and-tear theory must explain why some wear is reversible and other wear is not, and if it is really a theory of aging, its explanations must be compatible with its basic mechanistic assumption. Thus it must explain irrever-sibility by the wearing out of repair mechanisms that would have corrected wear in normal circumstances, and it must explain why these failures seem to follow a predictable pat-tern for given species. In principle, this mechanistic program of explaining aging in terms of physical forces could be car-ried out. But how many hypotheses can we add to the soup before the meal becomes indigestible? As noted, organisms that age are invariably also organisms that have great repair capabilities; if wear-and-tear theory is to be plausible, we must explain why wear and tear is not continually repaired. We know that there is, for example, a collagen repair mech-anism in the postpartum uterus, but we must understand why similar mechanisms fail to operate elsewhere. Clearly, it is something of a circularity to say that repair fails because the repair mechanisms wear out. Hierarchical systems are not perfectly integrated systems, no matter how varied and complex their feedback loops may be. They must have end points and starting points that give rise to pathways, and if wear occurs at these points, then systematicity is damaged also. But this fact by itself does not justify the wear-and-tear explanation. Wear-and-tear theory also must explain aging as *organic* wear, not simply as mechanical breakdown.

Accumulation theories, the final group of causal theories to be considered, explain aging as the result of deleterious substances that collect in the body. These substances can be such by-products of cellular metabolism as lipofuscin, free radicals, the various histones, aldehydes, and quinones. In this case aging is thought to result from an imperfect filtration of these substances out of the body. In other cases, foreign substances enter and accumulate in the body—for example, minerals such as aluminum that are found in higher concentrations in the cells of the elderly. Often accumulation theories are not theories at all but descriptions of aging cells that focus on the difference between young and old cells. Even as they postulate an aging agent, they lack an aging mechanism, unlike wear-and-tear theories that hinge on a specific mechanism but offer no clear idea of the agency involved. Mutation theories, in contrast with both accumulation and wear-and-tear theories, identify both a causal agent and a mechanism of action, but because they enter at a higher level of organic structure, they must explain the failure of corrective activity as well as the placement of deleterious agents. We can appreciate at this point the dilemma of theoretical gerontology: if one specifies simple poisonous agents operating in a simple fashion, one must still account for the apparent systematic or timed dimension of aging; if one specifies complex agents and processes, one must also account for the failure of a complex organism to overcome them.

Systematic Theories

Some gerontologists have maintained that it is pointless to seek the ultimate cause of aging as if aging were a unidirectional process with a single causal agent. Aging is systematic, they argue, and the aging mechanism must be systematic as well. They suggest that aging is programmed genetically: aging occurs because aging genes turn on the aging process once maturation is achieved. This argument for genetic programming has a strong evolutionary component. After all, why would there be genes for aging in the gene pool of a species if those genes had not been selected by the process of evolution?

Gene-level program theories set out to account for the programmed nature of aging as well as for the fact of inheritance in premature aging. If longevity runs in families, then causal theories must show how the same causal agents operate cross-generationally or else must show that longevity is not a true inheritable characteristic. Program theories often make use of the provocative findings of the experiments by Leonard Hayflick showing the limited clonal life of cells *in vitro*. In these experiments, when cells are allowed to grow (double) in a nutrient medium, they do not grow forever, no matter how much nutrient is available. Each generation produces fewer and fewer cells, which are more readily susceptible to malfunction in the synthesis of DNA and RNA. When cells from adults are grown in culture at the same time as cells from infants, these cells do not have the same lifespan. With support systems similar to those for the infant cells, the adult cells double in number in a shorter time and have less generational fecundity. Even cells frozen in liquid nitrogen somehow "remember" where they stand in the lifespan of their kind and pick up where they left off before freezing. And finally, young nuclei transplanted into old cells apparently rejuvenate, whereas the cytoplasmic constituents of old nuclei that are placed into young cells seem to age biologically. All of these experiments suggest that aging is a precisely timed genetic process controlled from within the genome. Both the process of development and the process of degeneration, including maximum lifespan, are programmed.

Such *in vitro* experiments suggest that the unit of aging is the cell and that the mechanism of aging is a genetic program. The macroscopic effects of cellular aging, then, are an arithmetic result of microscopic aging. It might be argued, however, that because cells contain genes and organisms contain cells, organisms contain genes. It might be argued further that evolution involves not only genetic variation but also natural selection, which involves whole organisms, their strength, vigor, fecundity, and general survivability. If one takes natural selection into account, *in vitro* cellular life is not natural cell life. Thus it may not be surprising that such isolated cells die off.

The program theorist might counter this explanation with two assertions: first, cells that develop abnormalities become "immortal" and only normal cells die off; and second, the cell does not know where it is as long as proper life conditions are maintained outside its walls. The first assertion rests on the claim that because immortal cell populations are possible—cells showing no decline in the ability to produce progeny forever—aging and immortal cells must be programmed differently: one cell must contain active aging genes; in the other, mutation must have turned off or destroyed aging genes. The program theorist's argument, however, commits the fallacy of affirming the consequent. Although it is true that if there are aging genes in the cells, then cells will appear to age, it does not follow that if cells appear to age there must be aging genes. As far as we know, the gene is the only constituent of the cell that is sufficiently "intelligent" for the task of controlling aging, but still we cannot infer that genes cause the results of the Hayflick experiments. Perhaps cells removed from the parent organism contain substances that are eventually and gradually used up and the depletion of these substances may cause populations to die off.

The program theorist's second assertion is open to considerable doubt because we cannot ascertain whether or not cells "know" where they are. The sequencing of cells in morphological development suggests that cells in a colony have something like positional information. Perhaps, then, the cells in a nutrient solution are themselves a reproducing "organism," whose programmed responses and growth patterns are continually thwarted by the experimenter's interventions. Separated from the chemical and electrical network of the living organism, the cell colony can only reproduce what it immediately knows.

Even if the cell colony reproduces without feedback from other levels of the organism, cellular aging might still mirror organic aging. But without feedback much can go wrong in the aging cell colony. If aging is in fact programmed, it may be programmed in some other manner, a possibility supported by the lack of correlation between doublings and organismic lifespan. Some human cells double only about sixty times, whereas the cells of certain small mammals with lifespans of only a few years can double up to 170 times!

Program theorists confront the additional problem of interpreting the timing of an aging process. The precise sense in which an organism can be said to contain or be governed by a clock is difficult to pin down. Gerontologists speak of an aging clock or of pacemakers or of aging hormones, but what clock ticks away during the aging process and how does that clock govern each stage of the process? From a commonsense point of view, one cannot imagine a clock operating without a mind counting away the seconds and marking the intervals passed. But it is possible to imagine that the body has a large complex clock, set at birth, that completes one cycle at natural death. At present, however, we know of no mechanism that works like this. If maximum lifespan is governed by a clock, then a series of small clocks that go through a number of full cycles in sequential order would not be equivalent to a master clock. A master clock for the lifespan must monitor the whole aging process and know when to end it. Such a master clock has been sought in chemical reaction times as well as in cosmic periods of radiation and magnetic force, but if one exists, it has not yet been found.

One response to the difficulties encountered in explaining programmed aging is to claim that aging is the result not so much of a program as a failure of programmed activity. In other words, the first part of life is programmed; in the second part the program gradually breaks down. At birth what is new about an organism is its software and the genetic mechanism to carry it out. With advancing chronological age, flaws develop in the hardware, and the software is imperfectly expressed, with aging as the result. In practice it is difficult to distinguish this view from wear-and-tear or genetic mutation theory, on the one hand, or, on the other hand, from program theories that postulate a master clock governing the ordered repression and activation of genetic information during an organism's lifespan. What is the difference between an activity that ceases because of mechanical problems with the hardware and one that is programmed to turn off at a certain point? In the first case, either a single causal agent operates or many agents act singly; in the second case, the agency is itself programmed and systematic. Has the program broken down when, for example, fetal proteins begin to appear in the bodies of the elderly, or do these proteins appear as part of the programmed aging process? Are they mistakes, or part of the aging process itself? One explanation for this appearance is that a previously inactive gene has become active: the normal program has been damaged and the cell is operating with improper information.

We should be careful about loosely using such terms as *genetic information* and *software* from cybernetics and information theory. When program theorists speak of software, they usually mean sequences of signals that are transferred from one structure to another. Humans program computers either by reading symbols and entering keyboard commands into the computer memory to gain access to certain capabilities or by entering impulses stored on a disk into the computer's memory. In the genetic process, by analogy, a master information source must come into contact with the executing functions of the genome to transfer the needed information, and this process must be disturbed when a system either gets the wrong information or gets no information at all. In the biochemical world this transfer takes place without the intervention of mind; its mechanism is chemical and ultimately electromagnetic. Thus when gerontologists say that a program "runs out" of information, they are only saying that the crucial genetic macromolecules have been damaged by some mechanical force. In what sense, then, can it be said that a gene "uses up" its information if there is nothing identifiable as software in the biochemical world?

Some system theories of aging attempt to avoid explaining the problem of information transfer on the molecular level by seeking a mechanism for aging on a more complex level of organismic life—for example, in the immune system or the endocrine system. Autoimmune theory postulates that a memory failure in the immune system leaves an organism unable to distinguish self from nonself, leading the organism to progressively attack itself: the immune system, instead of attacking only viruses, attacks the tissue surrounding them as well, thus weakening the entire organism. This hypothesis suggests a mechanism for aging but not a cause. Perhaps memory failure in the immune system results from somatic or genetic mutation or from a cross-linking of constituents involved in antibody production. But a decline in the normal capacity to produce antibodies occurs after the beginning of the aging process, so how can the dysfunction of the immune system serve as the basis for a theory of aging? To explain aging, the proponents of the autoimmune theory must be able to distinguish self-attack as a systematic response of the body from the overwhelming of the immune system by infection. The task of providing such an explanation is complicated by our unclear understanding of the limits and functions of the immune system itself: does it immunize *all* parts of the organism at all times and by the same set of rules? Until we understand the system better, we cannot be sure what it means to say that immune failure or self-attack is taking place.

What is the immune system's "concept of self"? Is it the memory bank of all those thousands of structural configurations of proteins that "belong to the self"; and if so, how is inclusion in that bank determined? If autoimmune theory is a genuine systematic theory, it must propose a systematic mechanism and not postulate that the external action of mutagens initiates the process of self-attack. It might conceivably postulate ubiquitous viral agents that present unprecedented problems for the immune system. Yet these agents would not be a truly systematic influence unless organism, virus, and immune system interacted within a larger supersystem. The immune system would then protect the organism for a period of time and kill it when that time had passed. But now we are, once again, forced to interpret a specific theory of aging, the autoimmune theory in this case, in terms of an even more macroscopically systematic theory, whose outlines are only vaguely apparent.

Once a systematic theory of aging is proposed, what are the upper limits of systematicity that must be considered? Can there be an endocrine theory of aging, or must the endocrine system be linked to the brain and nervous system and these with the metabolic system? In each system-level theory the problem of reversibility takes a different form. In causal theories the problem is why the organism fails to protect itself from foreign influences. In system theories the problem is why a return to homeostasis fails to take place. We cannot, simply because a system is complex and capable of departing from homeostasis, postulate departures beyond certain operating limits unless we introduce new outside factors. It has been suggested, for example, that ovarian function declines because of a degeneration of its immediate environment and that endocrine activity declines because of a depletion of the chemicals needed to facilitate neurotransmission in the hypothalamus. But to suggest these deficiencies requires an extension of the theory of aging. Systematic theories characteristically either reduce explanations to a causal mechanism or enhance them by comprehending higher levels of systematicity. Like other theories, these theories must determine the proper unit of aging. Do organisms age biologically because they contain a deteriorating component that drags the rest of the ship down with it, or does aging occur throughout an organism? To many clinical gerontologists, no doubt, this is a metaphysical question that admits of no empirical answer. But it may nonetheless be a crucial question if we are eventually to understand the aging process. We cannot, however, issue edicts about the appropriate level of conceptual generality until we have produced theories whose internal consistency is greater than that of currently available theories.

EVOLUTIONARY THEORIES

Perhaps the most confident aging theorists are the evolutionary theorists. Taking their cue from that great article of faith we know as modern evolutionary theory, these theorists worry less about the detailed mechanisms involved in

aging and more about the compatibility of those mechanisms with the tenets of evolutionary doctrine. In a nutshell
these theories assume that aging occurs because gene pools
with capabilities for aging are better able to survive than
those without them. Aging, however, conflicts with, or at
least challenges, one of the main tenets of evolutionary theory: that evolution selects what can best survive, given the
environment and genetic makeup of a species. But other
evolutionary goals enter the picture when aging is introduced. If, for example, aging is explained as a way to get rid
of members of a population of a highly entrenched and
adaptable species because their lingering on would prevent
the genetic variability that comes from breeding, then we
must explain why genetic variability need be a goal at all if
we already have a successful species, and why continued
life could produce such variability by continued breeding.

Evolutionary theories must ultimately rely on supporting
hypotheses that link aging and evolution. Thus theorists
claim that "intrinsic" biosenescent and antibiosenescent processes in organisms wage a tug-of-war to determine how well
the species fits into its ecological niche. Theorists explain the
extension of postmaturational life in higher animals by ar-
guing that "the vigour of the post-reproductive adult can be
attributed to beneficial effects of continued survival on the
survival and reproduction of descendents."[6] Nonsenescent
grandparents and great-grandparents, it is assumed, would
also compete with the young for the necessities and enjoy-
ments of life. These two processes would balance out in the
aging species, and indeed the extent of postmaturational life
reveals how well adapted a species is. If long life becomes a
threat to the gene pool, the pleiotropic effect of certain aging
genes or mechanisms comes into play; if it is potentially sup-
portable, those mechanisms are counterbalanced.

However, the evolutionary view leaves unanswered the
question whether intrinsic aging must serve that adaptive

6. W. D. Hamilton, "The Moulding of Senescence by Natural Selection," *Journal of Theoretical Biology* 12 (1966): 37.

function or whether some other mechanism, such as infection and disease, may do the job as well. Although evolutionary theories usually assume that the aging mechanism of each species is intrinsic, this intrinsic mechanism itself is at issue. The difficulty is revealed in a remark by Richard G. Cutler:

> The separation of the metazoan organism into soma and germ cell components represents an important means of avoiding intrinsic cellular biosenescent processes. This separation led to the evolution of the higher metazoan organisms, and to the origin of biosenescent processes for the soma, which can die with no serious consequence to the species. The biosenescence of the soma was merely the outcome of mechanisms used to ensure the continued preservation of the genetic information that can preserve itself. The separation of soma and germ cells might not have even taken place if intrinsic cellular biosenescent processes were not important or were a trivial matter to overcome.[7]

Cutler in one breath both denies and affirms intrinsic aging. The germ cell separates to be immune from intrinsic aging; at the same time the aging of the soma is an "outcome" of the process of protecting the germ cell. If there is an inadvertent but beneficial consequence of germ cell preservation—if the soma must be sacrificed for the sake of the species—how can aging be intrinsic? If new mechanisms are found for protecting both germ cell and soma, would there not be strong selective pressure for such protection? After all, germ cells do not exist as ends in themselves; they exist in reproducing organisms that also participate in the process of selection by their capabilities and liveliness.

Evolutionary theory may be rendered plausible by the hypothesis that the reproductive value of a member decreases with chronological age because the longer an organism lives, the greater the probability of accidental death. Presumably, it would be inefficient for a species to have long-lived mem-

7. Richard G. Cutler, "Evolutionary Biology of Senescence," in *The Biology of Aging*, ed. J. A. Behnke, C. E. Finch, and G. B. Moment (New York: Plenum Press, 1978), pp. 320–21.

bers when its goal is simply to preserve species-ness and not its specific manifestations. This is the assumption of James F. Fries and Lawrence M. Crapo:

> For species survival, granted hardship and variability, re- serve needs to be built into the individual. Thus, given the human age of puberty, one might speculate that most indi- viduals should live seventy years or so without serious mal- function. As in our automobile analogy, the body seems to be designed to outlast the warranty period (puberty) and the period of initial ownership (parenthood) with enough reserve to ensure that most individuals will survive these stages without a serious breakdown. After that, both you and your automobile are on linear lines of decay of performance of components, and on exponential lines of likelihood of total breakdown.[8]

The circularity of such an argument was long ago pointed out by Peter B. Medawar and doubtless by others since.[9] Instead of explaining aging in terms of evolution, part of the mechanism for evolution is being explained in terms of ag- ing. If species with an aging mechanism enjoy a selective advantage, that mechanism would also confer an advantage on species without it, which would have more opportunity to dominate and prey on the weak members of an aging species. What, then, is the advantage of aging?

Evolutionists have suggested that the earlier reproduction gets underway in a species, the fitter that species. If to de- sign a species that reproduces soon after reaching maturity requires mechanisms that also build in disadvantages for living much beyond maturity, then such a mechanism would be advantageous in a violent environment where death comes easily in mature life; its disadvantages would emerge only when that environment became pacified. But again this explanation fails to account for the need for any aging mechanism at all, particularly if it is assumed that the

8. James F. Fries and Lawrence M. Crapo, *Vitality and Aging* (San Fran- cisco: W. H. Freeman, 1981), p. 39.

9. Peter B. Medawar, *An Unsolved Problem in Biology* (London: Lewis, 1952).

older organism has a greater chance of dying violently any-way. It might be that nature did not design an organism as the best of all possible design options but built it piecemeal by trial and error, going from one problem to the next, and as a result it designed the organisms we associate with aging inadvertently, by a series of unlinked contingent processes whose necessary by-product was the degenerative process we call aging. In this case aging confers a selective disad-vantage on a species because it eliminates its members, but this disadvantage is outweighed by the advantages of the mechanism that finally emerged, including early reproduc-tion in maturity. Strictly speaking, of course, this explana-tion is not an evolutionary theory of aging at all; rather it is a structural-functional explanation with some evolutionary im-plications.

It has been argued that haploid organisms do not age because their opportunities for genetic variety are far less than those for diploid reproduction.[10] If the argument is jus-tified, aging would result from diploid reproduction confer-ring selective advantages by producing genetic variety as well as by making DNA repair possible. It would be a neces-sary consequence of the developmental response to the ad-vantages that subsequent selection in fact made possible. In conjunction with this view, it has been argued that we may account for degeneration on the basis of information theory alone: if longer-lived, more complex organisms result from natural selection and genetic variation, the information pro-cessors of these complex organisms must be maintained so that they work properly.[11] An increase in lifespan requires either an increase in genetic redundancy or an increase in repair capacity, or both. Thus if the maximum lifespan for a species is increasingly a function of organismic complexity, the greater the information transfer necessary both at con-

10. T. M. Sonneborn, "The Origin, Evolution, Nature, and Causes of Aging," in Behnke, Finch, and Moment, *The Biology of Aging*, pp. 361–74.

11. A. P. Miller, "A Computer Model of the Evolution of Specific Maxi-mum Lifespan," *Mechanisms of Ageing and Development* 16 (1981): 37–54.

ception and throughout organic life, the higher the probability of error during transmission. Biosenescence simply results from the accumulation of these errors.

Clearly the evolutionary account of aging poses as many problems for evolution as for aging. Are we to believe that the goal of evolution is the preservation of species-ness? Can we really believe that because any organism is bound to be seriously modified in its structure and overall function (if it has one) as a result of environmental assault, nature, knowing this, gives it a natural death in advance? Such fantastic beliefs have nothing to do with the notion of neo-Darwinian evolution, yet they are basic to the evolutionary theory of aging. If aging has a selective advantage it is not yet clear what it is. Do two imperatives propel the evolutionary machine, one to "increase reproductive values," the other to "increase variety in all ways possible"?

A PARADIGM OF AGING

We have examined some conceptual and theoretical problems of explaining aging. It might be useful at this point to ask ourselves what a good theory of aging might look like if we could simply dream one up, assuming that the concept of aging is biologically meaningful in the first place. Such a theory, which would be part of a general theory of organic function, would make no fundamental distinction between aging and disease. It would specify the beginnings of degenerative pathways and would indicate how those pathways could be closed off and degeneration reversed. As an empirically sound theory, it would also specify conditions that would keep mature adults alive forever, just as restored automobiles can now be kept in mint condition through changing times and circumstances. Currently the theory of aging most favored by theoretical gerontologists involves the failure of DNA repair. Although anything that works (in both senses of the word) can malfunction, organisms work exceedingly well. Only with aging do they begin to work less well. Do aging organisms encounter new problems, or do they lose old abilities? A good theory of aging must answer this question. Furthermore, that theory must solve the problem of reversibility discussed earlier. As it specifies the conditions for immortality, it must also say who can enjoy it and who cannot. Are all diseases correctable? Can the infirm elderly be revitalized? Can osteoporosis and arteriosclerosis be reversed? The theory must suggest not only whether these are practical possibilities but also whether they are theoretical possibilities as well. Only if it does so can it confidently treat the question of reversibility. As the infant science of theoretical gerontology advances toward answering these questions, it will change our traditional beliefs about life and death.

The Functional Theory of Aging

I have just suggested that aging should be analyzed in the context of the overall function of an organism. But does an organism have a single overall function? To answer this question we must decide on a proper description of biological activity. Individuals may be viewed as metabolizing beings or as information-processing systems or as gene-transferring vehicles. We cannot decide which view best explains aging without trying various hypotheses to see where they lead.

It is worth speculating that aging, from a functional point of view, may result not from a specific function or even from the general function of the entire organism but from a failure or breakdown of function. Perhaps the organism fails to utilize the entire potential of its organic inheritance. In this case aging would result from organic atrophy or boredom. In a world of perfect stimulation and nutrition no organism would age or decay, but all its components would be in full vigor and display. This mind-body or even teleological theory of aging would fully express our current insights about the relation between aging and illness, stress and depression. The extremes would be a life-denying, suicidal depression and a beatific excitement of full psychophysical stimulation; aging would occur in greater or lesser degree in a condition between extremes where some stimulation exists, though with increasing attenuation, and some boredom as well.

The teleological view assumes that organisms are designed to carry out functions but also recognizes that those functions may be thwarted in a finite world. How they are thwarted, however, is not entirely clear. We know that organisms compete with each other for finite resources, and we also know that changes in environment may threaten the overall health of the currently adapted species. But we have no inkling why such complex organisms as the highest species needed to be created in the first place. Perhaps we are nothing but a bio-chemical extravaganza run amok, though this suggestion is hard to accept when we reflect on the elegance of natural forms and the communication and symbiosis between them. We seem to have been created *as if* immortality is possible and is not realized only because the right circumstances have not come about.

As the teleological model suggests, the functional theory must specify the conditions that would accelerate aging, in-hibit it, or eliminate it altogether. As a starting point, we could study the correlation between mental habits and lon-gevity, and we might even be able to design experiments to ascertain the effect of aggressive stimulation on previous aging and to determine whether future aging had been re-tarded by the stimulation. Such studies and experiments might lead us to regard aging as an "intervening variable" between certain controllable influences and those conse-quences we normally associate with aging.

AGING AND CANCER

Apparently cancer can occur during all the ages of life, but generally incidences of cancer increase geometrically with increases in chronological age. The Hayflick experiments showed that normal cells can become immortal if they be-come cancerous cells by a process still not satisfactorily known. It is believed that cancer is a breakdown in regula-tory function, marked by the emergence of biological chaos and the vanquishing of biological law and order. Compare, for example, the behavior of normal and cancerous cells *in vitro*. Normal cells display contact inhibition; they line up in rows and cover a solid surface as if they were floor tiles. Cancerous cells grow in irregular masses and layers. They lose their biological identity and congregate where they do not belong. At least in some cases this neoplastic transformation is thought to be caused by the DNA or RNA of an invading virus, which tampers with the genetic code of the host cell nucleus and inhibits the normal action of enzymes. RNA viruses contain enzymes that can convert the RNA of the virus into a DNA double helix, which is then incorporated into the genome of the host to produce a cancerous cell. This is the only case we know of in nature in which genetic information flows from RNA to DNA.

How is cancer relevant to aging? We know that increasing susceptibility to degeneration accompanies biological aging and that cancer plays an important role in this degeneration. Common to cancer and aging is the gradual alienation of the body, which challenges our concepts of biological integrity and organismic unity. Thus the question of the units of aging may be tied to the question of the continuity or identity of the organism. As both a unity and a collection of unities, every organism has a peculiar complementarity. Functioning occurs on various levels at the same time. If I contract, say, hepatitis, I am aware of what is happening to me. But I am not aware of what is happening to my liver, which must fight this battle on its own. I can help it by not doing anything to make matters worse, but I cannot directly and specifically contribute to its effort. Biologically speaking, my liver and I are on different levels of reality.

Cancer is relevant to aging because it too takes place on another level of reality, but it marks a development that frees portions of the body from aging influences. If cancer cells lose contact inhibition and gain immortality, does this mean that factors producing such inhibitions, and probably other effects as well, also contribute to aging? The answer to this question depends on our definition of the units of cancer. Do cancer cells become immortal because they are constantly changing from one form to another in an apparently random fashion? Do they require a host that they must kill in order to die themselves? We tend to see aging as a particular stage in the life of a unified organism. But if we look at that organism at a lower level of reality, other perspectives come into play: now the organism is an environment whose individual cells are subject to violent aging hits and are preyed on by cunning viruses. This organism is like a country in which the political and cultural identity of various locations changes from one period to another. Only superficially does the country stay the same. Its soil and weather may be the same, but its population, constantly changing, is entirely different every century or so.

One might describe the organism in similar language. Not the single organism but rather a complex system of changing components ages. From this point of view, the period when cancer usually emerges may represent just another stage of biological function. Must an organism fulfill just one function throughout its entire life? Is reproductive value its only function? And must aging be only a mechanism for merciful departure from life? Perhaps what we call aging is just a transformation from the full systematicity of a unified organism to its fragmentation into more or less isolated systems. Intuitively this is how we usually see aging: the organism is falling apart. Perhaps instead we should cease looking at the aging organism as something useless or degenerate, an imperfect copy of its past real self, and begin to think of it as a new biological reality.

There may be symmetry in living from birth to death. During development, a genetic program assembles nonorganic components into systems that progressively gain more control and encompass more of the organism as a totality. At maturity full systematicity is attained, as determined by the genetic program. But does nature then just discard this work? If we picture the function of an organism in neo-Darwinian terms as the maintenance of selfish genes, then the answer must be yes. The experiences of the organism after its genes have been passed on must die with it.

However, there is another way of looking at the matter. The manner in which postmaturational organisms experience gradual involution may still influence biological destiny. For example, when viruses attack organisms whose genes have already been passed on, evolution continues to work on the gene-virus level, though whether this working is adaptive or maladaptive for the aging organism itself is far from clear. It is generally assumed that evolutionary value is fully achieved at the onset of maturity, as soon as the germ cell is ready for fertilization. Yet procreation can take place well into late life, particularly in the case of males. Thus an organism that passes along genes modified by the action of various viral mutagens may serve an evolutionary function. We know that the likelihood of birth defects increases as mating humans grow older, but this likelihood may not mean that their mating has no benefit whatsoever. Although by the standards of normal, young, healthy members of the species the process of procreation appears to have gone astray, with nothing good coming from it, such a conclusion requires that other possible functions for the aging organism be ruled out. Nature is not likely to discard its great investment in protoplasm and structure as if the aging organism were an empty bottle. Moreover, the increasing likelihood of cancer raises an intriguing possibility: the organism may take on a new role as a biological laboratory, a workshop where primary cellular constituents are modified and reworked into new possibilities and inventions.

These speculations seem improbable only because we are accustomed to thinking about organisms with the prejudices of the anatomist—as ideal forms with a set of fixed, ideal functions. In fact organisms may have radically different functions in relation to the entire biological kingdom at different phases of life, so much so that it is possible to think of each organism as several different organisms or systems of organisms. We easily think of a child as a developing adult, but it is difficult for us to regard an aged adult as less than fully an adult as well. The reasons for this difficulty have much to do with our common social and moral beliefs about personhood, but these beliefs are not developments in biological knowledge. Already the discovery of even relatively simple mechanisms of gene action has changed our view of the life of cells. We increasingly think of the cell not simply as a building block, but as a marvel of nature in its own right, which becomes more marvelous as our knowledge of it grows. No longer is the cell merely a factory. The very idea of a "selfish" gene suggests that genes too may be like cells and that the individual body may be a locus of thousands of these individuals, wise little computers that operate more or less in symbiotic harmony with the totality of the individual person.[12]

THE METHUSELAH DEBATE

The more we learn about the mechanisms of aging, the more we confront new problems, philosophical problems at first but later technical problems as well. Should we try to slow the aging process as much as possible? Should we try to extend the maximum lifespan? Should we try to overcome death entirely? Some gerontologists argue that we cannot prolong the maximum lifespan; we can only keep the organism healthy to the end of life: "Death does not require disease or accident. If all disease and all trauma were eliminated, death would still occur, at an average age not much older than at present. If premature death were eliminated . . . we would still face the prospect of a natural death."[13] But clearly this view of aging as natural rests on special meanings of the terms *disease* and *premature death.* The contrast between disease and aging depends on our ability to detect specific causes. If we could find a specific

12. Richard Dawkins, *The Selfish Gene* (Oxford: Oxford University Press, 1976).
13. Fries and Crapo, *Vitality and Aging,* p. 3.

cause for aging, we could regard it as merely a pervasive state of bodily disease. Similarly, we could regard all death as premature if we could imagine a realizable bodily condition whose occurrence would have postponed death. Our notion of death as premature is not a medical notion but a psychological one. The young are said to die prematurely because they have so much left to do; the old die in their time because they have ceased to matter to society.

The anti-immortalists defend their position by reference to the Hayflick limit—and specifically to the presence of aging genes or hormones—or to holistic thermodynamic conditions of complex organization, or to the theoretical limit of the biological clock.[14] Strehler, however, described the limitations of life in evolutionary and functional terms:

> It appears to me that there is no inherent contradiction, no inherent property of cells or of metazoa which precludes their organization into perceptually functioning and self-replenishing individuals. On the other hand, the evolutionary dereliction is probably so manifold and so deeply ingrained in the physiology and biochemistry of existing forms, including man, that the abolition of the process is a practical impossibility.[15]

By contrast, the immortalists maintain that all disease is curable, that humans will genetically control aging, that artificial organs will replace defective natural ones, and that brain cell transplants will make longevity potentially unlimited. From a historical perspective, of course, the immortalists have the upper hand. Scientific knowledge must always produce experimental implications if it is to be verified by other experimenters. By its very nature it must be a knowledge of

14. Daniel Hershey and Hsuan-Hsien Wang, *A New Age-Scale for Humans* (Lexington, Mass.: Lexington Books, 1980). See also Zsolt Harsany and Richard Hutton, *Genetic Prophecy: Beyond the Double Helix* (New York: Rawson, Wade, 1981); John Langone, *Long Life: What We Know and Are Learning About the Aging Process* (Boston: Little, Brown, 1978); Durk Pearson and Sandy Shaw, *Life Extension: A Practical Scientific Approach* (New York: Warner Books, 1982).

15. Strehler, *Time, Cells, and Aging*, pp. 224–25.

things we can control. So according to our standing definition of science, what we cannot control we cannot know.
Strehler's distinction between theoretical clarity and practical
impossibility cannot be cashed out in scientific terms where
theoretical clarity always must be translatable into practical
conditions. Where there is no practical control, there is no
theoretical clarity.

Are there theoretical limits to human life? That is, can we,
in spite of our ignorance, say that we will never conquer
aging and death? If we think of the organism as a machine of
vast complexity and variability, it is easy to imagine that immortality must be possible. All we have to do is label all
processes as either life-enhancing or life-endangering, conceive that instantaneous diagnosis is possible, and assume
that the means exist to reverse immediately the effect of life-
endangering processes. We could imagine a limit in principle
only if the very process of enlightenment produced a pleiotropic secondary effect that neutralized the potentially beneficial effects of that enlightenment. But only if this effect is
necessary and automatic would it be intractable to scientific
control.

Scientific knowledge often produces conditions that nullify the benefits of that knowledge: wonder drugs and toxic
chemicals, space exploration and atomic warfare. The litany
is well known today. But few believe that the proliferation of
both goods and evils is inevitable, for we credit scientists
with the former and blame politicians for the latter. If there
is a mechanism that makes aging inevitable, it would have
to be located at the heart of scientific knowing; that is, the
very source of knowledge must somehow extinguish itself.
Suppose that a prerequisite level of knowledge is required
for the solution to the riddle of aging but that as soon as that
level of knowledge is attained, the knower is directly—by
the very act of knowing—caused to die before storing that
knowledge in some symbolic (presumably nonlethal) form
accessible to other minds. Or less implausibly, imagine another possibility based on the way science itself advances: to
understand the aging mechanism we need a mind more com-

plex and powerful than either the individual human mind or the scientific social mind of periodicals, printouts, abstracts, lectures, and the like. All the data stored in a computer may contain the answer but humans could not get at it either because they would not know where to find it or because they would not recognize it if they did find it. Unable to reach the requisite level of understanding, humans would continue aging forever.

These theoretical possibilities seem far less plausible than those proposed by the immortalists, who assume that single minds can solve the riddle simply because they have solved clearly defined scientific problems this way in the past. A further advantage for the immortalists is that a cure for aging in the form of some miracle drug might be discovered without in any way extending our knowledge of how or why it works. Some future "gerovital" might really work, producing rejuvenation and the potential for great longevity. The immortalists need only point to the current practice of medicine—where the effects of medication are known but the mechanism often takes place in a "black box"—to support the plausibility of this option.

The practical implications of the Methuselah debate, however, are much clearer. On the one hand, if we cannot extend life, should we try to "put more life into our years, rather than more years into our life" or should we rethink what it means to live a life, regarding organic degeneration as a degeneration of the entire person? On the other hand, if immortality is possible, should we embrace it, and if so in what manner? The biological conception of aging by itself does not help us resolve these questions, and we postpone them for a later chapter.

2

The Aging Psyche

Human beings not only age biologically but can also conceive of themselves as aging. Perhaps this capacity distinguishes us truly from the rest of the animal kingdom. When animals are terrified by the sudden death of kin, they may recognize that they too can experience such death. But can these animals also conceive of life as a progressive degeneration of living capacity?

Although nothing may seem more obvious than that we know ourselves as aging beings, on further reflection that cognition is something of a mystery. We could easily know as much as we do about biological forms yet have no conception of aging. When we judge a biological entity to be undergoing a degenerative, irreversible process, do we do so independently of our notions of human goals and feelings of failure? Our concept of aging seems to be tied to a sense of self-awareness, in particular to a feeling that increasingly things are not going as well as they used to. Vision blurs, taste muddies, steps slow, breathing is more labored—these are cognitive experiences as well as physiological events. Because of this element of cognition it is doubtful that the young could know what it is like to *feel* aging. When they gaze at the pictures of their own parents taken many years before, they may know in some abstract way that their fate is to become adults, but they may think only rarely that the process of becoming a middle-aged adult involves aging as well as growth.

What, then, is the experience of aging? And what is it in that experience that ages? In the preceding chapter I described the contrast between the mechanistic processes of chronological aging and the organic processes of biological aging. Is there also psychological aging? Are there states of mind and feeling that are old? Does the mind age? And if so, is there a pattern of mental aging? These are the questions for consideration in this chapter.

THE PSYCHOSOCIAL ORIGINS OF AGING

Let us attempt to sort out the various factors that contribute to our concept of aging. In particular, let us imagine various states of nature, first among them the fiction of one person in the wild. The wild child witnesses death around him and sees himself gradually change in the reflection of the pool from which he drinks. But does he know that he too is mortal and that each day brings him closer to his own death? If he does not have photographs of himself and if he is not able to witness aging by, say, comparing the images of actors in old movies with their present appearance, he may not be struck by the dramatic changes that aging eventually produces. But he is still likely to suspect that the deer he chased in his youth did not run more slowly than those he chases now in later life. This psychosomatic sense of decline may be as close to a sense of aging as the wild child comes. But it is always possible that he may think himself chronically ill and believe that someday soon he will recover and run down the fastest deer in the forest.

A small tribal society inhabits the second state of nature. This society comprehends the origin and destiny of individual life. Infants are born into it and members die, either through accident or from withering away, losing their physical and mental capabilities with time. Although this society, like the wild child, may lack photographs and other cultural artifacts, the ways in which its members become aware of aging are nonetheless increased. The young may compare the abilities of their parents at different times, and the old may have an overview of the life of the community. They recall the elderly of their youth, and, seeing how the cycle of age and youth repeats itself, they perceive life as a process and time as a destroyer and restorer—a prominent theme in ancient Greek lyric poetry. The tribal elders begin to analyze and express these conceptions in mythic forms. Their images contain useful information not only about the psychodynamics of everyday life but also about various alternative states of existence: states beyond time (the gods), states within time but unaffected by it (the demigods), and states subject to time (the mortals).

The small tribal society can fully conceive of human life as an ongoing aging process; our own recognition of aging probably differs little from that of, say, the ancient Sumerians. Already in the writings of Plato and Aristotle we see a prominent place given to philosophical questions raised by the reality of the aging self. These questions are seldom, if ever, directly asked in connection with aging, but they are motivated by such a connection nonetheless. The whole preoccupation with the issues of permanence and change from the pre-Socratics to Plato and Aristotle may have been motivated by amazement that the marvel of the philosopher's own mental capacity should hinge on a process of eventual physical destruction.

As social reality has changed, our conception of aging has reflected the changes. Tribal societies may recognize aging as such and, because few people live even into the fourth decade of life, these societies may value old age as an accomplishment. Indeed, the traditional image of the philosopher has been that of someone ancient in years who has a magical commerce with a past that few contemporaries know. And traditionally the aged have been those who know the larger cycles of things and can help place events in a wider perspective. Socratic wisdom sought to elaborate the wider true context, in contrast with the narrower false one. Socrates usually undermined his critics' arguments by showing that from a higher or wider perspective a lower level became inconsistent. So Greek philosophy, in a fundamental way, was tied to experiences seldom available to the young.

In a society that can express its images in an external, preservable form, however, we can study the process of aging in great detail. The ancient Greek *korai* and *kouroi*, statues representing, respectively, a young, naked woman and man—whatever their religious connotations—transmitted a sense of life as it was really meant to be: youthful, powerful, joyful, confident. In giving the statues symbolic importance the ancient Hellenes were worshipping life itself. Once these statues were created, the concepts of beauty and perfection had a vehicle for public discourse. Indeed, the concept itself may have evolved from an original abstract reference to images or states to a more concrete sense of some *thing* that contained beauty or was beautiful. And this change of meaning might have given rise to the age-old contrast between youthful beauty and ugly old age.

Since Hellenic times social life has emerged as a complex network of roles and interactions. The proliferation of both artifacts and their uses has added layers of significance to our earlier conceptions of life and value. At first the qualities of individuals were transferred from creator to object created; the living imagination of a genius such as Phidias could be seen in his few unique creations. As the making of artifacts became more systematic and impersonal, the qualities of the objects could be transferred to their users. A powerful weapon made the user powerful, an expensive chariot made its owner feel that his own worth was higher. Nowadays, artifacts do not control our lives by themselves, but they do control indirectly our thinking about our lives. Only after the Industrial Revolution could we have had a firm idea of the aged as obsolete, rendered useless to society both because of their physical deterioration and because of their outmoded capabilities. How much of our current conception of the old is borrowed unwittingly from our recognition of the fate of artifacts that become useless in a consumer society?

Aesthetic objects as well as utilitarian objects, however, influence thought. We can greatly refine the distinctions of aging as we are able to record the fine details of its progress. Portraiture, at least from the sixteenth century, was the first great advance in such recording, followed by photography and motion pictures. It is well known that movie stars do not cope well with aging. They see themselves and moviegoers see them as heavenly bodies, untouched by earthly corruption. A particular film is like a long-running play in which the actors never age; each performance is identical to the last. Taken in by the dramatic illusion and accustomed to identifying actors with the characters they portray, we think of the actors themselves as eternal, and if we see them off-screen, we become acutely aware of their aging. This experience may not be unique to modern society, but it is far more prevalent in a society surfeited with such portrayals of human existence.

In our age movie stars serve as images of the elusive solidity of life much as did the *korai* and *kouroi* of the Hellenes. They have a transcendent character that defies particularization and limitation. "Elvis," fans say, "will always be Elvis." When Marilyn Monroe's photographs began to reveal signs of aging, the popular media interpreted them as signs that her skin was silky and delicate, thus preserving her ethereal standing. In the past twenty-five years more and more people, convinced that they too can achieve a personal stardom, have used the mirror as their standard, preserving a changeless image of the self with cosmetics and with surgery if necessary.

AGING AND THE BODY

The experience of aging has been a silent influence in the ancient problem of the relation between the mind and the body. I can easily conceive of myself in a variety of physical forms, but I cannot conceive of myself without my thoughts. The inevitable bodily change of aging poses a particularly acute problem here. If my body merely changed, being one day this way, another day that way, then I might imagine that I am not really my body, as it would have all of the continuity and variety I experience as my mind. Aging, however, signals a subtle but gradual diminution of bodily life and does so in a manner we cannot measure as corresponding to any change in mental life.

In the general philosophical treatment of the mind-body

problem the central issue is the linking of two ontological realms, one material, the other spiritual. But more particularly, there is also the problem of uniting my mind with a specific body. If I can conceive of myself as having some other body, could it be *any* other body whatsoever? Descartes's point was that I could not conceive, in any logical sense, of my not having my own mind, for if I had someone else's mind, it could not be I who was thinking. My thoughts inevitably are my own, he argued. Although in some mental disorders (schizophrenia, for example) patients claim to hear voices, these are presumably signals they themselves are sending. What is to stop the normal person from applying this notion to undermine all mental experiences? Why can't a person say, "All my thoughts are really those of someone else who is so radically deceived that he now thinks he is me." Perhaps what Descartes assumed about "my" thoughts was that they were mine to the extent that they were familiar to me. I recognize my memories as mine either because I recognize myself in them or because I have grown accustomed to reflecting on them. Even before we have attained a state of mental development sufficient to allow Cartesian reflection, we have become familiar with many thoughts and thought patterns that are part of our mental history. It is not the bare thinking of them that establishes them as ours but the continued thinking of them. When we think a thought for the first time, it is new and fascinating. We say, "It occurred to me." Rather than thinking of thought as a process that is carried on entirely inside of us by an invisible thinking substance like a soul or homunculus, we may just as easily, though unfamiliarly, think of new thoughts as entities that travel through space and are picked up by instruments called minds that store them, play them back, and send them on.

When we examine our notions of the body, we observe similar possibilities. I may experience disembodied (nonkinesthetic) states of awareness as, for example, when I am dreaming. But when I experience bodily states, I still do not settle for any body at all. There are limits to what could familiarly be my body yet not the specific body I currently have. I may accept myself as having hair or eyes of a different color. What shifts would I have to make to imagine myself with skin of a different color? Would I become unfamiliar to myself at that point? Or what about imagining myself as a large beetle? When Gregor Samsa changes into a beetle overnight in Kafka's story "The Metamorphosis," there is no question at all that Gregor's personality remains the same. But we are sure that this is possible only because we imagine our mind in a beetle's body while at the same time remaining in the familiar confines of our own body. To test whether the mind retains its identity, we would have to transplant a human brain into a beetle, letting that "self" experience life somatically as a beetle does. How would we feel about expressing love if we had to do so with a beetle's body? Isn't our concept of love connected not only with what we see—what does a beetle see?—but also with what we smell, hear, and feel?

Focusing on the acts of a "thinking thing," Descartes gave little attention to the reason it was so important that those acts of cognition should be regarded as the acts of a self. The self can isolate those acts from one another and can doubt their reality, but not in a manner that leaves the self devoid of all content. The self cannot be neatly divided into its pure (mental) state and its impure (bodily) manifestation because it involves both to the core, though, as Descartes suggests, that core is not susceptible to clear and distinct analysis—at least not yet.

The experience of aging is only one dimension of the general problem of body image. Children only gradually come to grasp that they have a body. Even after they have good motor control over many body parts and can mimic the motions of others, they still do not have a clear notion of what they are as embodied selves. Indeed it may be that we never really know our body as it appears to others or to ourselves in photographs. People often cannot distinguish silhouettes of their own faces from others', or they cannot accurately visualize the size of parts of their bodies. At times it may be possible for people to think of a part of their body as not, or as no longer, belonging to them. This phenomenon of depersonalization is found not only among acute schizophrenics, who can spend hours carefully scrutinizing their image in a mirror, but also among normal people who suddenly discover something on their body that was not previously theirs. This normal depersonalization reflects a time lag in our body image. What we think we are today is what we were yesterday. And when we discover a small change, in most cases we can reverse it. We can snip the first gray hairs and have a mole or two removed. But as the changes increase, we must change to remain the same. As gray hairs proliferate, we can counter by cutting or dyeing our hair. With these multiplying changes in mind, we can see more clearly why cancer can be so terrifying. It is not merely an illness or a disease of our organs and tissues but marks the emergence of a new body growing within us. Its effects are not simply that the affected organs are substandard in form and function but that a new form and a new function are taking hold with a power all their own. From the point of view of the aging body, cancer is just the temporally localized extreme of the depersonalization that takes place generally in the aging process.

A number of phenomenologists, most recently Richard Zaner,[1] have attempted to overcome the false position of Cartesian dualists. Rather than simply "having" a body, Zaner argues, we are more accurately "embodied" selves, selves with a particular spatial orientation and with continually shifting subject-object orientations toward our body. Descartes's ontological dualism cannot account for an entity that is neither mind nor matter but instead embodied self. Although Zaner does not deny the possibility of alienation from one's body, he does deny that in becoming alienated one attains a disembodied state:

1. Richard M. Zaner, *The Context of Self* (Athens, Ohio: Ohio University Press, 1981). See also Zaner's *Problem of Embodiment: Some Contributions to Phenomenology of the Body* (The Hague: Martinus Nijhoff, 1968); and Hans Jonas, *The Phenomenon of Life: Towards a Philosophical Biology* (New York: Dell, 1966).

> If there is a sense in which my own-body is "intimately mine," there is, furthermore, an equally decisive sense in which I belong to it—in which I am at its disposal or mercy, if you will. My body, like the world in which I live, has its own nature, functions, structures, and biological conditions; since it embodies me, I thus experience myself as implicated by my body and those various conditions, functions, etc. I am exposed to whatever can influence, threaten, inhibit, alter, or benefit my biological organism.[2]

How is dualism overcome in such a view? Descartes may have failed to consider the marvel of that "intimate" connection between body and mind, but that failure does not mean that the connection could not be undone. Zaner admits that "embodiment" requires effort and ceases with death,[3] and this admission suggests that the body is a vehicle of self-expression that sometimes fails the self. And if I experience myself as implicated in the trials and tribulations of my body, must I feel owned by it? If my car breaks down in the center of Death Valley, I am likely to become anxious about my situation; but only if I am in a paranoid state might I think that my car has taken charge of my life and now takes full possession of me. Although the "I" in this context is an embodied "I" who may be thirsty and exhausted, this "I" experiences the same feeling of vulnerable reliance that occurs during illness, when my body takes on an alien otherness. The more desperate our situation, the happier we would be to jettison our diseased body for a new, healthy one. It is not embodiment we seek at all cost but consciousness and feeling. That so many people are willing to replace their own hearts either with someone else's or with a mechanical device suggests the limits to our sentimentality about our bodies when conscious life itself is at stake.

Most philosophies of the body analyze the feeling of alienation in the context of health and illness but seldom in the context of aging. There is a crucial distinction between these. Health and illness involve particular psychological states of

---

2. Zaner, *The Context of Self*, p. 52.
3. Ibid., p. 59.

the embodied self and for each illness there is the hope of regained health. But in the case of aging we are speaking of a pervasive change of embodiment. The body is mysterious and problematic not only because of its vast impersonal network of biochemical processes and interactions but also because such processes are organic in a way that affects all organisms—that is, they support a life that first develops and then withers away.

What, then, should be the proper philosophical attitude toward the body? Perhaps we should look on it with a combination of tough-minded dualism and tender-minded monism. The monism of embodiment means nothing if it does not mean that we feel a special relation to our own body, even a certain pride in it when it gets us through difficult periods. Perhaps we may even speak of our body as a "self" in its own right, like a friend that has served us well, and we may feel that we have betrayed our body if we must choose to disfigure it significantly in order to survive. Perhaps, on the tender-minded side, we may even feel an obligation to die along with it. On the dualist side, however, we recognize that the body, ever-changing and beyond our ultimate control, does not comprise our essence. In a sense the sentimentality of the monist view is akin to that of adolescents who believe their first love has no match. All they know of love is what they now experience. Similarly, I know only my body, and the multifarious contingencies of that body undeniably make me what I am in many important respects. But nonetheless, should it be physically possible, I might choose another body. Would a victim of birth defects not choose to have functioning limbs or eyes? Our body is not the same as our body image, and in our judging our body according to norms of beauty and excellence, we have evidence of the tough-minded stance in everyday life.

The process of living involves a fundamental disappointment philosophy has not yet been able to explain. The unfolding of consciousness does not seem to bring with it the willingness to embrace extinction as well. This is not the mere vanity of the living so eloquently described by Lucre-

tius and Schopenhauer but an awareness of the sheer delight of conscious life and of the restless addiction to sensation. Aging casts over this sensory delight a shadow that
illness could never cast. We can always hope that illness will
pass us by, but we have no such hope for aging. As soon as
we fall ill, our sensation is clouded and disturbed, but even
before we are aged we worry that the beautiful sensations
we experience will attenuate and that indeed they may have
already attenuated in comparison with our past experience.
In this respect, at least, the psychological effects of aging are
chronic and pervasive.

Does dualism require the existence of disembodied spirits? The belief that the child leaves behind its Platonic
heaven and enters the world "trailing clouds of glory" may
express the core insight of dualism. But one may just as well
embrace a functional dualism that rests on a materialist
monism, though it is hard to see how such an answer can be
ultimate in any sense. How brute matter could have formed
itself into libraries and museums without the aid of eternal
spirits is a mystery materialism has not even partially explained. Yet the materialism we know which allows us to
speak of physical bodies as material substances does give us
a way to explain the rise and fall of mind: in the beginning
there was matter and its capacity to be energetic relative to
itself; out of this matter emerged forms that made the trans-
ference of energy more and more habitual. This habitualness
eventually produced me but in doing so tied me to a set of
conditions that traverse the entire history of matter. Thus
while emerging out of matter generally, I am free to control
to whatever extent possible its effect on me.

In recent years we have come to apprehend if not a philosophical at least a pragmatic justification for this view. The
computer and biological revolutions give concrete evidence
that someday human minds may travel from one bodily condition to another. The view that mind is just organized matter may not be the ultimate explanation, but the functional
dualist at least is not burdened with the task of explaining a
bootstrap ascent of mind over matter.

AGING AND DEATH

We face death in two ways: as an imminent possibility, a violent event that can end our life at any moment; and as a destiny, a condition we cannot help entering someday, if not now. But we have not yet died; why are we so convinced that we shall? For us living is the rule, not the exception. If we ask what analogical reasoning convinces us we shall die, the answer must lie ultimately in the pattern of life that *includes* death as part of the design. No analysis of probability by itself will convince us that we must die sooner or later because the likelihood of violent destruction approaches unity as time approaches infinity. There is always a chance, no matter how slight, that our fate will depart from the norm. When we think about the biological stages of life that have invariably included the death of all previous members of our species, however, and when we observe these stages in ourselves, then we can only infer that death must be our fate too. Dying, in other words, is one of the things complex biological organisms do, and regardless of particular fates, the process of aging brings us ever closer to dying.

If aging did not exist, dying would be as paradoxical as philosophers have always said it is. But in fact it is hardly paradoxical. Philosophers have chosen to focus on the incomprehensibility of our death—if we imagine we are dead, we only imagine ourselves in a quiet, inert state, unresponsive to others, as children imagine the inner life of the dead—rather than on the quiet process of dying that the aged experience, the closing up of the world, the eventual graying of sensation and desire in the very old. From the standpoint of the pure thinking self, death is always an infinity away. "As soon as you are born you are old enough to die," Jean-Paul Sartre said, thereby giving us courage to believe that the self is timeless, existing in a full-blown state as long as it exists at all. So a man of sixty is no closer to death than a child of several years. Both are an entire world apart from death, and both may enter its realm at a moment's notice.

How should we compare the philosophers' transcendental view of death with the commonsense view? Even if philosophers have neglected the philosophical importance of aging and the developmental view of life, and have instead discussed the adventures of the energetic mind in relation to its timeless "body" as merely a reality external to other minds, is there not something changeless about the self throughout life so that it is always an infinity away from death? In her study of aging, Simone de Beauvoir does not resolve these perspectives. Although she views aging as only a character of the self-for-others—the "I" literally never ages—she also claims that "for the aged person death is no longer a general, abstract fate: it is a personal event, an event that is near at hand."[4] Yet she also says, "The idea of death's coming closer is mistaken. Death is neither near nor far: it is not."[5] And finally she remarks that "it is old age, rather than death, that is to be contrasted with life."[6] The last remark shows a begrudging willingness to accept advancing age as a state of being-toward-death different from the abstract being-toward-death that all who are alive must confront. To be alive is to be no longer in the process of being born; we cannot speak of being-toward-birth when we speak of living. Thus if we regard life from a "digital" point of view in which we are machines that are either off or on, our only options are to live or die. From an "analog" point of view, however, life is a matter of degrees, of more or less.

Although the transcendentalists never puzzle over the emergence of the pure self—there is really no room in their vocabulary for the phrases *I grow* or *I emerge*—nevertheless growing and emerging are what I continually feel myself doing. If so, why not also include the phrases *I decline, I age?* Philosophers traditionally have seen asymmetry between emergence and decline. They are willing to concede the emer-

4. Simone de Beauvoir, *The Coming of Age*, trans. P. O'Brian (New York: G. P. Putnam, 1972), p. 440.
5. Ibid., p. 442.
6. Ibid., p. 539.

gence of the self, even though its rise from contingency to autonomy is incomprehensible, but they assert that the self, once existing, is forever fully itself and does not lose itself piece by piece, like hair falling from a balding head. Do philosophers intend to describe the life of the self or do they prescribe what we should think regarding the self in the living process, including the aging process?

The paradigm of the self's life is its awareness of its consciousness of an object of thought. But this life is hardly continuous within the restrictions of the paradigm. There are moments when the self seems to have no life, yet the self can resurrect itself and proclaim that its life has been temporarily dormant. For the ancient Greeks, Hypnos and Thanatos could be brothers because in neither sleep nor death does the self die. So the philosophical view relies on the common experience of the "return" to self-awareness as a basis for the claim that no matter how decrepit a person may be, the self can grasp that unity of all previous selves and, in effect, like the fittest of adolescents, clearly apprehend its individuality.

The difficulty with the evidence for the transcendental standpoint, whether articulated by philosophers such as Descartes and Fichte or by such commonsense statements as "I will always be myself" and "You can never leave yourself behind," is that we can never be sure we have avoided illusion and deception. For at any moment when I claim I am still myself, I must assume that all my evidence—perceptual, intellectual, somatic, and so forth—accurately describes my previous selves as well. But this assumption rests on relatively unstable beliefs: that my own body image has not changed or that other people, changeless themselves, have not detected a serious change in my character. For short intervals of a lifespan these beliefs constitute a workable hypothesis, but they may not hold for longer periods.

Our language has a number of words for the stages of youth—neonate, infant, baby, child, youth—but we have no names for the stages of aging. Like a machine that either functions or does not, the aging human has no characteristics that require a modification of the concept of person-hood. A machine may perform well or badly, but we do not describe malfunctions as part of its proper life and character. Similarly, there are many pathologies of the life of the self, but these are not usually regarded as intrinsically related to age. Even in Freudian analysis old age is a period of regression to infantile behavior—not a new state but a falling back on earlier habits.

As long as the continuity or identity of the self is elusive, the proper perspective on death is difficult to attain. Death happens to "me," yet as long as I remain me it is no real part of me. In this vein Paul Weiss writes:

> If I lose interest in living, I make it easier to be overcome by other actualities. But I do not cease to be until I lose hold of the being I had possessed. Things and animals, instead, have being withdrawn from them; what had intruded is no longer countered by them. They never did possess it. Only men possess their beings, though only for short periods.[7]

Weiss invites us to imagine a tug-of-war between death and the self, the "surrendering" of the soul either by force (the arrow of Apollo or Artemis that strikes one down) or by deception (the predicament of Faust). One *enters* the state of death. Death is the beginning of nonexistence and the end of being alive. But that it is also the end of dying suggests other possibilities. We could, for example, think of the self as an achievement of nature. It slowly unfolds, reaches its pinnacle of flowering, and then recedes. Being a self means, as Hegel describes it, being in a state of autonomy and acute awareness. It means that selfhood ebbs and flows throughout the living organism, dynamic in it but not identified with it.

Common sense and the prescriptions built on it demand another view, one that accepts the coming-to-be of the self but the passing away of only the organism. The self is fully alive to the very end; indeed, as its extinction becomes more

7. Paul Weiss, *You, I, and the Others* (Carbondale, Ill.: Southern Illinois University Press, 1980), p. 218.

probable, its resistance to it increases. It puts up a fight; in its anxiety and terror it marks itself as a powerful, indignant autonomy that cries out for a higher principle to rescue it from its organic fate. The aged and the soon-to-be-aged do not want to submerge this response in a predefined period of "decline" wherein manifestations of selfhood are no longer taken seriously by other selves.

Is there a middle ground between the transcendental view of an ageless self and the commonsense recognition that aging is a decline of all aspects of living, a decline of the self? On the one hand, we readily allow talk about decline and grant that we are likely to become pale shadows of our former selves as we grow older. The elderly who remain active and alert are beautiful in part because they reflect dynamic personalities that have managed to live on despite all adversity; the young admire in them what they repre-sent—the continuation of brilliant selves of former times. Thus, many an aged actress remains beautiful as the descen-dant and possessor of the glorious being that she was previ-ously. On the other hand, we reject the prospect of embed-ding in our understanding of and discourse about the self any notion of gradualism. By law and custom the self is a full possessor of rights once it achieves autonomy.

How could we weigh the plausibility of each view? In the former view death is a slow, prolonged process that ends life; it goes on during life and in the instant when it is said to "occur," it actually ceases to occur. Death is the process of dying. In the latter view death "greets" the self; it is a new terror, a novel experience. It is a murderer of the self, as if a personified antiself. Both views are specific conse-quences of their corresponding pictures of the self. Which view of death is more desirable? Is aging as slow death pre-ferable to aging as a war against death?

In the second view, more prevalent today, aging repre-sents a failure of biological integrity at once tragic and comic: tragic because the aging self resists it and comic because with the odds so great resistance is foolish. Value is invested primarily in the self and only secondarily in the embodied self. The aging body is an enfeebled friend of the self, a friend who increasingly fails to reciprocate affection. As an object of the self's concern, the body is cared for, but eventually its condition becomes hopeless. Throughout, the self remains unassailed. The benefit of this view is its adamant seriousness about the status of the self; its drawback is its great psychological cost. Projecting aging as a tragic process that subjects the self to a biological fate of the cruelest, most unjust kind is essentially an age-denying view that assumes that the self is fundamentally immune from the effects of aging. To protect the self's status in all of its ages we make an abstraction of the self, a mere holder of moral and legal rights. In so doing we neglect the particularity of life and the feelings of the aged, who must embrace the prevalent view that they are not really changed "in essence." Understandably, the elderly become demoralized as it becomes apparent that they will lose the war against death. Those who are younger increasingly see them as victims, people to be avoided and shut away from the mainstream of social life.

If we accept the view of aging as slow death, we incorporate into the life of the embodied self the process of dying. The self begins to die not long after it matures—a tragic but dignified process. In this monistic perspective it is the self that declines and dies. Each day its individuality grows but is increasingly in jeopardy. In later life the self experiences more and more losses; its familiar world and friends and abilities begin to disappear. Yet as its facilities decline in value, its status rises. We recognize this when we think the elderly are to be respected. Of his father Michelangelo wrote in a poem: "By your dying you taught me to die." The elderly are pioneers not of the chronological future but of the psychological future. They have already arrived at the place where we are going. Moreover, they are travelers from a real past into a real future (now past or present). They are a dying breed, the remainder of a dwindling cohort. They represent a specific period of history and a worldview that is dying with them.

Although this view grants dignity to the aging, it has

drawbacks as well. Are we to take seriously the image of a self that begins to decline in status even though it has more years to live? What are the implications of the claim that a person is only an imperfect reflection of a former self? Should the elderly be given two-thirds of a vote if they are regarded as only two-thirds of the person they used to be? To answer affirmatively would be to misconstrue the position of the monist, who argues that the status of selfhood is defined in terms of both intrapersonal and interpersonal experience. As the personal life of an individual declines—in ways that only the individual at first recognizes—social status rises. The individual ascends from personal, domestic life to historical, social life. If we do not recognize that the elderly of modern industrial society fit this description, it may be that we are unwilling to accept that persons age, not simply bodies.

AGING, TIME, AND NOVELTY

In the previous chapter I examined the relation between time and aging. If time is a relative measurement and if aging is a temporal process, then in some respects aging is relative also. But in what respects? To an insect whose lifespan encompasses a day, humans might seem as eternal as the gods; to the mountains, however, we are ephemera. In short, there is no single answer to the question of how long it takes to live one's life. One answer is that one lives as long as it takes to die a natural death. But death is often "untimely." So we are confronted with a series of confused norms.

We usually mark the biological process of living from birth to maturity to senescence as an objective process that takes the number of years indicated as the maximum lifespan. All members of the species must die within that period, many sooner but none later. A person murdered in adolescence dies an untimely death because that person had "more time" to live. Not the manner of dying but the comparison of lifetime against life expectancy makes the death untimely. Those who criticize abortion as murder imagine an entire lifetime disappearing, as if the fetus possessed this lifetime as one of its attributes, whereas an aged man murdered on his deathbed does not die in an untimely way because "his time was up" anyway. We tend to think of time as an objective quantity that manifests itself in the maximum lifespan of one's species.

But how does time manifest itself to the self? And how does it look in retrospect? Is it radically subjective—that is, can one person at age sixty-five feel that he or she has lived ninety-five years although another that age feels that he or she has lived only thirty-five years? What is the basis for such different feelings? How does one measure whether life is "too long" or "too short"? Embedded in our elementary physical notions is a conception of time that is tied to our everyday experiences. For example, we can measure time in terms of work (the force needed to move an object across a certain distance) and power (the rate at which the force does work). We can then form an equation:

$$time = work \div power$$

For any given quantity of work to be done, time is inversely related to power: the less power, the longer the time required to do the work; the more power, the less time needed. This is a simple, objective relationship, and the units of time involved are of equal duration. But the objective relationship between time and power also gives us insight into their psychological relationship, one noticed by anyone who considers the energy one must expend to accomplish a given task. For machines no such relationship exists. But for psychological beings who plan a task and review their performance of it, time can come to characterize the work experience itself. If much power is available and the task is completed quickly, then it takes only a "short" time. If that same work becomes routine, it would soon take its "normal" time because it would no longer be surprising that it could be done so quickly. Expectancy would no longer affect our sense of duration.

Time, then, is a comparative measure of work effort against past experience. If we are to think about it in a temporal way, an activity must have some element of discovery in it, something we are in the process of learning about. Thinking of activity as a process of discovery helps us to measure our power or output. First we assess how long a task will take, based on past experience; then we execute the task; and finally we observe how easy or difficult it was to carry out relative to our expectations. We measure how powerful or feeble we have become based on the difference between present and past experience.

The problem confronted by the psychologist of time perception is that time values may be the same for different circumstances because time itself is a relative or comparative variable. We measure time by our sense of power, but also power by our sense of time (work ÷ time). If our sense of the duration of fixed time intervals were to increase, our sense of power would decrease in proportion, and vice versa. This reciprocity raises a number of questions. Do the senses of power and time harmonize in an individual at all times? Are there objective criteria for power as well as for time?

We begin with the idea of power. As described in physics, power is the rate at which a worker overcomes both gravity and inertia. However powerful a person may feel, the amount of work actually done can be determined objectively. A child may feel powerful in picking up a brick, but the child does less work than the father who picks up ten bricks in the same period of time. But there is another, subjective, sense of power—the idea that one is powerful enough for the task at hand. One can remain equally powerful (in this sense) throughout life if one continually redefines the tasks to be done. This is what B. F. Skinner advised in a lecture entitled "Intellectual Self-Management in Old Age": "Possibly you like complicated puzzles, or chess, or other demanding intellectual games. Give them up. If you want to continue to be intellectually productive you must risk the contempt of your younger acquaintances and freely admit

that you read detective stories."[8] Clearly this subjective
sense of power does not affect one's real power at different
times. If the notion of power is tied to goals and expectations and those goals and expectations are clearly set before-
hand, however, one can say whether one acts to achieve
those goals more or less powerfully than before.

The passage of time, like the sense of power, relates to
expectation, but is it also relative in a strictly age-related
way? A psychological line is said to divide life into two
periods, the first focusing on progress from birth, the second on the time remaining until death. Once that line is
crossed, concern increases that time is running out. Suddenly the individual feels old. Self-doubt arises, along with
regret for having squandered time and opportunity. Previous standards of progress and growth no longer seem adequate. These feelings are fairly typical of the first crisis of
maturity. They result not from an objective assessment of
the basis for maximum lifespan but from an inductive assumption that our lives are no different from that of other
members of our species and that as a result we can expect at
most another thirty-five years, years that will increasingly
seem to fly by before we can experience them fully.

It is possible to look on the future in yet another way,
however, as utterly unknown. From this skeptical Humean
view, we cannot know the future no matter how confident
we are that our inductive inferences are valid. New discoveries may enable us to live for many more years, for decades
or even centuries. At the same time, no one of any age can
be sure of being alive beyond the next hour. Although the
violent world of the past has been pacified, it has not been
entirely subdued; and even if we could subdue it, we could
not be certain it would remain subdued.

Because it is possible to adopt either the closed inductivist
or the open skeptical perspective, attitudes may differ with
respect to personal time. The inductivist sees future time

8. B. F. Skinner, lecture delivered at the annual convention of the
American Psychological Association in Washington, D.C., 1981.

diminishing as the present and future turn into the past. Then as individuals age and their past expands, their focus shifts from action in the future to recollection of the past. The skeptical perspective is psychologically timeless, and it is tempting to describe it as forever young. It has been called a perspective of cognitive futurity, open and always available as a tool for abstract, hypothetical reasoning.[9] We all possess this future, no matter what our age.

In describing the character of the aging psyche, we have considered instances of relativity that can be traced to the acceptance of certain assumptions, in particular those involving clock time, maximum lifespan, the uniformity of past and future, and the radical severance of past and future. To the extent that the individual does not recognize the influence of these assumptions, we may say that he or she is being deceived. Once the assumptions are recognized, an individual can consider alternative beliefs. But are there even more radical—that is, irradicable—forms of subjectivity and relativity with respect to time and aging? Let us consider some other commonly observed phenomena.

It is often noted that time seems to speed up with advancing years: the years pass by more quickly, and birthdays seem to come more frequently. It is also observed that older adults tend to underestimate the duration of temporal intervals; that is, what seems like a half hour to a younger person may seem like twenty minutes to an older person. When time is socially punctuated (by bells, alarms, and holidays), no wonder the elderly think it is literally fleeting. To underestimate the length of a duration, however, is still to recognize the objective nature of an interval. Our discovery that time has passed quickly is such that we recognize the difference between our experience and what it should have been. Most important, it is we who make the discovery. Even in a controlled psychological experiment, the investigator does

9. R. Kastenbaum, "Cognitive and Personal Futurity in Later Life," *Journal of Individual Psychology* 19 (1963): 216–22; and his "On the Meaning of Time in Later Life," *Journal of Genetic Psychology* 109 (1966): 9–25.

not need to convince the subject being tested that an interval was longer than the subject had thought. The subject accepts the error upon learning what time it is. The discovery that time has passed more quickly than the subject had realized, however, is based on an inference: if this is really the time, then I have been mistaken in believing it earlier than in fact it was. Even if the investigator moved the clock ahead and the subject accurately guessed the time, the investigator still might be able to deceive the subject because of the subject's inductive belief that clocks are usually left to their own devices. This possibility of deceiving the subject suggests that someone who underestimates an interval of time can reassess that estimate solely on the basis of a cognitive belief that a clock measures the objective duration of the interval more accurately. In this belief the elderly are no different from anybody else. They are not locked into a different physio-psychological system of time reckoning.

Why, then, do the aged seem to underestimate more frequently? To answer this question, it might be useful once more to tie together time and action. If the experimental episode involves waiting, perhaps the elderly underestimate the interval because they are more patient. What seems like only a few minutes to them may be much longer because they are able to put themselves physically on hold. And this ability, in turn, may be a function more of training and experience than of age. It is not surprising that as cognitive temporal beings live longer, their time perspective changes. This change seems to result from a growing comprehension of life's processes, particularly the relation between effort and result and between plan and effort. Undeniably, life holds less novelty for the aged than for the young. If life and nature were more volatile, persons regardless of age would react similarly in situations of equal degrees of novelty. Perhaps as the percentage of often-repeated activities increases, it becomes difficult to recognize novelty when it appears. This difficulty should not be considered an unfortunate tendency of the elderly alone, however, but a rational response to unfulfilled expectation.

Anyone who explains that the elderly underestimate duration because of variations in an internal metabolic clock must account for the ability of the elderly to comprehend their mistakes. As the metabolic chemical clock slows down, mechanical time seems to speed up. Conversely, as metabolism is increased, mechanical time appears to decrease. As Klaus F. Riegel suggests,

> Slowing of oxygen consumption observed in aging organisms would be congruent with the observation that time passes more quickly with increasing age. If the temperature of an organism were lowered, metabolism would slow down. Time, defined by the reciprocal of metabolism, should pass more quickly for the organism. Therefore energy transformation and metabolic processes provide a reasonable definition of time-dependent change in the organism.[10]

Can we assume from Riegel's analysis that at some point metabolic and mechanical time are in perfect synchrony and that time is then perceived at its true pace? Can we assume, in other words, that the mature adult lives a full hour every hour of the day, that a child lives several hours in that period, and that the aged live but a fraction of an hour? If the assumption is valid, at the end of the hour the child has an abundance of riches, the adult has gotten what is due, and the aged have been robbed. Again, Riegel:

> Raising the internal body temperature increases the speed of reaction such that the chemical clock runs faster than a laboratory clock: about two minutes of performance time equals one minute of clock time. Lowering the body temperature makes clock time seem faster: about one minute of performance time equals two minutes of clock time.[11]

Riegel is seeking an "interaction between biological and psychological event sequences." But has he established such an interaction? Consider children who during the first hour

10. Klaus F. Riegel, "The Dialectics of Time," in *Life-Span Developmental Psychology*, ed. N. Datan and H. W. Reese (New York: Academic Press, 1977), p. 13.
11. Ibid.

of classroom time have experienced several hours of life. Do they experience that duration as one in which they have extra time at their disposal? Not at all. They cannot even comprehend that in some objective sense "more" time is left between the onset of boredom or distraction and the end of the period announced by the school bell. They know only that they would rather be doing something else but must remain still. This relative sense of duration results not from a metabolic difference between teacher and pupil but from a direct experience that there is something else of more importance to be done. The teacher who designs the learning situation does not experience real time because of a properly synchronized chemical clock; rather the teacher has filled the hour with tasks required for the purpose at hand. Thus we are not correlating performance time with clock time but rather one scale of performance time (the teacher's) with another (the particular student's).

We are inclined to think that the units of clock time are entirely natural as units of living in time because of their regular mathematical properties and the astronomical calibrations on which we base them. However, our choice of units is largely conventional. We define an hour as a twenty-fourth of a day; we could just as well define it as a thirtieth of a day or modify it seasonally the way the ancient Romans did. The "day," with its natural circadian rhythms, is naturally suited to a marking of human living. The "hour" is simply a rough estimate of a workable unit with which to measure many performances in daily life. It is too long for some, too short for others.

Instead of speaking of "time-dependent change[s] in the organism," we should focus upon experience-dependent changes, asking about the tasks at hand—What are they? How interesting are they to the performers? And what about the performers' abilities? Both the young and old suffer from some deficiencies relative to the competent mature adult. That they easily grow bored because a task is too difficult or not challenging enough simply means that the task has been chosen for someone with a different threshold of stimulation (in the case I described above, the teacher's). Children do not construct a world of children but live in the adult world. The elderly too live in the adult world—not the one they themselves created but the one the next generation has established, which reflects that generation's standard of performance, its units of space and time.

A further correlation between time and interest is suggested by experiments whose subjects, under hypnosis, were asked to consider the present of great significance and the past and future of much less significance. Even those who simply were asked to give the present a greater importance showed test results similar to those for the hypnotized subjects. In both cases subjects lost their inhibitions about concrete, present experience, as if they had been given permission to forget social norms and responsibilities. Rather than attacking these norms directly, the experimenter undermined the structure that coordinates them in consciousness. The success of this effort indicates the reciprocity of time and our sense of the nature and appropriateness of norms of conduct. If the norms—that is, our ideas of worthwhile action, career goals, and life plans—change, so does our sense of the pace or timing of life. Likewise if our sense of such pacing changes, our prevalent norms of conduct would be transformed into other norms.

The authors of the experiment suggest the implications of manipulating the time perspective for those in the later years of life: "We would expect that techniques (hypnotic and other) which might induce a sense of expanded present or future in old people would be an antidote to retrograde amnesia phenomena and might even increase longevity."[12] They also suggest that psychic disorders affecting the sense of time might be treatable, like the spatial disorders claustrophobia or agoraphobia. The problem here is that aging is not a space-bound variable. There is no place that all the elderly,

12. P. G. Zimbardo, G. Marshall, C. Maslach, "Liberating Behavior from Time-Bound Control: Expanding the Present Through Hypnosis," *Journal of Applied Social Psychology* 1 (1971): 322.

like dying elephants, go. We mark the progress of life in years, not in miles. When the elderly suffer from temporal claustrophobia, they have more grounds to complain than do the young who suffer from phobias. The inductive facts of maximum lifespan make the elderly person's fear of a narrowing temporal horizon a real fear.

Simone de Beauvoir has given another explanation for the variability of time perception in the old and the young. She argues that because we measure time against the duration of our entire life, the fixed mechanical units of day and year measure different durations, depending on our age. "If a single year amounts to a fifth of our total age, then it seems ten times longer to us than if it represents only a fiftieth part."[13] Two apparently conflicting assumptions seem to be at work here: (1) that the experiential content of a year of life is the same for persons of any age, and (2) that persons of all ages have an absolute sense of the length of a year. According to the first assumption, the five-year-old child whose experience of the year is ten times longer than the fifty-year-old grandfather's must be experiencing that year with the mind of a fifty-year-old who is biologically only five years old. Without such a starting point, how could we determine how much longer the year is to the child? If we speak instead of a centenarian, the child's year becomes twenty times as long. According to the second assumption, as my age increases, the ratio of one year to my sense of the totality of years lived decreases, but this only happens if the temporal value of each year remains the same. Let us consider the case of a person able to expand the content of life experience—by drugs, meditation, travel, hypnosis, and so forth. If, say, the last two years seemed to that person twice as long as the previous four, this experience would reverse the trend of the decreasing value of a year's temporal duration.

Although we should not take de Beauvoir's analysis too literally, it contains nonetheless some valuable insights. For she seems to say that as we age we lose interest in the

13. De Beauvoir, *The Coming of Age*, p. 375.

typical activities of our year. We have, so to speak, seen it all already. Then because we know how the parts of the year go together and because we have mastered those feelings of boredom that torment the five-year-old, we are already living in a stretched-out temporal zone, a zone with no surprises, in which the present is a canvas of varying shades of gray.

THE PSYCHOLOGY OF THE LIFE CYCLE

I have suggested that humans may be the only creatures of nature who conceptualize life as a totality ending in death. Although we are not certain we will die, our natural humility coaxes us to accept our death as inevitable. And although we do not know whether our consciousness will live on beyond bodily decay, our observation that the dead stay dead is so painfully persuasive as to have inspired traditional religious beliefs: if we did not progressively and systematically die, then our interest in the possibility of an afterlife would just be like our interest in science fiction. Religion instead suggests that something miraculous must take place for life after death to continue.

To conceive of life as a totality, however, does not require religious assumptions. Even before we reach middle age, we have ample opportunity to witness life in its final stages. Family and social life provide images of the light slowly dimming in a life. Memories and photographs help us compare past vitality with present infirmity. Aging, as noted, is a way of marking life as a process of slow death. In its broad contours this commonsense image of life is probably as old as civilization. Childhood may have been discovered only in the last several centuries and adolescence only in this century, but the image of life as a journey from birth to death can be found in the literature of ancient civilizations—in ancient Egyptian and Sumerian poetry and in the epics of the Hebrews and Greeks. Indeed the very premise of Plato's *Republic* is that social continuity and stability require a system of government guaranteeing that the process which produces leaders cannot be interrupted by demographic changes or generational conflicts.

In describing the image of the life cycle we must identify the things that comprise the ontology of life—traditionally, persons and their activities. Persons, like all living creatures, manifest life by their activity. That activity itself comprises intentionality, decision, struggle, fulfillment, and compromise. Not all living creatures give equal evidence of these qualities in their activity. And presumably none besides humans know either of finite life or of being alive. Yet even people have no single image of the life process but many images, depending on their interpretations of life's meaning and the various choices of human behavior. When Shakespeare used the metaphor of theater to describe the course of life in the "all the world's a stage" speech in *As You Like It*, he used biological, psychological, and sociological categories to describe the seven ages of man: puking infant, whining schoolboy, lover, soldier, magistrate, comfortable but declining gentleman, and finally decrepit old man in a second childhood, "sans teeth, sans eyes, sans taste, sans everything."

If we must read something into this speech, perhaps it is that the course of life begins with the biological (puking), moves to the psychological (whining and loving), then to the sociological (success) and returns to the biological (infirmity) once more. Herein is captured the popular notion of life as a cycle from "dust to dust." Strictly speaking, of course, we do not experience life as a cycle. Life is cumulative, and only in the very last days of most people does it even approach the primitive condition of the first days of life. And even then the very structure of the older person's experience must be essentially different: the child is sans teeth but doesn't miss them!

Psychologists during the past century have developed the casual observations of Shakespeare's witty character to suit their own purposes. To produce a theory of the life cycle, we must investigate the ontology of being alive and must establish categories that characterize the entire process of living from birth to death. One can be a painter as well as a soldier;

if so, the theory of living must account for both pursuits. When Friedrich Schlegel wrote his *Philosophy of Life*, his standpoint was "the soul" as timeless spirit in its relation to truth and eternity. The same may be said for Hegel in the *Phenomenology of Spirit*. In these works "consciousness" is an ageless activity that only abstractly reflects upon the contingencies that influence it. Subsequently philosophers have failed to consider the effect of the realization that life follows a pattern, thinking, perhaps, that their fundamental studies were as impervious to a psychology of knowledge as to a sociology of knowledge. It remains to be seen whether their thinking is justified. Perhaps a thought, taken in isolation, cannot be said to be young or old, but does this mean that wisdom in the final analysis is not to be distinguished from knowledge?

Psychologists, unlike philosophers, have made at least a tentative start in the direction of producing a theory of life. Karl Bühler delineated five stages of life based on his investigation of biographies: home life (birth to fifteen years), experimental self-determination (fifteen to twenty-five years), culmination of goals (twenty-five to forty-five years), self-assessment (forty-five to sixty-five years), and fulfillment or failure (after age sixty-five).[14] Thus for Bühler life is a great task to be undertaken in some specific form, as if it were a work of art to be prepared for, completed, and then judged. Just as we devised the notion of a maker-god from our own creation of artifacts, we have come to construe life as a labor upon some product whose value may be said to measure our net worth. It is moot whether Bühler himself shaped the analysis to fit this assumption; his own subjects held to it, as we would expect in a study restricted to figures worthy of a biography.

Jung's analysis of the stages of life also contains the notion of life as a goal-directed striving, but in this case the

---

14. For a discussion of Bühler's theory, see Douglas C. Kimmel, *Adulthood and Aging: An Interdisciplinary Developmental View* (New York: Wiley, 1979).

goal is more obscure: "Life is an energy-process. Like every energy-process, it is in principle irreversible and is therefore directed towards a goal. That goal is a state of rest. In the long run everything that happens is, as it were, no more than the initial disturbance of a perpetual state of rest which forever attempts to re-establish itself."[15] Jung conceives of life as a temporary departure from equilibrium. The cyclic dimension is even broader than Shakespeare's: we begin at rest, depart from it, but continually strive to attain it once more, eventually getting our wish.

Jung uses a physicalistic image of life: "The curve of life is like the parabola of a projectile which, disturbed from its initial state of rest, rises and then returns to a state of repose."[16] In that process, however, the "psychological curve of life" often departs from the inevitable trajectory. Jung deplores the attempt to depart from what one is supposed to be at each point in the journey. Youth should not be in descent and old age in ascent. Being in step with the natural curve of life means not attempting to circumvent the unconscious wisdom of human nature. We begin to die, Jung asserts, long before actual death takes place—in the dreams and images the unconscious produces for the conscious self—and we would be better off surrendering to this unconscious force.

Jung's description of the stages of life follows the parabolic curve from rest (unconsciousness) to action (consciousness) and back to rest. In the first stage primal consciousness is born: we compare two states of psychic awareness in a sporadic, unsystematic way. This is the stage of childhood. In the second stage the ego is born out of the recognition that to compare psychic states requires an observer. This is the period of ego energy (from puberty to middle age). In the third stage the complexity of consciousness greatly increases. Ego recognition is no longer satisfying. The testing

15. Carl G. Jung, *The Structure and Dynamics of the Psyche,* vol. 8 of *The Collected Works of C. G. Jung,* trans. R. F. C. Hall (Princeton, N.J.: Princeton University Press, 1978), pp. 405–6.
16. Ibid., p. 406.

of ego strength in new situations begins to wear thin as opportunities to experience novelty decrease. Now the ego recognizes the possibility of its isolation from experience itself; self-awareness becomes more than an awareness of acting, and the question to act or not act comes before it. At this point the person may choose either to act inauthentically, taking on a purely social role and thereby risking diminution of personality, or to recognize that the journey of self-consciousness will come to an end.

Inasmuch as Jung sees consciousness itself as the problem, there can be no conscious solution to this dilemma; both courses lead to frustration. Once we foreclose the possibility of a happy consciousness for the socially integrated self, we are left with only the meanspirited social climber and the underground man. This dilemma is the reason, Jung suggests, that depression and neurosis are so common in men and women entering middle age. One result is an ossification of personality, an unlifelike rigidity in manners and morals. At such a point in life it is important that individuals not look back at their active selves, that they not become hypochondriacs, pedants, applauders of the past, or eternal adolescents. A final and fourth stage of life (extreme old age) may now begin. In this stage one looks beyond the ego to psychic life in general and to a generous life for the individual. Just as the mind of the child emerges out of consciousness, the mind of the aged person sinks back into unconsciousness and the problems of life disappear as well.

Jung's image of the life cycle fails to provide a detailed prescription for everyday life. Other than to recommend primitive existence according to natural instincts, he does not guide us toward a practical philosophy of life applicable to all the rich experiences of growing old. Because his contrasts are too stark and his vision leaves little to hope for, we should characterize his theory of life as cosmic, not psychic. For a better example of psychic theory we should turn to Freud and his progeny.

Freud devoted remarkably little time to the study of the

psyche in relation to lifespan. In 1896 he described to Wilhelm Fliess the four periods of life: preconscious (birth to four years), infantile (four to eight years), prepubertal (eight to fourteen), and mature (after age fourteen). Most repression must occur between the second and third and the third and fourth periods if "normal" psychosexual development is to take place. Once sexual maturity is reached, the psyche is fully developed in its essentials. Freud's early theories explain deviations from normal psychological development—manifested in hysteria, neuroses, and psychoses—as the result of poor integration either of psyche and soma or of various other psychic structures. Sexual drives not excited or channeled properly block psychic energy, thus "poisoning" psychosexual energy or causing it to hemorrhage.

In his early writings Freud also attempted to devise a general theory of nervous activity. Its model was the image of the psyche as a vast piece of neurological machinery whose gears and levers were attached to powerful natural sources of energy that often could not be dampened properly. Unfortunately, the mechanistic model did not satisfactorily explain to him why the psyche was so crafty. A machine may be as intelligent as we can imagine, but could it also be guilty of self-deception? Because Freud needed to answer this question, he had to begin a new analysis of defense mechanisms and repression.

For the mechanistic model Freud substituted a biogenetic law derived from Ernst Haeckel and others, according to which "ontogeny recapitulates phylogeny." The development of individual organisms, in other words, follows the same series of stages as the development of all ancestral species of that organism. The biogenetic law thus encapsulated a method for assessing the normalcy of individual psychic development. The mechanistic model postulated inhibitory and excitatory structures and processes but could not explain how the processes were orchestrated. In broad outline the biogenetic law provided the answer: each individual was born not only with a legacy of instincts and drives but also with patterns of response and strategies for resolving conflict.

This change of perspective from individual to species and from physics to historical evolution enabled Freud to explain psychoneurosis as the manifestation of either arrested development or regression to an earlier stage of development. Neuroses had their socioevolutionary parallels in societies that either became sterile and ceased to change or lapsed into barbarism. Freud assumed that although the natural course for an individual was to develop, this was not necessarily its fate. Rather, fate was determined by particular circumstances, especially early experience, and the physiological makeup of the individual's system. Normal development meant the orderly progression of phases, from oral to anal to genital.

Freud also relied on the biogenetic law to explain the mechanism of repression. Once one stage of development has been surpassed by another, the purposes of the former may be nullified but not its operation, which must be censored to keep the previous stage from reactivating. Freud considered this censoring an altogether healthy response. For example, as we learn that certain smells are pleasing or revolting, we open and foreclose certain avenues of psychosexual exploration.

The stages of life, then, were conceived by Freud as the stages of historical evolution from the amoeba to civilized industrialized society. In a letter to Sándor Ferenczi, Freud presented one particular scenario for this process:

> What are now neuroses were once phases in human conditions. With the appearance of privations in the glacial period men became apprehensive: they had every reason for transforming libido into anxiety. Having learned that propagation was now the enemy of self-preservation and must be restricted, they became—still in the time before speech—hysterical. . . . After they developed speech and intelligence in the hard school of the glacial period, they formed primal hordes under the two prohibitions of the primal father, their love life having to remain egoistic and aggressive. Compulsion, as in the obsessional neurosis, struggled against any

return to the former state. The neuroses that followed belong to the new epic and were acquired by the sons.[17]

Neuroses were no longer considered misfirings of neurons
but the results of a structured social repression of instincts
and prior strategies. Once compulsion was established in
civilized life, dementia praecox, narcissism, and mania became possible. From this perspective on psychosexual development Freud concluded that a person who displayed deviant behavior was a throwback to a level of development no
longer reflected in the most up-to-date form of social organization. His conclusion reflects our commonsense idea of normalcy—something that follows the prevalent social norm.
But with such a transition from neurology to social analysis,
Freud was unable to unify his early clinical work with his
later works of social theory and advocacy.

Adherence to the biogenetic law, however, raised a profound question: if evolution drives psychic development, insofar as this development is an accommodation of the psyche
to the conditions of contingent natural and social history, what
drives evolution itself? In short, how can human psychic development be looked on as a response when what it responds
to is at least in part the world of human creation? As Marx may
have understood, the biogenetic law is itself a good recapitulation of the relation between ontogeny and phylogeny, but it
begins to break down in the most recent phases of evolution.
We cannot postulate internal mechanisms of recapitulation
and thereby account for the wide variety of human psychic
response. Active, living forces were needed to create the imbalances and resolutions experienced in the present and to fuel
evolution into the future. This need for a living dynamism in
psychic development may have led Freud to postulate the
struggle of the individual (ontogenetic) psyche between id,
ego, and superego and the contest on the social (phylogenetic)
level between eros and thanatos, love and death.

17. Sigmund Freud, letter to Sándor Ferenczi, July 12, 1915, quoted in
Frank J. Sulloway, *Freud: Biologist of the Mind* (New York: Basic Books, 1979),
pp. 387–88.

Freud did not formulate a psychoanalytic theory of the life cycle, yet all evidence indicates that he surely wanted to construct one. His later papers on the death instinct and the psychological origins of social structures may have been efforts to describe the phylogenetic counterparts of the later phases of life. What seems clear is that Freud had relatively little interest in the aging individual but great interest in the evolutionary and sociological meaning of postmaturational life. From among his scant observations on aging, however, the following, not entirely coherent, picture may be constructed. The "sexual time of life" is the period between childhood and old age.[18] After that time the decline of reproductive potency produces anxiety neuroses and a relative increase of libido, which in turn produces so much "somatic excitation that the psyche proves relatively insufficient to master it."[19] Thus, he who is the dreaded primal father to later generations of offspring is in fact a fragile, childlike confusion of unfulfilled emotions and desires.

In *Beyond the Pleasure Principle* Freud speculated about the process that sustains and eventually overturns object-centered genital sexuality. He postulated an internalized death instinct that in effect made the individual want to give up its sexual mastery. In a characteristic mixture of psychological and biological concepts, Freud postulated that all cellular creatures contain a mechanism that regulates and harmonizes growth and senescence on the basis of the recognition and participation of each cell in its community of cells:

> We might suppose that the life instincts or sexual instincts which are active in each cell take the other cells as their object, that they partly neutralize the death instincts (that is, the processes set up by them) in those cells and thus preserve their life; while the other cells do the same for them, and still others sacrifice themselves in the performance of this libidinal function.[20]

18. *The Standard Edition of the Complete Psychological Works of Sigmund Freud,* 23 vols., trans. J. Strachey (London: Hogarth Press, 1953–1974), 1:214.

19. Ibid., 3:101–2, 110.

20. Ibid., 18:50.

Freud believed that experimentation with protozoa had shown both that rejuvenation could occur when separate organisms "conjugated" and then separated and that eventually such organisms would have to succumb to the injurious influences of their own metabolic by-products in the immediate environment.

Freud embraced the cell-organism analogy with some trepidation, yet he could not break its hold on him. He realized, for example, that a single-cell animal might live forever if its environment was continually rejuvenated and it had ample opportunity for conjugation. Yet it must have impressed him that these conditions do not exist in nature, and he must have wondered why metabolizing organisms did not evolve that could purify their environment. The most plausible answer was that as conditions for phylogenetic development changed, communities of individuals became established, not just the solitary individual. Because organisms developed in communities, one needed immunity not only from one's own by-products but from those of all others as well. In effect, a biological compromise was forged whereby some deleterious influence was allowed in the community in exchange for certain rejuvenating mechanisms based on specifically communal activities. In so many words, Freud accepted this hypothesis of compromise in his description of the life-enhancing (erotic) character of cell intermingling.

Cellular cooperation kept the chemical activity of each cell from running to final completion, thus continuing the translation of erotic drive from the cellular to the organic level as each composite grew into a unity with each phylogenetic advance. Because libido was literally "stored" in the cellular structure of the organism,[21] the erotic and destructive influences would have to be preserved at each level of organization. Higher organisms with progressively greater opportunities to thwart the original compromise between cell and environment thus had to develop more sophisticated methods of preserving the death instinct as well. Once an organ-

21. Ibid., p. 52.

ism experiences sexual rejuvenation, it is theoretically possible for it to continue reproducing the conditions that make rejuvenation possible. Yet this does not occur in Freud's scheme:

> The life process of the individual leads for internal reasons to an abolition of chemical tensions, that is to say, to death, whereas union with the living substance of a different individual increases those tensions, introducing what may be described as fresh "vital differences" which must then be lived off. . . . The dominating tendency of mental life, and perhaps of nervous life in general, is the effort to reduce, to keep constant or to remove internal tension due to stimuli . . . a tendency which finds expression in the pleasure principle.[22]

In short, the organism desires both stimulation and the cessation of stimulation, moving automatically from one desire to the other. But has Freud explained why it was also necessary for new organisms to replace those already established? Why couldn't established organisms continue indefinitely, moving from pleasure to pain and back again?

Perhaps Freud thought he had answered this question when he postulated the two instincts as tendencies to restore organic life to an *earlier* state of things. The adult becomes childlike, the child animal-like; the multicellular entity becomes unicellular, the organic inorganic. But it was also necessary to explain how the mind could be kept in control by the more basic death instinct. Freud set to work on this problem in *The Ego and the Id*, where he constructed the model of mind as a triumvirate of conscious ego; the atavistic ego, or id; and the ideally constructed ego, or superego. The ego "withdraws libido from the id and transforms the object-cathexes of the id into ego-structures."[23] The id, which includes the aggregate of primitive experiences, is simply the latent phylogenetic reservoir of the organism that governs psychosexual development; the ego represents the actual experienced opportunities of an organism perceptually open to

22. Ibid., pp. 55–56.
23. Ibid., 19:55.

the external world. Evolution requires that an organism react to its environment for selection—and, for Freud, Lamarckian selection—to occur. But the organism is burdened by a past that includes even its connection with "much simpler organisms." Finally, the superego or "ideal" ego is the product of early ontogenetic development, including both our history as "open," experiencing organisms in primitive biological form and the more recent period when our primitive ancestors developed. Due to this development id and superego are closely related, the former as nonmental, amorphous libidinal energy, the latter as a specific "reincarnation of former ego-structures."[24] That reincarnation, for Freud, took the form of the father or father figure. The child, once it recognizes that it has a father, can no longer experience innocent pleasure. A desexualization results that in the young is more obstinately resisted but eventually wins out in the adult as the influence of the superego increases. Through the superego, then, the death instinct works in the higher creative organisms to foreclose unlimited sexual experience.

That Freud believed the superego resulted from the Oedipal struggle and was reinforced through generations of patriarchal organization committed him to the idea that the superego was unique to homo sapiens. If, as he argued, death was not a late phylogenetic development, the same could not be said of the superego. We may then wonder why he thought the superego was a necessary condition for the operation of the death instinct when the instinct had operated so effectively in the lower organisms. And did Freud also believe that desexualization by itself was sufficient to produce death? In more primitive times spontaneous forms of aggression, sadism, and rape may have temporarily harmonized the erotic and death instincts, but eventually the harmony was disrupted by competition between generations for scarce desired objects. During such competition death was violent and natural, and the superego grew out of the frustration of the vanquished.

24. Ibid., p. 48.

In summary, the Freudian life cycle begins with the growth of raw cellular libido, emerges into human ontogenetic form, and progresses by the phylogenetic law through the oral, anal, genital, ego-conscious, and superego-conscious stages. The last two stages involve more loss of function than acquisition of new abilities. Freud argued in *Moses and Monotheism* that the destiny of aging individuals is to become living symbols of dead ancestors and to be drawn down by guilt or a "dull malaise" for having survived their progenitors.[25] Clearly, however, this argument assumes that progenitors must die in the first place; the growth of self-consciousness and the super-ego does not cause death, but vice versa.

Because Freud refused to separate death from the development of the psyche, he was committed to explaining death psychologically. Had he considered any of the biomolecular or physiological theories discussed in the previous chapter, a psychological explanation would have not been necessary. Having been impressed by the power of sexual development as an organizing instrument of psychosocial life, he must have thought that such power required its "match" in an equally powerful and circuitous device. Yet his acceptance of the phylogenetic law suggested to him that all influences on ontogenetic development were already confined within narrow limits. And this limitation must have suggested that the human person represented a terminal phase of evolution. The "dull malaise" he attributed to ancient Mediterranean civilizations, suffering guilt for having killed the ancient primal Father, may have represented the phylogenetic counterpart of the senescence of individual organisms. If so, there was no need for a detailed psychology of later life. Old age was merely a period of psychic exhaustion when cellular libido glowed like a dying coal in a furnace, unresponsive to any stoking or fanning by an ego now fully at the service of the superego.

These speculations must have been troubling to Freud. Why should the "murderous id" kill the vehicle that gives it

25. Ibid., 23:135.

release? This question is the Freudian counterpart to the Darwinian question of why sexually reproducing creatures must grow old and die rather than merely curtail reproduction to harmonize with rates of accidental death. Perhaps senescence really is "murder" by active agents in nature, not just the result of neglect. If so, the whole Freudian universe, with its sun of radiant sexual energy, becomes chilled. After more than thirty years of research, Freud wrote in *Beyond the Pleasure Principle*: "Science has so little to tell us about the origin of sexuality that we can liken the problem to a darkness into which not so much as a ray of a hypothesis has penetrated."[26]

Perhaps Freud's greatest legacy to us is not the collection of theories he formulated but the reminder that psychological life requires complex explanations including variables from all or nearly all of the life sciences and social sciences. We cannot say that he has overrationalized human life and development until we have a better understanding of such ordinary and pervasive phenomena as childhood sexual curiosity and identification, the need for sexual privacy, the love-hate dimension of sexual pursuit, the need for fantasy, the embarrassment of bodily illness, and the fear of death. Freud's theory, with its limited number of theoretical variables, was unified, though not fully convincing.

More recent theoreticians who have sought to explain the psychology of aging as regression from the genital phase of mature adulthood have been less successful than Freud himself in evading circularity. They have argued that the preoccupation of the aged with food and bowel movements signals the reemergence of oral and anal characteristics latent since the beginning of the genital phase. Moreover, bodily preoccupations of the aged and their supposed desire to find parental surrogates in doctors and spouses are said to be other indications of regression to childhood. Hence "the need for regression arises out of the inexorable fact that genital primacy, which was the maturational goal arrived at,

26. Ibid., 18:57.

now diminishes to varying degrees, sometimes disappearing altogether." Yet somehow "many aged people refuse to give up genital primacy and seek to prove they are what they once were. In consequence, we sometimes see aging people trying to behave both sexually and occupationally as if they had not changed."[27] It seems to make no difference to such theorists that the childhood preoccupation with food and feces may be quite different in function from the overtly similar preoccupation among the aged. What is more, the "inexorable fact" of genital decline cannot be used to explain other psychological episodes but itself needs explanation, as our reading of Freud himself suggests. We cannot point to the failure to give up genital primacy as pathological until we can define the normal course. And Freud himself left this area open to investigation.

Attempts to link psychological development with the changing experience of our bodies or of the passage of time seem more worthwhile additions to Freud's observations.[28] Our bodily experiences of childhood and old age are radically different. In old age we watch our bodies gradually deteriorate and recognize the limited future before us. Even if regression takes place, it occurs not because old habits or attitudes once more emerge but because new problems make regressive response one of the possible alternative strategies.

A more systematic extension of Freudian psychology has been proposed by John Gedo and Arnold Goldberg.[29] Instead of looking on psychosexual development as a parabolic trajectory, they postulate a hierarchical process of simultaneous progressive and regressive modes of psychic functioning throughout the life cycle. Genital primacy is not

27. I. Kaufman and N. E. Zinberg, eds., *Normal Psychology of the Aging Process* (New York: International Universities Press, 1978), pp. 81–83.

28. See, for example, Robert Seidenberg and Hortence S. Cochrane, *Mind and Destiny: A Social Approach to Psychoanalytic Theory* (Syracuse, N.Y.: Syracuse University Press, 1964).

29. John E. Gedo and Arnold Goldberg, *Models of the Mind: A Psychoanalytic Theory* (Chicago: University of Chicago Press, 1973).

the end of the story in this scheme, for new chapters may be written after maturity has been attained. In the early stages of development reversibility is possible. With the attainment of maturity, however, development becomes irreversible in the sense that new functions change the operations of previous functions, and therapies applicable to earlier stages are inapplicable to later stages even where regression seems to produce the same symptoms.

In Gedo and Goldberg's approach the child is no longer "father of the man": "We see the increasing complexity of mental life with each transition from one phase to the next as a sequence of shifts of a qualitative nature, with the psyche progressively acquiring the capacity to function in an increasing number of modes, arranged in hierarchical fashion."[30] Ontogenetic development consists of five phases governed by five principles: phase 1, the period after birth, governed by the "unpleasure principle" to avoid disagreeable stimuli; phase 2, the period of ego emergence, governed by the principle of self-determination; phase 3, the period of ego development, governed by the pleasure principle; phase 4, the period of superego function, governed by the reality principle; and phase 5, the period of "adult" response to living, governed by the "creative principle." In the last phase anxiety is more a signal than an uncontrollable affliction, and narcissism takes the form of wisdom, humor, and creativity. This is the level of "expectable adult functioning" for Gedo and Goldberg.

The hierarchical model utilizes the major categories of Freud's work, though not the phylogenetic framework. As a result it eliminates the problem of the psychological significance of aging. It is worthwhile to ask whether the model is open-ended at the top or whether there is an overall developmental contour, including a completion to growth. This question is not so urgent to Gedo and Goldberg because they construe their proposal as a structural-genetic model, not as a causal-explanatory theory—in other words, as a

30. Ibid., p. 173.

description of the various normal phases of psychic life and the pathologies and psychoanalytic techniques associated with them, not as an explanation of the emergence of the psyche.

The most popular extension of Freud's work on the life cycle is that of Erik Erikson. Erikson's model is based on an epigenetic principle: "Anything that grows has a ground plan, and . . . out of this ground plan the parts arise, each part having its time of special ascendency, until all parts have arisen to form a functioning whole."[31] For Erikson the person is born an organism and dies a member of a society. Living is a three-tiered process of change involving physical, psychological, and sociological dimensions. This process consists of six psychosexual stages: oral-respiratory, anal-urethral, infantile-genital, latent, pubescent, and genital. These stages, in turn, correspond to six psychosocial modalities: get/give, hold/let go, pursuit/pretend, make/complete, reflect/share, love/bond. To these Erikson adds two later stages that are no longer part of sexual development: accomplish/take care of and reminisce/reconcile. At each stage the personality confronts a series of crises, which must be mastered for full development to proceed. Ascent to the next stage always represents an achievement, an adaptive response. Rather than being phylogenetically driven, Erikson's model is ego-driven. Each stage is a heterogeneous construction of aspects of the former stage and aspects of the next stage held together in a dialectic dynamic.

Erikson gives greater weight than many of Freud's followers to social factors in psychic development. We live most of our chronological lives as social beings even if we traverse half of life's psychosexual journey before puberty. Our psychosocial adaptation takes place not against a state of nature but against a changing social panorama. We experience simultaneously changes in the individual life cycle and changes in the social-generational life cycle that is the

31. Erik H. Erikson, *Identity and the Life Cycle* (New York: Norton, 1980), p. 53.

particular milieu of our social existence. Freud's image of the relation between personal and social development was essentially the Victorian image of a society that changes at a glacial pace: the weight of stored ego energy in living libidinal forms was hard to budge.

For Erikson, however, the social cycle is more volatile; at times it falls out of phase with individual development, producing people out of season—children without childhoods, elderly persons with no tolerance for getting old. In the typical situation, however, "man's psychosocial survival is safeguarded only by vital virtues which develop in the interplay of successive and overlapping generations, living together in organized settings. Here living together means . . . that the individual's life-stages are 'interliving,' cogwheeling with the stages of others which move him along as he moves them." If these virtues of communication and confidence are preserved, new meanings and opportunities for personal development become possible: "Once we have grasped this interlocking of human life stages, we understand that adult man is so constituted as to need to be needed lest he suffer the mental deformation of self-absorption, in which he becomes his own infant and pet."[32]

Erikson offers this image of "living for society" in his description of the eight psychosocial crises corresponding to each of the stages of life: trust/mistrust, autonomy/doubt, initiative/guilt, industry/inferiority, identity cohesion/identity diffusion, intimacy/isolation, generativity/self-absorption, integrity/despair. Healthy middle-aged development means desiring to be productive, to make a contribution to the ongoing tasks of one's generation; it means not being preoccupied with one's self, not being neurotic or narcissistic. Healthy development in late life means being relatively satisfied and accepting of one's course of life, presumably regardless of the outcome, recognizing that no one escapes the limitations of living life contingently—missing opportunities and meeting

32. Erik H. Erikson, *Insight and Responsibility* (London: Faber and Faber, 1964), pp. 114, 130.

misfortunes by the sheer fixedness of spatiotemporal existence. One acquires during the generative stage an interest in
preparing the world for, and guiding, the next generation;
during this time one works and raises children. Thus if wisdom is to emerge in late life, it must be prepared for in the
seventh stage. Erikson defines wisdom as "the detached and
yet active concern with life itself in the face of death itself, . . . that . . . maintains and conveys the integrity of experience in spite of the Disdain over human failing and the
Dread of ultimate nonbeing."[33]

In Freud's dark picture the superego and id conspire to
vanquish the ego; in Erikson's picture the superego and ego
form a partnership, leaving behind the id, to perpetuate the
social values of the superego. Older persons accept their one
and only life and embrace a comradeship with humanity
past and present. Old age need not surrender to childhood:

> If the cycle . . . turns back on its own beginning, so that the
> very old become again like children, the question is whether
> the return is to a childlikeness seasoned with wisdom—or to
> a finite childishness. This is not only important within the
> cycle of individual life, but also within that of generations, for
> it can only weaken the vital fiber of the younger generation if
> the evidence of daily living verifies man's prolonged last
> phase as a sanctioned period of childishness.[34]

If Freud could reply to Erikson from the grave, he might ask
if a being who develops sexually, with all that that implies,
is capable of living the last half of life without further genital
expression and exploration. Freud imagined a sexual organism that progressively broke down under the strains of libido and society; Erikson recognizes that such strains exist,
but he nonetheless believes they may be eased.

Robert C. Peck has divided Erikson's eighth stage—integ-

33. Erik H. Erikson, "Reflections on Dr. Borg's Life Cycle," in David D.
Van Tassel, *Aging, Death, and the Completion of Being* (Philadelphia: University of Pennsylvania Press, 1979), p. 60; and Erikson, *Insight and Responsibility,* pp. 133–34.

34. Erikson, *Insight and Responsibility,* p. 133. See also his *Life History and
the Historical Moment* (New York: Norton, 1975), p. 128.

rity/despair—into several parts.[35] He argues that as one ages, the maintenance of integrity takes different forms. One must reconcile one's sense of wholeness with the first signs of bodily deterioration. Integrity in this case means valuing mental rather than physical powers. As climacteric approaches, it also means giving priority to social rather than sexual relations. Psychologically, integrity means attaining new emotional and mental flexibility, specifically the ability to shift emotional and creedal allegiance, to be open to new experiences. In later middle age and old age Peck delineates other needed adjustments: the need to differentiate the ego beyond the context of one's work role, the need to transcend the body rather than be preoccupied with it, and finally the need to transcend the ego itself by thinking of future generations and by contributing to the well-being of descendents.

LIFE BEYOND THE LIFE CYCLE

Whereas Freud struggled to combine evolutionary and developmental biology with the clinical problems of psychopathology, hoping to forge out of this amalgam a new scientific theory of psychic emergence, Erikson seemed less concerned with this project than with prescribing proper modes of social and intellectual conduct for the individual at specific periods of life. But does Erikson's approach beg the question? Are there really stages of life once the individual is fully matured? From a biological standpoint there are ontogenetic phases of development, and from a psychological standpoint there are forms of intellectual and emotional development specific to each phase. But what grounds do we have to say that psychological development continues after maturity? Here we face the paradox of personality: personality appears to be a unified continuity of experience but is also supposed to be composed of a variety of experiences.

35. Robert C. Peck, "Psychological Development in the Second Half of Life," in *Psychological Aspects of Aging*, ed. J. E. Anderson (Washington, D.C.: American Psychological Association, 1956), pp. 44–49.

Persons have experiences and are also shaped by them. From the biological point of view, using the same body throughout life means experiencing the world differently at different periods. One feels the stiffness of muscles, for example, and objects seem heavier than they once did. Distances appear longer, staircases higher. Do these feelings and appearances indicate a *personality* shift? Or does the same personality simply recognize that the world has changed? Do a person's complaints about the effects of infirmity give evidence of a new personality in the making or only of the old one confronting new situations?

If what we call the stages of life consist of new sets of problems that occur predictably, then we may not have true stages at all but only a social construct that seems innate. Each person goes through all the stages because each person confronts the same sequence of problems, whose origins are predominantly biological and sociological rather than psychological. Yet there are no problems without the psychological reality that gives them contour and draws out their fearful implications. So once again we are back to the paradox.

Consider the mechanism of transition from one stage to another. Either the transition is abrupt and a structural, holistic change occurs, or it is gradual and the personality, if it changes at all, changes gradually. But just as in biological aging we find it difficult to answer the question of what ages when we contrast the biological organism with its physico-chemical components, so in personality development we find it difficult to answer the question of who changes when we contrast personality and self with the biological and social individual. Perhaps we need to distinguish self from personality: the self reacts to experience; personality results from the self's encounters. Still, however, we confront on an ontogenetic scale the problem of the self's emergence from slime and on a phylogenetic scale the problem of the origins of life and particularly of self-conscious life. But granting that this is a problem for any theory one may choose to adopt, one may separate the phylogenetic question from that of the self's ontology while the self does exist.

Perhaps the paradox of personality may be resolved by saying that the self never changes, that to a remarkable degree the young man who feels for the first time the confusion of a new romance is the same *self* who is buried sixty years later—though a different *person*. What is the self, then? At a minimum it is the total sentient capacity of an organism, the capacity to perceive a unified world. Thus I perceive the sounds I hear as sounds in a world whose objects manifest the colors I see and the shapes I feel. When all the outlets of sentient experience are open and coordinated, we may say a self is operating. Furthermore, however, a self is the reflective capacity to make plans and arrive at conclusions; it constitutes the entire intellectual capacity of an organism. Its foundation is the entire genetic structure of organic life, and in this respect it is not unique. Nor are its circumstances early in life unique. Throughout much of its developmental phase, the protoself gives only standardized responses. Sentient capacity is a necessary but not sufficient condition for selfhood. Full sentience, an accurate sense of the world, and rational behavior according to our notions of it would not make up a self unless memories, plans, and intentions were added. A "self" without the additions might be said to have a personality, as robots that do not behave uniformly might be said to have quirks or personalities. Assuming that a personality manifests the self, something robots presumably do not possess, we might wonder whether robots, with their quirks, have true personalities.

If the personality has a self that is externalized both to itself and to other selves, does the self have a personality? Surely it could not have one at the outset of organic life; its uniqueness cannot be guaranteed for eternity like that of an original idea in the mind of an eternal god. And when the self emerges, must it not be driven externally throughout its life, moving from phase to phase without controlling the act of living an entire life? Because we know that the biological organism exercises no control over its growth from conception, we may find it easy to bring this developmental perspective to bear in our thinking about the self—to assume, in other words, that the lifespan is a series of episodes that happen to the self. If we think this way, however, we take an external view of the self: we compare a child with an adult so that the child seems only a portion of its adult self-to-be. If we take an internal view, then we see the self as something that makes things happen. Even the tiniest zygote, by engaging in metabolic exchanges with its environment, alters the immediate environment around it. This cybernetic interchange seems universally to characterize selfhood. As the organism develops biologically, it produces a pattern of experiences that becomes increasingly unique in the sense that the organism interprets later experiences in light of previous ones.

If we accept this perspective, we can divide the lifespan into just two stages: the emergence of the ultimate self and the maintenance of the ultimate self. During the first stage the community of hierarchical selves that constitute an entire organism is at work. The sum total of these selves is the organism's personality, which already shows signs of uniqueness to an outside observer who is already an ultimate self. Out of this amalgam the ultimate self finally emerges—generally, in our present culture, during the third decade of life. In this second period a person for the first time recognizes personality as a contingent product of experience and an unformed self that may be accepted *or changed*. In this period one also begins to have a relatively consistent, though not necessarily a clearly articulated, philosophy of life. Unless one develops early the skill to analyze the assumptions of this philosophy, one may have to live out the rest of life to recognize all its implications fully.

A philosophy of life may be looked on as a manifestation of Jean Piaget's fourth stage of cognitive development, formal operational thought (the others are sensorimotor, intuitive, and concrete operational thought). At first a person builds with such thought specific models of experience— what kind of person to love, what kind of task to do, and the like. Then a person establishes guidelines for assessing alternatives entailing commitments longer than months or weeks. Earlier in life, a person makes commitments self-lessly. After discovering that alternatives to such selfless-ness exist, that person scrutinizes and evaluates them, ac-cepts or rejects them. This process follows no timetable. Piaget suggests that formal operational thought is possible after age eleven. More determinative than mere mental ca-pacity is the opportunity to experience a variety of life con-ditions. That in wartime we find out who we are may well be true, perhaps because in wartime we must abandon tra-ditional careers and make staying alive and sane our career.

Once the ultimate self emerges, it maintains itself time-lessly. It has no chronological age but marks the passage of time by what it discovers or believes. It is not old or young but only wise or foolish. Wisdom, a function of mental dis-cipline and experience, is related to chronological age only to the extent that the longer a self exists, the more *likely* it is to be able to think wisely—as long as it has the energy to think at all. The young are rarely wise because they have not had the experiences that are needed for a broad per-spective.

Because our moral and social intuitions recognize the exis-tence of an ultimate self, we distinguish between acts com-mitted by children and acts committed by adults. We also recognize impaired capacity to function mentally and emo-tionally; in the last years of a long life such impairment may be conspicuous. Yet for most of one's life as an adult, law and convention recognize a singular responsible self, not a changing panorama of selves. Although it is almost a truism to say that a self that goes through stages is a self nonethe-less, perceptive scholars continually deny it. James K. Fei-bleman, for example, argues that the journey through life is punctuated by "abrupt transitional stages" for which we cannot be prepared and which yield markedly different per-spectives.[36] These different perspectives are formed as we accept different philosophies of life. Each of us is supposed

36. James K. Feibleman, *The Stages of Human Life: A Biography of Entire Man* (The Hague: Martinus Nijhoff, 1975), pp. 14–19.

to have such a philosophy, a product of our position in the life cycle rather than an outgrowth of our individual temperament, reflection, or personality.

Feibleman sees even traditional philosophies as products of particular stages of the life cycle: "Thus it is legitimate to speak of Heideggerian gestation, Humean infancy, Husserlian childhood, Herbartian early school years, Schopenhaurian adolescence, Cartesian youth, Deweyan manhood, Aristotelian and Hegelian maturity, Stoic later middle age, Bergsonian and Heraclitean old age, and Kierkegaardian senescence."[37] Philosophies are like mental forms of biological adaptations, each taken up in turn as the individual confronts a new "environment" in the form of a changed body and social group. This confrontation is always resolved *ex post facto*. According to Feibleman, philosophies are formed to describe new feelings and problems that suddenly appear:

> Life proceeds for the individual as though it were a series of static frames, very much like a motion picture film. The individual always exists for himself as a kind of static self, arrested as it were in the very act he is in the process of performing. He is unaware of any continuity but moves imperceptibly from one static frame to another. Each frame he imagines to be the permanent condition in which he exists. He awakens each morning, in his own view at least, always the same person. Thus he is unaware of maturing or later of declining. He is young; he is mature; he is old; each all of a sudden and altogether.[38]

Yet who is this "he" but the ultimate self? And how does this self make these discoveries within each frame? Are they factual discoveries? Are they discoveries at all, or are they instead resolutions and beliefs that derive from an essentially social conception of human life? Would the desert island survivor have such experiences? And do all persons have the same experiences in all societies? These are questions seldom explored in accounts of the psychology of the life cycle. In fact

37. Ibid., p. 22.
38. Ibid., pp. 219–20.

the failure to agree on what happens in the stages of life suggests that writers who claim to describe various stages are in fact describing frames of mind and prescriptions for coping with different problems. The problems of being the father of a teenage son are not the problems of being a young married man. But the difference has less to do with the passage of time than with the structural conflicts inherent in such different relations.

It may be possible to make some broad generalizations about living. For example, it is probably true, as Feibleman notes, that "old age is an accretion and an increasing formalization at the expense of the interchange. The open system tends to become more closed."[39] The closure may have less to do with being old, however, than with growing old in a static social scene with little opportunity for new experiences. In a finite world, the longer we live, the less opportunity there is; and if we could live as long as Methuselah, we might justly grow bored with everything around us. Deterioration of the sensory processes in late life no doubt contributes in some measure to growing quiescence. Most likely, however, the phenomenon is social and medical, not inherently psychological. If there were genuinely "old thoughts," Descartes could not have produced in middle age what Feibleman describes as an adolescent document, nor would Kierkegaard have written *Either/Or* at age thirty.

Instead of looking at living as an opportunity for continually increasing one's alternatives, most psychologists who study the lifespan agree that middle age should be one's productive period and old age one's reflective period. This model goes back to G. Stanley Hall, who observed that "the function of competent old age is to sum up, keep perspective, draw lessons, particularly moral lessons."[40] (Hall also counseled that it was wise to give up all desire for sexual stimulation in later life.)

39. Ibid., p. 220.
40. G. Stanley Hall, *Senescence: The Last Half of Life* (New York: Appleton, 1923), p. 419.

More recently, Robert Kegan has argued that living is a process of rebalancing the self between phases of acute subjectivity and acute objectivity. He describes six stages of ego progression: incorporative, impulsive, imperial, interpersonal, institutional, and interindividual.[41] The ego moves from the practical to the theoretical: "The community is for the first time a 'universal' one in that all persons, by virtue of their being persons, are eligible for membership. The group which this self knows as 'its own' is not a pseudo-species, but the species."[42] In particular it moves from identifying with the social roles of a career to distinguishing one's career activity from the self that has chosen that particular pursuit. Kegan attempts to provide a psychology of aging that does not require fixed, age-related stages of development. In fact he sketches a picture that represents the emergence of what I have designated the ultimate self, a self capable of autonomy and intimacy, principled action and flexibility. For him personality has a basic unity that activates the struggle to rebalance the relation between person and world. Once the interindividual self becomes possible, it can adopt the dynamics of a previous stage, but "at a whole new level of complexity."[43] Henceforth this self is "ageless"; it chooses how it wants to be, it orders the personality to change or conform, it resolutely takes a vacation from responsibility and surrenders to impulsivity, and it decides when the vacation is over.

Kegan's picture of the evolving self, like Erikson's, is an essentially normative one. It prescribes the "proper" way to grow to full maturity and offers a standard for measuring deviation from "normal" aging but does not prescribe specific behavior that might characterize each period of life. Presumably the same pattern should occur regardless of the social setting in which the evolution of self takes place. The

41. Robert Kegan, *The Evolving Self: Problem and Process in Human Development* (Cambridge: Harvard University Press, 1982), p. 104.
42. Ibid.
43. Ibid., p. 109.

self that achieves institutional, that is, social, reality has further to travel and will be incomplete if that final step to communal reality, interindividuality, is not taken. Like most other psychologists of the life cycle, Kegan assumes that development must be dialectical, progressive, and hierarchical. Yet to what extent is even this assumption valid? If we do not ground psychic development on biological development, as Freud attempted to do, then should we ground it on sociology, as Marx may have hoped to do?

A better perspective is one that recognizes both the contingency of development toward maturity and the need to postulate the existence of the entire person or ultimate self—the subject of moral discourse—who is open to experience, who increasingly controls the conditions of contingency either physically or mentally, and who chooses from a variety of options how to be and what to do. Strictly speaking, therefore, there are no stages after the onset of maturity but rather revelations, discoveries, confusions, and inconsistencies. Among other things, the perspective I propose requires those who investigate the dimensions of aging to study the sociohistorical factors that provide the milieu for such possibilities. After all, how can we develop a psychology of the entire life cycle without first becoming acquainted with the nuts-and-bolts experience of living to see whether sociohistorical variables influence the formation and reformations of self-identity?

3

The Social Clock

The more differentiated a social life form becomes, the more age grading—the association of age with social roles—seems to affect further differentiation. But before age grading can have an effect, individuals must be able to live long enough to occupy several socially graded levels. Primitive societies included the young, the mature, and a few aged patriarchs. Traditional societies revered the elderly, because there were so few of them, as authorities. Today we confront the possibility that entire generations of people will reach old age together. An increasing proportion of the members of advanced industrial/service societies are over sixty years of age.

THE SOCIAL AND HISTORICAL CLOCK

To investigate the social dimension of aging we must first look at the internal dynamics of a society. But before beginning that investigation, we must look at the natural lifespan of a society. Individuals age socially as well as biologically and chronologically. Sociological age is the social meaning given to chronological and biological age. A professional football player is too old for his sport at the age of thirty-eight. But if he retires from playing he might become, overnight, a relatively young entrepreneur.

How is the social clock calibrated? In Plato's *Republic* individuals progressed in a fixed course of education until personal differences in skill and intelligence began to appear. Then each individual was assigned the role that was best suited to his or her abilities. Greater ability required more education. Thus, Plato structured roles and tasks according to his belief in a fixed system of hierarchically structured

truths. Because complex truths require more time to comprehend fully, in his republic those who achieved the greatest
breadth of mind were the older members of society. Plato's
social clock, then, was calibrated by absolute ideals, the ab-
stractions of intellectual study.

In reality, however, the Athenian social clock was much
more primitive. Leadership and power had diverse sources.
A young man hardly in his twenties could become king of
the Hellenes and sit with the elders. In Plutarch's account of
a meeting between the young Alexander and Diogenes the
Cynic, then in his seventies, Alexander and his large en-
tourage approached Diogenes, who was sunning himself.
"You're blocking my sun," the Cynic said, unimpressed by
the swagger of state power. Though made to look foolish for
a moment, Alexander recovered and expressed his admira-
tion for the old seer. The irony of this scene could not have
been lost on Plutarch, who took every opportunity to lament
the disappearance of the Hellenic Golden Age. Here was
wisdom prostrate, but with dignity. It was this impotency of
wisdom Plato's *Republic* was designed to preclude.

Like physical mechanisms, the social clock must be regulated. The processes whereby individuals' roles shift during
their lives cannot be too rapid or chaotic. Yet political revolutions often produce abrupt changes in social roles and timing. Just before despotism emerges, Plato says, there is a
period of anarchy when "the parent falls into the habit of
behaving like a child, and the child like a parent."[1] Here the
social clock seriously malfunctions: the conditions that keep
it ticking regularly are disrupted; individuals are no longer
sure of their "proper" place or role in society as a new order
is established. Even the political designations of Left and
Right may be distinguished by views on how to regulate
social timing. Conservatives see nature and human nature
as the ultimate calibrators of the social clock; leftists see history and economics as the true timing mechanisms.

1. Plato, *The Republic*, trans. F. M. Cornford (London: Oxford University
Press, 1967), p. 289.

Is it necessary to investigate the nature of human social life before the social meaning of aging can be clarified? If aging is a universal human phenomenon, then in any social system the old are old, their perspectives are broad, their personal losses many. Although being old is not merely a social conception, the social meaning of aging is determined by a society's beliefs about persons and the meaning of life. However a society may define old age chronologically, being old invariably means being less useful to society than one once was.

Consider the conservative viewpoint. If society is a fixed milieu that remains, or ought to remain, unchanged from one generation to the next, then social roles result from the natural progression of individual life from birth to maturity. Nature determines when responsible parenting should begin, when love is true love, and when work and play should take place. Society simply provides individuals with the opportunities to fit into existing biological and psychological niches and should be as unmanipulative as possible. The conservative believes abortion is a crime not only because it kills an innocent person (in fact opponents of abortion seldom condemn wars for killing innocent civilians) but also because women of childbearing age ought to have the children they conceive and people in general ought to preserve the results of the natural powers that work through them. If one then regards living as a process that consumes natural forces, the older people become, the more exhausted they become. Because women lose their procreative power earlier than men and may be more easily worn out by continual childrearing, it has been easy for conservatives to represent the male as a powerful life-giver who dominates and controls the raw material of social life—women and children. And from this vision of male power flows the conservatives' romantic fixation with oligarchy and patriarchy.

If society is a slowly evolving organism that in dialectical fashion both affects and is affected by its environment, the focus shifts to the stage of life of the social organism under consideration. Just as new biological capacities emerge suddenly after a slow process of growth, so new social roles or modifications in the timing of established roles may develop overnight once the infrastructure is in place. The culture of old age that has appeared in the past two decades follows the slow development of a medical and scientific infrastructure. We cannot interpret the significance of this culture properly unless we know whether to regard the workings of the social clock as natural or historical.

Perhaps there is a third possibility that combines the conservative and Marxist views. In this case, social evolution does occur; the social clock for a given generation is itself driven by an intergenerational social clock, which in turn is driven by changeless natural rhythms. Civilizations rise and fall just as organisms live and die. This was Arnold Toynbee's view but not that of Hegel, who thought that what emerged—civilized, full-blown human life—could eventually control the very conditions of emergence. Historically, societies have risen and fallen. The earliest societies in Sumer had a fragile basis in nature, appearing and disappearing as crops and livestock flourished or died. The direct impact of nature attenuated, however, as the smaller city-state societies became complex, diversified cultures. And as complex cultures developed, the historical social clock—the consciousness of tradition, the sense of cultural forms as continuous—came to dominate.

Plato's educational system was an attempt to transcend the historical social clock, but he recognized that an element of narrow selfishness that entered the system would easily be compounded and would overturn the entire apparatus in one or two generations. In reality the cause of social decay may be much less insidious. Civilizations may rise because novelty and adventure are powerful motivators, and they may fall because duty and repetition are not. A vital civilization must continually rebuild from the ground up. A nation of great natural wealth can easily become an industrial giant but cannot maintain that standing by simply doing over again what has been done well. Only when a worker has been chastened by unemployment will he or she return happily to the assembly line or desk. The entrepreneur faces a similar problem, but on a larger scale. If a business is successful in its early years, the owner has two choices: diversify or stagnate. If, as is more likely, the enterprise flourishes only when the owner is in early middle age, the owner's later years may be filled with satisfaction and pride of accomplishment. For workers not there at its creation, however, the thriving enterprise becomes a vehicle for repetition and monotony.

Both conservatives and Marxists must confront the problem of novelty and repetition. The conservative must posit a natural society with enough enterprises to keep social stagnation at bay. The conservative usually finds sufficient energy for growth in scientific innovation and an undying profit motive. Marxists, however, argue that the conservative overlooks the problem of economic scale: individual entrepreneurs have increasingly less opportunity to establish new businesses as larger corporate enterprises systematically investigate the frontiers of innovation. The entrepreneur is increasingly limited to offering services for the new products produced by established corporate operations.

Marxists propose, in contrast, to reinterpret social labor and enterprise as a serious ritual whose boundaries are subject ultimately to control. They would make work an end in itself and sociality the reward for individual effort. Recognizing that repetition is inherent in labor, they would attempt to keep repetition within tolerable limits. Even though socialism recognizes that monotony is the greatest threat to social equilibrium, it neglects the greatest source of energy in new cultural forms and societies: the zeal to discover. Ultimately these opposing forces—the desire for novelty and adventure, on the one hand, and for structure and routine, on the other—one centripetal, the other centrifugal, must be balanced by controlling the outward impulse and disciplining the inward impulse.

In modern industrial societies the burden of repetition falls on the managers and workers who carry out the projects of the dreamers and schemers. Marx suggested that workers become alienated from nature, from themselves, and from their fellow workers when tasks do not keep them interested in the process of labor at each stage of production. The more they take from nature, the less there is for them to take without first going through an act of commodity exchange. But the experiences of entrepreneurs are similar: the more successful they are, the more they reduce the opportunities for further success and for practicing the abilities that most satisfy them. A version of Machiavelli's warning to the prince— that the more generous he is, the more he deprives himself of the opportunity for further generosity—also applies to entrepreneurs. They become managers or they withdraw their energy from the structures they created. In either case that structure takes on a life of its own. Its energies become contained in a preestablished structure, and it becomes part of a static economic world.

As the units of economic exchange grow larger, it becomes more difficult to modify the social roles of the individual during the life cycle. In the economic state of nature—that is, in preindustrial society—the periodicity of the historical clock was hardly detectable. The long wave rhythms of nature— climate and global temperature variations—profoundly affected population density and cultural intensity, but social roles were fixed by the hunting and gathering operations necessary to sustain social life. In such a society the elderly were a "luxury" to keep around as long as younger members did not have to pay too high a cost to care for them. They served as story tellers, healers, and teachers when times were tolerably good.[2] Because a long life allowed them to observe the consequences of actions and events, the elderly naturally served as educators in preindustrial society. Their long expe-

2. Accounts of aging in both relatively prosperous and harsh subsistence societies are included in Pamela T. Amoss and Stevan Harrell, eds., *Other Ways of Growing Old* (Stanford, Calif.: Stanford University Press, 1981). In "The Old People Give You Life: Aging Among !Kung Hunter-Gatherers," Megan Biesele and Nancy Howell describe a picture of useful later life; in "Old Age Among the Chipewyan," H. S. Sharp describes a society in which the old are looked on as burdens.

rience also enabled them to take on priestly functions and to segregate generations and control their exchanges. In gerontocracies the elderly typically controlled access to marriageable women, a practice continued more covertly in modern societies that regulate sexual relations by law.

As industrial society developed, with its characteristically rapid emergence of unprecedented situations, the knowledge of the elderly became less important. During the late nineteenth and early twentieth centuries the social value of the elderly began to decline. Young workers, who presumably could do a better job, replaced older ones. A new class of elderly persons emerged who had retained inherited and accumulated wealth no longer available to young working families.[3] Others among the elderly began taking pensions, living lives of poverty or near poverty yet at the same time burdening productive economic life.

Today the elderly are generally thought to make up the third stage in a three-stage process of urban socialization: education, work, and retirement. Their roles are fixed by education that is segregated by age, by personnel management policies, and by pension and social security systems. Being old by and large means being retired. And being retired increasingly means living among other retirees in the Sunbelt of America. If current trends hold, by the end of this century slightly more than 12 percent of all Americans will be sixty-five or older, increasing to nearly 20 percent, one in five, between the years 2020 and 2030. If there is a historical precedent for such percentages, it has gone unnoticed by historians and social anthropologists.

Simone de Beauvoir ascribes the decline of the status of the elderly to the rise of property rights that began in the late Hellenistic period, particularly the rise of a money economy. Once such an economy took root in Hellenistic Asia

3. For detailed discussions, see David H. Fischer, *Growing Old in America* (New York: Oxford University Press, 1977); W. Andrew Achenbaum, *Old Age in the New Land* (Baltimore: Johns Hopkins University Press, 1978); Jill S. Quadagno, *Aging in Early Industrial Society* (New York: Academic Press, 1982).

Minor, however, it still had a slow, lingering development through the Roman period and the Middle Ages as counterbalancing influences and traditions came into play. Roman society rewarded old age through the patrician system but also ridiculed it through its poets. Perhaps only because the old *were* so powerful could they have been ridiculed by poets such as Lucan, Ovid, and Juvenal. Property rights and money made possible the division of the elderly into rich and poor and changed their status from that of educators to that of plutocrats. As Socrates confronts Cephalus in *The Republic* we see these two roles side by side: Socrates the educator and Cephalus the wealthy retired businessman. While welcoming Socrates, Cephalus tells him what life in old age is like:

> Some of us old men often meet, true to the old saying that people of the same age like to be together. Most of our company are very sorry for themselves, looking back with regret to the pleasure of their young days, all the delights connected with love affairs and merry-making. They are vexed at being deprived of what seems to them so important; life was good in those days, they think, and now they have no life at all. Some complain that their families have no respect for their years, and make that a reason for harping on all the miseries old age has brought. But to my mind, Socrates, they are laying the blame on the wrong shoulders. If the fault were in old age, so far as that goes, I and all who have ever reached my time of life would have the same experience; but in point of fact, I have met many who felt quite differently.[4]

That difference, as Socrates notes, is a matter of wealth, which Cephalus admits is necessary for virtuous living in late life. Such a distinction would have been unthinkable in a society that did not allow the accumulation of wealth as well as the exercise of power.

Two cross-cultural conceptions useful for systematically analyzing the role of the elderly in society have been proposed: the balance between the costs of maintaining the elderly and their contribution to the productive society; and the degree of

4. Plato, *The Republic*, pp. 4–5.

control the elderly have over the resources necessary to sat-isfy the needs of younger members.[5] It is questionable, how-ever, whether such conceptions can apply to industrial and postindustrial culture. As long as a significant number of the elderly can control a considerable proportion of a society's wealth, they might also be able to control the very balancing mechanism in the first, cost-benefit, measure. Most revolu-tions have to some extent pitted youth against old age. It is reasonable to assume that no matter how bad the living con-ditions were for the minority of aristocratic elderly protected in their eighteenth-century palaces, they were decidedly bet-ter than conditions on the street. In democratic societies younger members can reduce government-controlled sub-sidies of the elderly through legislation, but it is unlikely that this curtailment of wealth could proceed very far as long as the current concept of ownership prevails in Western soci-eties. We do not think it immoral that an elderly widow or widower controls a large investment portfolio, just as we do not usually consider bringing moral or even nationalistic con-siderations to bear on the financial strategies of investors of any age.

Besides posing a problem for social theory, increasing lon-gevity has also raised new problems for political and moral philosophy. Should a society attempt not only to keep each citizen alive and healthy but also to guarantee that citizens of all ages will be actively represented in that society? Should the elderly constitute only a limited percentage of a society for fear that beyond that percentage they threaten the society with economic contraction and cultural decline? Perhaps, as I suggested above, socialism may be looked on as a somewhat heavy-handed attempt to deal humanely with this question. A capitalist always prefers a young society, if given a choice between two societies, one young, the other old, and each with equivalent spendable wealth. Younger consumers prom-ise profits over a longer period of time. Under socialism, however, as the very name suggests, social relations are a

5. Pamela T. Amoss and Stevan Harrell, "Introduction: An Anthropo-logical Perspective on Aging," in *Other Ways of Growing Old,* p. 5.

greater good than commodity exchange relations. Thus, as the median age of a society increases, opportunity for capital expansion seems to lessen. Furthermore, as the members of a society live longer, the likelihood increases that they will confront the problem of boredom and repetition noted earlier. (The younger person, regardless of objective conditions, has more opportunities because that person has had so little experience.) Socialism recognizes and seeks to treat this problem primarily by socializing the activities that constitute work. Thus Marx's belief that he had discovered the laws of history in economic relations really amounts to a somewhat pompous boast: we ought to be able to control the nature and meaning of social roles at the point where the mechanisms of the social clock interact with those of the historical clock.

MODERNITY AND DISENGAGEMENT

The friends of Cephalus complained that life was better in earlier times and that "they had no life at all" in the present. Perhaps this complaint has something to do with the saying Cephalus mentioned to Socrates to the effect that people like to socialize with others their own age. We say that people who socialize in this way have "something in common." What could it be? Are we not all just separate selves living in the same real world?

Understandably, a forty-year-old man, recognizing how different he is from teenagers, would not want to keep company only with them or try to befriend them as he might, perhaps, someone his own age from a different culture. The reason for this preference appears to relate to the sensitization that takes place in early maturity when a person finally comes of age. To come of age means to recognize that the present is your time and to make that present the model for reality. The experience has individual and social dimensions because individuals both define and are shaped by their time. The historical context of their early life provides the conditions and raw material—the economic circumstances, the mode of artistic expression, the political beliefs, and the social expectations. With these, individuals produce their own particularized world. Because of the generational nature of biological reproduction in socially organized structures, each cohort thinks of the established world in which they mature as the world of their parents. When they have changed that world, it becomes *their* world, which will be marred by the next generation.

A sense of temporal belonging may be even more important than a sense of spatial belonging. A cohort may move from one place to another and to some degree recreate the place they left, calling it *New* England or *Little* Italy. But they are given only one time to cherish in memory as the time when the world first became unified as a nexus of *their* interests and opportunities. To such persons there is only one president, only one musical style, only one way to be married, and so forth; all the subsequent ones are variations on the major chords but are mere approximations at best.

From the perspective of a fading authentic world we can distinguish several more refined dimensions of the tripartite social life cycle of the individual: life without a world (from birth to adolescence), discovery of the world (early maturity), adventure in the world (maturity), and contraction of the world (late life). During the final process, as the world of the individual contracts, memorabilia, pictures, and idealized memories come to symbolize original lived experience. Consider the following recent description of the inhabitants of Sun City, Florida, a retirement community:

> Sun Citians keep their houses with the same fanatical tidiness: the fibers in the carpets are stiff from vacuuming; the tables reflect one's face. . . . But the interiors of Sun City houses are not anonymous, for Sun Citians are collectors; their houses are showcases for family treasures and the bric-a-brac collected over a lifetime. . . . Almost every living room has a cabinet filled with pieces of antique china and gold-rimmed glass. On the tables are ship models, sports trophies, carved animals, china figurines, or trees made of semi-precious stones.[6]

6. Frances FitzGerald, "A Reporter at Large (Sun City Center)," *New Yorker*, April 25, 1983, p. 86.

Sun Citians may not be as well off as Cephalus, but they too have achieved a happy accommodation with a present that is not fully their own. It may not be true that they have "no life at all," but the life they have is a highly rarefied and protected one. It lacks robustness of the sort possessed by young active families able to move from job to job and to rebound from crises. When the means are available, life appears to have only a museum-like, alienated quality for many older individuals.

Does modernization produce this alienation of the elderly, or does each generation's discovery of the world mark it with a historically contingent uniqueness that eventually sets off the forces leading to modernization and rejection of the previous generation's world? Subsequent generations that perceive older people as part of a cohort or a generation (for example, the "lost generation," the Beat generation, the generation of the sixties) feel an increasing obligation to produce a culture of their own. And they pass on the knowledge of their own achievement to younger generations, beginning many a lesson by telling how things were done "in our day." Each generation prides itself on its unique achievement. And each generation covertly conveys to the next the value of breaking with the past even while overtly advocating conformity to the status quo it has achieved.

The alienation of the generations is a phenomenon tied almost exclusively to industrial and postindustrial society and at bottom may be driven by economic forces. The opportunities for technological innovation have accelerated in the past century and will probably accelerate even more in the computer age. The hardware one generation uses—the pots and pans and appliances and clothes—seems to characterize the activity and identity of that generation for a while. Although innovation occurs rapidly, the new hardware becomes obsolete just as rapidly.

Even revolutions in artistic styles and fashions have occurred with accelerating frequency. The American Revolution and the French Revolution brought about the first systematic and conscious revival of classical (Greco-Roman) art forms, but since the beginning of the nineteenth century revolutions in style have, with increasing frequency, revitalized the forms of more recent periods. A single generation may now experience several styles as belonging to their world as long as they can identify the source of the innovation among themselves. In the arts as in technology, the causes of innovation are essentially economic. Music, for example, is no longer the isolated concert-hall experience now supported primarily by generations that knew such concerts as a bona fide part of their world. For recent generations music exists in the form of an electronic commodity, just as drama for these generations exists as film and now video. Art permeates the culture, increasing the opportunity for its consumption and widening its impact.

Does this harnessing of art by salesmanship mean, then, that the Sun Citians are temporal émigrés, whose world has fled them and whose alienation is primarily economic in nature? Or does it suggest that generational marking is an inevitable and natural (evolutionary?) trait, built into each generation of our species as a mechanism for reducing errors? Consider some implications of the second possibility. If curiosity is built into each new generation as an adaptive mechanism, then a species can question innovations and impartially investigate alternatives. If rebellion is built into each new generation, also as an adaptive mechanism, then the cost of constant change does not exceed its evolutionary benefits for a species, and a decision to produce a creature in perpetual revolution must have been made eons ago in our biological heritage. In the first case, where only curiosity is natural, generational marking is not inevitable because a fair questioning *may* reveal at some point that innovation for its own sake is no longer necessary; in the second case, where rebellion is natural, such marking is inevitable but only on the assumption either that there is an irrational element in adaptation or that the environment changes so rapidly that generational as well as species adaptation is necessary. Whatever plausibility the evolutionary option has may be less a function of nature than of society in general. Thus the economic interpretation of social aging ultimately seems sounder. From this perspective a dialectic emerges with the onset of accelerated technological innovation. First, technological innovation makes changes in material comfort possible; second, changes in basic comfort produce changes in general lifestyle; and finally, changes in lifestyle lead to an ideology that marks each generation—a system of beliefs about work, leisure time, and ultimately, even if it is never clearly articulated, the meaning of life itself.

This economic perspective gives a historical contingency to the process of discovering the world. Even though it is a brute biological fact that individuals must enter a world not of their own making, there is no reason individuals must associate that world with the efforts of the previous generation. Instead, they may take a broader perspective even *during* the period when they are discovering the world and they may see the world as a product of many generations and many conditions. Such individuals remember fondly in later life the time of their life, the years of sexual discovery, and the first taste of accomplishment and social esteem, but they neither regard particular cultural products as exclusively their own nor feel disenfranchised by the products of later generations.

This broad perspective, however, requires a view of culture and humanity that assumes that whatever is preserved is up to date, including the Parthenon, Mozart's symphonies, and the music of the Beatles. We regard as antique the works we think of as creations of a particular psyche in a unique time. But antiquity is a formal, not a substantive, quality. To define something as antique means accepting the psychology of modernity that marks something as new simply because it is proclaimed as new even if it is a form clearly revived from an earlier time. The motivation for such a proclamation—it is now well known—is economic. Although fashion designers and artists desire to leave their own lasting mark on the world of style and art, their efforts to produce mass changes in current fashion are motivated primarily by the great rewards of social esteem—the fame and mobility and freedom that only money and monied connections make possible.

In recent years discussion of social obsolescence has centered on the much-debated theory of disengagement proposed by Elaine Cumming and William Henry. They described disengagement as "an inevitable process in which many of the relationships between a person and other members of society are severed, and those remaining are altered in quality."[7] The theory itself consists of nine hypotheses: (1) Inevitable death and the eventual decline of ability lead to a mutual severing of ties between a person and others in the society; (2) Release from interaction leads to freedom from control by norms and thus to further disengagement; (3) Disengagement of men and women differs to the extent that their social roles differ; (4) In modern industrial society disengagement may be initiated by the individual or by "organizational imperatives," or both; (5) Society has a great influence in determining when disengagement is acceptable for an individual; (6) Disengagement leads to reduced social life space, resulting in crises and loss of morale; (7) Decline in ego energy, life space, and a sense of an open future indicate that the internal disengagement of an individual is beginning; (8) Disengaging roles are less hierarchical, normative, and symbolic and are more egalitarian; and (9) Disengagement is a culture-free concept, though its precise cultural form varies.

The controversy has focused on the normative impact of the theory: is the theory based on biological realities (1) and does it really describe culture-free conditions (9)? And if individuals do not fit the model, are they anomalies or are they resisting disengagement? On the methodological level one might doubt that the theory can define the nature of the role from which disengagement is supposed to occur. If death is ultimate disengagement, is the corporate chief ex-

7. Elaine Cumming and William E. Henry, *Growing Old: The Process of Disengagement* (New York: Basic Books, 1961), p. 211.

ecutive officer with many daily contacts and interactions ultimately engaged or actually less engaged than the coterie of old men who sit in the parks of urban America and argue furiously about politics and life? For example, as a measure of "life space" Cumming and Henry proposed the frequency of contacts with relatives, close friends, neighbors, and co-workers; they measured "ego energy" according to subjects' interpretations of ambiguous pictures (thematic apperception tests), interpretations that Cumming and Henry claimed show an inclination to either activity or passivity. They measured "morale" by responses to questions such as "What age would you like to be?" and "If you could live your life over again, in what ways would you like it to be different?" Yet each of these measures might give false readings and might leave the investigator to choose among them.

Disengagement theory also has been criticized for not considering sufficiently the psychological dimensions of aging.[8] A socially disengaged person may be highly engaged psychologically; or disengagement may wax and wane in old age. A person mistakenly diagnosed as dying of cancer may disengage, only to engage once more when the diagnosis is corrected. Finally, one's interpretation of the meaning of work— as a necessary evil or a personal fulfillment—will determine one's attitude toward retirement. For someone who has disliked working, retirement may be a time of reengagement.

The problem of assessing disengagement is similar to that of assessing the factors that produce life satisfaction.[9] We

8. See, for example, Arlie R. Hochschild, "Disengagement Theory: A Logical, Empirical, and Phenomenological Critique," in *Time, Roles, and Self in Old Age,* ed. J. F. Gubrium (New York: Human Sciences Press, 1976), pp. 54–79. See also the paper by David Gutmann in the same volume, "Alternatives to Disengagement: The Old Men of the Highland Druze."

9. For an example, unfortunately typical, of such a problem of assessment, see Joeylan T. Mortimer, Michael D. Finch, and Donald Kumke, "Persistence and Change in Development: The Multidimensional Self-Concept," in *Life-Span Development and Behavior,* vol. 4, ed. P. B. Baltes and Orville G. Brim, Jr. (New York: Academic Press, 1982), pp. 263–313.

cannot measure such satisfaction by asking respondents how much autonomy they have on the job or whether their jobs give them opportunities to exercise their skills. A person with a positive self-image may be highly satisfied in later life, but perhaps only because that person took the course of action promising the least tension. In other words, people may have a positive self-image not because they are high achievers but because they take few risks. The issue is not whether social scientists can measure perceived life satisfaction but whether their analyses include accounts of the context and meaning of respondents' descriptions. It may seem democratic to leave to individuals the analysis of their own sense of autonomy, but social science cannot disregard the nagging question of whether personal assessments are accurate.

A similar abstraction from any context characterizes analyses of the normative nature of social timing. It is understandable that individuals believe there is a proper time to experience such predictable events as leaving home, getting married, having children, being promoted, and retiring; it is also undeniable that many of these events have biological determinates. But again we must take care not to regard the events of life as if they themselves were causal factors,[10] something we do when we consider the possibility of a time-disordered social relationship—for example, a mother who returns to school, an executive who retires at forty to take up competitive sailing, a worker who refuses to retire. In R. K. Merton's model of social timing, five relationships between age and social role are possible: conformity (having the right goals at the right time), innovation (having the right goals but not in the right order), retreatism (rejecting both goals and timing), rebellion (redirecting both goals and timing), and ritualism (timed behavior but without goals).[11]

10. This point is made by Orville G. Brim, Jr., "On the Properties of Life Events," in Baltes and Brim, Life-Span Development and Behavior, vol. 3 (1980), pp. 367–88.

11. Merton cited in Mildred M. Seltzer, "Suggestions for the Examination of Time-Disordered Relationships," in Gubrium, Time, Roles, and Self in Old Age, pp. 112–25.

Such a model, as it is generally used, provides empty explanations or even psuedo-explanations of concrete behavior
and choice. We could not, for example, take seriously the
argument that teenagers drop out of school because their
sense of social timing is off. Instead, we would insist on
examining their social class, environment, and beliefs.

Economists turn increasingly to macroeconomic investiga-
tions of aging as the implications of aging populations for
social and economic relations become more pronounced. Fertility rates are thought to have a greater impact on the percentage of the population over sixty-five than longer lifespans.
Barring a reduction in life expectancy because of disease or
war, a population will age if its young members have fewer
children, because an increasing percentage of its members
will arrive at age sixty-five. If replacement equals mortality
in a population, then about 59 percent of that population
would be eighteen to sixty-four years old. If the cost of care
per individual is greater for members over sixty-five than for
members under eighteen, a given population will have to
spend more per capita to care for the estimated 17–19 percent over sixty-five than for the 22–24 percent under eighteen. Such a shift is bound to affect productivity and the
gross national product.

Given the current arrangement of sovereign nation-states
and the great disparity of wealth in the world, a nation could
support an even higher percentage of people over sixty-five if
it controlled and imported wealth from younger, poorer
countries. Such a possibility, however, becomes increasingly
unlikely as colonialism diminishes. At present economic relations influence the patterns of social timing by affecting the
aggregate distribution of wealth. Originally, as more wealth
became available during the period of industrial expansion,
mortality decreased among both infants and the elderly, but
as wealth stabilized and became concentrated in the hands of
a few, fertility began to decline. As the median age increased,
the effects of an older population on production and consumption further changed the economy. Five such changes
have been suggested: decline of productivity, decline of both

vertical and horizontal mobility, decline of typical patterns of consumption in favor of more specialized patterns, increase in savings, and decrease in investment.[12] Translated, these changes mean that more and more service and white-collar professionals are locked into dead-end positions, unable to advance as rapidly as their superiors did; more and more manufacturers are going out of business or catering to an older clientele; and more and more people are saving for reasons of security and investing in low-risk, government-backed financial instruments.

Such a situation is bound to produce a variety of strains on the normal, or traditional, pattern of social timing. Retirement would have to be postponed to increase the productivity of the older population; and trade-oriented education for the young would have to be emphasized to get them into useful positions and to socialize them rapidly for a long productive work life. The value of the very old would be debated once more, as it was in earlier times.

SOCIAL IMAGE AND AGE TABOOS

Human beings now recognize each other as belonging to a single species. Such recognition, however, is not innate. Only a few centuries ago Spanish explorers doubted that the natives of South America were really human beings. The question that shaped the debate was rather abstract: did the natives possess immortal souls? More concretely, it must have been obvious to the explorers that the natives possessed enough human qualities—language, emotion, sexual attractiveness—to render the theological question all but moot. Perhaps humans did not recognize their own kind so readily at times when, for example, issues of cannibalism and bestiality were not clearly defined. When we consider the elaborate mechanisms of species recognition in the higher animals, however, this possibility seems unlikely. It

12. Robert J. Clark and Joseph J. Spengler, *The Economics of Individual and Population Aging* (Cambridge: Cambridge University Press, 1980), chap. 9.

is far more likely that the recognition of the social species presented, as it continues to present, the greatest source of confusion and suspicion. The social species is the subclass of humans belonging to a specific group—"us" as opposed to "them."

Two kinds of markings delineate the social species—those for the outer boundary of each group and those for internal rankings within each group. Historically, spoken language and physical appearance distinguished one group from another until adults realized that it was possible to learn foreign tongues rapidly and systematically. Children always took to language, and no doubt the existence of bilingual adolescents must have done more to advance the cause of assimilation than anything else. Intragroup signals, by contrast, were historically more varied, ranging from those with natural origins whose interpretations were socially bound to those whose origins and interpretations both were socially bound.

The social valuation of the individual's physical appearance is partly personal and subjective, partly social and conventional. Because gross physical deformities have always seemed to signal a deformity of personality, they have marked individuals for exclusion from group membership. Within a range of variation, social species implicitly sense how a whole and entire person ought to look. Physical ability and coloration are additional natural signals with social and conventional meanings. The preference for blond hair as a symbol for ethereal beauty might be akin to the preference for gold and silver as symbols of value; the preference for dark hair and red hair as symbols of power and fertility may be akin to the preference for iron and copper as symbols of strength and power. No doubt these metaphors cannot be traced to a simple source but to shifting experiences and perceptions—the light of the sun, the darkness of night and of caves, personality traits associated with hair coloring, and so forth. Metaphors of skin coloring are similarly complex, but because human behavior affects the degree of darkness possible in light-skinned populations, coloration is a symbol of behavior as well as personality. For example, when peasants are dark, the bourgeoisie prefers to be white and stay indoors. But when the peasants leave the fields for the factory, the bourgeoisie comes outdoors, using coloration to signal its ability to be a sun-loving leisure class.

For civilized humans the variety of signals becomes increasingly more refined as civilization becomes more complex. What could be said by wearing good, clean, functional clothing in earlier times now requires the latest designer fashions. The imperative of choice cannot be avoided. No matter how casual one might wish to seem about matters of style, one's appearance still tells about one's self-image and values. Even among primitive cultures some fine distinctions are necessary; these are regulated by the rituals of body painting and scarring. Paint highlights the facial and muscular features and signals rites of passage and social stature. Australian aborigines cover their bodies with mourning paint when a loved one dies; Maori women tattoo their faces to disguise wrinkles and make themselves look younger; Papuan women are tattooed in stages to mark their progress toward the age of marriage; some Japanese practice *irezumi,* or body tattooing, to "clothe" the body and mark its owner as unique and desirable. On their dark skin, where tattooing is not effective, Africans use scarification to mark tribal and clan membership, social status, and personal feelings. Sexual attraction and social status are the two functions, not always separate, of body art and clothing. In Anglo-American culture high cheekbones and a strong chin are marks of authority and stature in both sexes, as are beards on men and short hair on women; dimpled chins, slender faces, and long hair are signs of submission and gentility.

Where bodily social signals are important, the process of aging presents a series of opportunities and problems. Indeed, because ontogenetic development and aging occur in the first place, in societies that continually measure status—that is, in nearly all the societies that have ever been studied—the struggle to maintain or acquire status continues as individuals age. And insofar as women have been

marked traditionally for attractiveness and men for authority, the aging process has had a greater impact on women.
Older women become obsolete as women, whereas men
acquire greater stature with age. In primitive gerontocracies, where old age confers increased privileges, the elders
control marriageable women by increasing the number of
their own wives and producing daughters by them, whom
they can then dispense to the younger men.[13] In modern
society the situation is far less contrived, but there is a parallel effect. Men retain the potential for reproduction and
so may be encouraged to consider themselves suitors of
young females. In other words, age constitutes no barrier
to them, and the male-dominated society provides an opportunity. Women, by contrast, have faced a "terror" in
getting older because they have accepted the sexual double
standard.[14]

It has been argued that the process of measuring social
status by age, age grading, is an attempt to create structural
social order amid the inherent flux of biological reality:

> Age-systems give ageing a cultural stamp. Insofar as age-
> systems allocate status to named segments of the population
> who share the same, culturally defined, segment of time,
> and that status incremented through time, age-systems are a
> device to make the cruel descent through life to decay as if
> it were an ascent to a superior, because senior, condition.[15]

Because societies reproduce themselves biologically, they
must value individuals qua individuals at least by giving
them equal opportunity. We cannot measure individual social worth until a person has lived a good part of life. During
youth and initiation we have no way of knowing what that

13. Uri Almagor, "Gerontocracy, Polygyny, and Scarce Resources," in
Sex and Age as Principles of Social Differentiation, ed. J. S. Fortaine (London:
Academic Press, 1978), pp. 139–58.

14. Elissa Melamed, *Mirror, Mirror: The Terror of Not Being Young* (New
York: Linden Press, 1983).

15. P. T. W. Baxter and Uri Almagor, "Observations About Generations," in Fortaine, *Sex and Age as Principles of Social Differentiation*, p. 176.

social worth will be, so we confer worth automatically and try to justify what we have done through education. Yet plainly because individuals age and continually lose their value—according to current attitudes—societal norms are bound by a double standard: because persons are valued a priori, they must retain their worth even when it declines. As I have noted, traditional gerontocracies have attempted to control this problem of declining social value by ritualizing authority. Present Western societies confer status partly according to traditional cultural norms and partly according to economic power. A woman can jump back several age grades by having cosmetic surgery. Her social self is measured by the company she keeps rather than by her chronological age, as in traditional gerontocracies. It is questionable, however, whether postindustrial society would endorse this novel departure from traditional roles and expectations.

Cosmetic surgery gives an older person a younger appearance. Because of better medical care and the nature of labor in the service economy, it is plausible to think that individuals in their fifties and sixties who have not had a catastrophic illness might genuinely feel young by the standards of their parents' generation. Cosmetic surgery could bring the appearance of such persons into conformity with their attitudes. But should those same persons truly believe themselves to be young, they would be deluded. And if, thus deluded, they insisted not on a younger *look* but on a transformation into a genuinely younger self, they would risk social disapprobation even in societies relatively free of age grading. Such a transformation would have to be total and not superficial to diffuse the suspicion of fraud. The attempt to maintain a frozen image of an earlier self eventually leads to tragedy because the contrast between inner and outer, form and function, grows with the years. "If we know a thing to be useless and fictitious," Santayana wrote, "the uncomfortable haunting sense of waste and trickery prevents all enjoyment, and therefore banishes beauty."[16]

16. George Santayana, *The Sense of Beauty* (New York: Dover, 1955), p. 98.

There is another sense in which beauty may be "banished" by cosmetic surgery meant to correct the deterioration of normal aging. Beauty may be in the eye of the beholder, but regardless of the beholder beauty always emerges as both scarce and highly particular—scarce because not all experiences contain it (indeed only a small number do) and particular because the person possessing it has a "beatific" status: few persons are so fortunate as to be beautiful, and those so blessed are presumed to have a special status, almost the status of the divine. Cosmetic surgery, however, works against these intuitions. It renders beauty a purely phenomenal and mechanical reality. With enough surgeons and enough money we could make beauty plentiful; but in so doing we would transform it into only an ersatz elegance that we would soon tire of.

In postindustrial societies cognitive control over the processes of what might be called person turnover is achieved by age grading in the earlier stages of the life cycle and by cultural age stereotyping in the later stages. Individuals have a remarkably clear idea of the appropriate age at which to be a student, father, mother, productive worker, and so forth. Personnel managers cut through the difficulty of judging personal ability with such rules of thumb. Furthermore, each society maintains an image of a typical member of each age-graded group—an image on which casting departments in Hollywood rely. In tradition-bound domains such as education and religion, gray hair is a mantle of respectability, whereas in innovative domains such as business it signals fixed habits and mitigated ambition. What is the function of these images? Perhaps in domains where roles count more than individuals, the stereotype tells prospective initiates how to replicate established role behavior even as it tells those responsible for fitting individuals to roles who the best candidates are. Dress and appearance are codes that help individuals decipher the essentially intractable mystery of self-knowledge, personality, and motivation.

When the social image to be preserved is crucial, an age taboo traditionally has helped to preserve it. Increasingly, however, age taboos are losing force. Although age may restrict roles in the military, in the wider world of daily commerce we assume that age without reference to ability is not the key factor in most occupations. We make similar assumptions about the world of politics even though we accept constitutional limits on age for officeholders. Because we know age does not automatically confer wisdom, we cannot justify such restrictions regardless of the likelihood that age and wisdom will coincide. In the world of personal relations, too, individuals can evade stereotyping by age. Friendship is theoretically possible between mature individuals of disparate ages, but as we have seen in the previous chapter, to achieve such a meeting of worlds requires great sympathetic and analytic abilities on the part of both individuals.

Why do individuals make so little effort at friendships that cross generations? Perhaps they find unsettling the asymmetry in the greater need of old for young than of young for old. The young, after all, expect to inherit the wealth of the old no matter what happens. The young neither need to know nor care to know the internal life history of the old. Although the old need the young to keep the wheels of socioeconomic life turning, any comfort and support they receive comes from their own cohort. Thus the cohort allegiance of the young may signal a recognition, however dim, that each cohort sinks or swims together and its members must be for one another the primary source of support.

I have isolated two asymmetries relating to social age grading: that between male and female reproductive periods and that between the life expectancy of young and old generally. But are these essentially biological differences the *entire* basis for social age grading? I have also noted that age grading in early life is partly justified because it allocates social labor efficiently. But after maturity it may on balance be more counterproductive than useful. Surely the business world is less productive when workers become demoralized because their status has not kept pace with their age. If age discrimination can be overcome, older workers may remain more involved and productive.

By and large, however, considerations of efficiency may dominate when all aspects of social life are considered. The business of society is not simply business and social production but self-preservation and continuity. If children are grouped by age, then at puberty they will be likely to direct reproductive desires to those around them who are also novices and have similiar life experiences. With this grouping by age and experience as the dominant mode of mating behavior, the rest of the life cycle is locked into place— marriage, work, children—and society is preserved from the ground up. The need to segregate generations may be one reason for the persistent controversy over issues affecting adolescent sexual behavior, and it may explain why the culture of romantic love is so cherished. If late adolescents are led to believe that they alone are situated to experience true love, then it is reasonable for them to waste no time in pursuing that goal. Adults conspire here by keeping from adolescents the deep dark secret that sexual passion at forty and fifty can be just as intense as at twenty.

The taboos that prohibit intergenerational sexual contacts and specify proper sexual behavior at each stage of the life cycle help regulate the social clock and maintain the full sequence: sex, marriage, work, children. Traditional societal norms accept as genuine only the sexuality that is expressed in this sequence. But sex outside the norms continues in the private lives of individuals.[17] Older men in disproportionate numbers rely on the fantasies and images of pornographic art, having been judged sexually superfluous by the culture of romantic love. Retirees of both sexes, feeling free from the threat of strictures, may engage in sexual relations with whomever they feel close to. This unofficial sex life is allowed as long as it does not disrupt the main sequence and its goals: the production of children by adults who in being responsible for their progeny must also be socially responsible.

17. Judith Brier and Dan Rubenstein, "Sex for the Elderly? Why Not?" in *The Age of Aging: A Reader in Social Gerontology*, ed. Abraham Monk (Buffalo, N.Y.: Prometheus, 1979), pp. 195–213. The literature in this area has grown rapidly in recent years.

RESETTING THE SOCIAL CLOCK

I have suggested that socialism confronts the problem of the mechanized social clock by discovering the historical conditions that produced the structure in the first place. Thus it seeks to transfer the social *modus operandi* from maximizing profit to maximizing dignity. From an economic standpoint, to desire dignity is far less efficient than to desire profit. Similarly inefficient, however, is the intermeshing of nature and society that produces creatures who age while they are still socially active and worthwhile, creatures who are considered a burden, forgotten, and thought to belong to times past. One of the supreme ironies of political philosophy has been the association of socialism with collectivism and capitalism with individualism. Capitalism is socialistic in its belief that individuals in the aggregate automatically and systematically working to maximize utility produce on balance the society with the greatest personal freedom and social justice. (Only in the heyday of social Darwinism did capitalists believe that a superior energetic minority benefited from capitalism and that this situation was all we could ever hope for.) Socialism, in contrast, is individualistic in postulating the need for a mechanism that makes particular individuals watchdogs over the main economic trends of a society. And the clash between the two systems has really come down to being a clash between individuals—the rich and the revolutionary—who know what is at stake. In this struggle candor has not been a virtue on either side. On the capitalist side it has been more severely trampled, however, for capitalists have announced their commitment to a free society of individual pursuits even though they have known the cost of this commitment to the workers. The workers who serve another's cause and expect their own reward in the aggregate increase of wealth in the total system pay in lost opportunity far beyond the direct compensation they receive for their labor. Capitalists have also recognized that being at the center of decision-making power allows them to benefit from the latest developments.

Capitalist opposition to socialism has been caused by the threat of socialism to this privileged placement, not by disagreement over the proper (more just) mechanism for creating social happiness.

Thus the difference between these opposing views turns on the question of whether the basic unit of concern in a political economy ought to be the living human individual in *all* phases of life—from birth to old age and death. Capitalism's answer has always been that the genuine social entity is the individual at the maturity of productive and consumptive power, bidding in the marketplace, responsive to trends, moving with energy from one opportunity to another. An individual successful in this sphere will have the wealth to raise other healthy, well-adjusted individuals and will be secure in old age. Because modern capitalism has not fulfilled this promise, the welfare state was created to help pay the social costs of the system.[18] The alliance between capitalism and welfare programs, however, is clearly unstable. If aggregate wealth does not increase, if the rate of profit declines, then the welfare state and capitalism will come into conflict and one or the other must be sacrificed.

The socialist option turns everything on its head. The dignity of individuals is the master yardstick against which all economic strategies must be measured. The energies of adventuresome entrepreneurs must be channeled into pursuits that bear no harmful social costs in either the present or the near future. Unfortunately, socialists have not articulated this contrast clearly or often enough. Indeed socialism has seemed to care little about the last stages of life. Marx spoke often against the exploitation of the young, and in socialist folklore promoted at every opportunity the image of the new communist youth unfettered by the bad habits of their elders. Mao Tse-tung's communism attacked the Confucian philosophy that granted inherent status to the old

18. Michael Harrington, *The Twilight of Capitalism* (New York: Simon and Schuster, 1976).

and turned the youthful Red Guards against the entrenched cultural leadership.[19]

Socialism, however, represents only a necessary, not a sufficient, condition for adopting a new attitude toward the social clock. It is a necessary condition because it recognizes the possibility that humans can manipulate the hitherto quasi-natural realm of culture and society. Marx's historical materialism assumed that history could be transcended by an awareness of the economic driving force of historical change. But socialism is not a sufficient condition for change inasmuch as its focus remains the economic sphere; if the attitude toward the social clock is to change, a cultural revolution is required also. Maximizing dignity means scrutinizing all phases of the lifespan to isolate and eliminate sources of repression and injustice. In concrete terms dignity depends on the recognition that children and the elderly have rights hitherto ignored or denied them. If socialism means thoroughly self-conscious economic planning, it should also mean thoroughly self-conscious cultural planning. The planned society of a segregated retirement community is not the answer. Both the elderly and the young should retain full social value, and both should be fully integrated into the network of social relations, into "real" society.

What is ultimately social about socialism, then, is its recognition that the primary product of society is sociability; the production of goods and services only in part helps to achieve this end. Under traditional monarchies the few privileged elderly enjoyed great stature; old kings and queens enjoyed the services of young bodies and minds. In that society the author of *The Passionate Pilgrim* could complain that "crabbed age and youth cannot live together." Under capitalism the stature of the few increased to the stature of the several. But proportionately the number of elderly also increased and so now nothing less than a thorough retinkering of the social clock may be necessary to expand that stature once more.

19. Thomas W. Granshow, "The Aged in a Revolutionary Milieu: China," in *Aging and the Elderly: Humanistic Perspectives in Gerontology,* ed. Stuart F. Spicker, Kathleen M. Woodward, and David D. Van Tassel (Atlantic Highlands, N.J.: Humanities Press, 1978), pp. 303–20.

4

Ageism and Social Justice

The first three chapters of this study looked at the process of living through time from biological, psychological, and sociological perspectives, each discipline providing a perspective on human activity from birth to death. Like the plants that spring up, spread their leaves, and eventually wilt and decay, we are at least and always biological beings. The mystery of birth is no less mysterious for us than it was for our ancient ancestors. We are biologically part of a vast network of generations, each linked to another.

The moments of our individual lives are also linked biologically as moments of living exertion—of breathing, moving, eating, hurting, and feeling well—that make up an intricate system. Our own bodies are mysterious to us—that is, we may wonder not just about our race and local lineage but also about our particular physiology and physiognomy. The more we understand the body and the influence on it of our behavior, temperament, and environment, the more we can see how the ultimate self, the self that remains the same through aging, molds the body to its needs. The modern aging body is not just a biological kingdom but a moral kingdom as well, so that one can plausibly argue that only part of human aging occurs naturally; the remainder individuals themselves produce. If the aging program can be modified by new information that triggers subroutines, then the living person contributes to his or her own aging process in a slow but continuous way.

We are psychological as well as biological beings with a philosophy of living. Most of us see life as a multistage affair with excitement and enthusiasm at the early stages, reflection and resignation at the final stages. Popularly conceived,

life is a journey, a march through time from birth to death
marked by, and subdivided into, periods of growing, matur-
ing, and aging. Those who journey measure their progress
against the experiences of their own cohort and their ancestors. But the relation of the ultimate self and the psyche, like
the relation of the ultimate self and the body, is not always
harmonious.

If we do not decide in our early life that we will "think
young," on what grounds can we decide to "think old"?
Does the ultimate self have the power to accept and proclaim that it is now time to be old, or does it simply begin to
feel old and then discover itself becoming old and worn to
the bone? If every determination is a negation, as Spinoza
observed, then being old is *not* being young. Memory preserves for the elderly, however crudely, the experiences of
their long lives, and the successive arrival of new generations destroys for them any pretense of youth.

Psychologically, graying human beings often look on their
transformation as a magical happening, an almost alien intervention, but in fact no aging can take place without a
mind to interpret that transformation precisely as aging. If
we lived in small social units, this psychological transformation would be harder to accomplish than it is now in postindustrial society. The old patriarch did not give up without a
fight, and we can imagine that once he was dethroned, his
life was over. As sociological beings, we invariably age in
public. The anonymous strangers who see us know our age,
and even if we do not, for the moment, show it, we know
that eventually we will.

The ultimate self confronts not only the tensions of biological and psychological aging but also the stress of aging in
modern society. Because modern society since the industrial
revolution has been structured primarily according to criteria
of efficiency, the pattern of programmed social development
has been dictated by cultural and economic and, lately, bureaucratic norms that define one's place and role with respect to one's age. Yet the social system is not geared to
efficiency alone. If it were, it would favor the old over the

young and would value the ability to do just one job—the one best suited to each person—throughout an entire life. Instead, it favors advancement and change as the essence of life itself. Efficiency must be balanced against continuity. New arrivals must be added to the social system and earlier ones moved along, eventually to the periphery. In response, a whole culture has arisen in which individuals seek and take rewards, slow down and take time off, and disengage. Today a young Michelangelo will not become an old Michelangelo, but only an old man.

What are the implications both for social justice and for a philosophy of aging of the issues raised in the first three chapters of the book? Knowledge creates not only technical choice but also moral anguish. If aging is fully natural only in the state of nature, then a person can be morally implicated in the process of biological aging and a society morally implicated in the process of sociological aging. And it is necessary to ascertain the limits of responsibility, apportioning that responsibility between persons and nature. In other words, the legal notion of contributory negligence on the part of a victim needs to be brought into play at the very outset as we consider the moral dimensions of aging.

Except in rare situations, there has been little historical inclination to blame individuals for aging as we blame criminals for their actions. Even in Genesis, Eve's punishment was to die, but not specifically to die of old age. Aristotle attributed physical corruption to the "imperfect" motion of the earth relative to the sun, which produced seasons of generation (spring) and corruption (fall). Nowadays we consider aging a primarily natural phenomenon, and although we might partially blame alcoholics for the physical degeneration and aged appearance of their bodies, we would never blame a child for being born with progeria.

We have no choice but to continue looking on aging as a blameless, nonnegligent process, at least until we can reverse it entirely and control it at will. At such time, we might blame a person for the consequences of actions or the failures of performance that result in aging. Overcoming natural aging, however, would not preclude our passing judgment on the negligent behavior of persons in cases of physical self-abuse. The opposite of the progeria case—in which an unknowing victim suffers from a genetic disease—in a nonaging society would be people willfully poisoning or infecting their bodies with agents that bring about natural aging. Such an act would be entirely moral. We can, however, distinguish between the responsibility of such a person and that of the young victim of progeria, though the line of demarcation will move with our ability to control the fundamental processes involved. The biological theory we adopt will affect the moral judgments we make about a person's aging. If we adopt program theories, for example, rather than wear-and-tear theories, we will believe individuals to be far less culpable for their conduct.

What can be said about biological aging cannot be said so easily about psychological aging, in which humans are more fully implicated. That individuals feel old and useless cannot be attributed entirely, if at all, to a condition of nature. One recent author has suggested that although we may be living longer than ever before and feeling physically younger at a later time in life, we are also being made to feel socially older sooner than ever before: "If old age is that point in the life cycle when redundant and socially irrelevant individuals are to be removed from active participation in social life, it is clear that old age is occurring at a relatively earlier age now than ever before."[1] No organic changes need occur to indicate the onset of old age, for it begins in the collective social mind as reflected in the minds of those individuals—politicians, judges, educators, entrepreneurs—whose thinking accords with prevalent social norms.

However, before we can make the treatment of the elderly a standard for criticism of the social structure, we must

1. David E. Stannard, "Growing Up and Growing Old: Dilemmas of Aging in Bureaucratic America," in *Aging and the Elderly: Humanistic Perspectives in Gerontology,* ed. Stuart F. Spicker, Kathleen M. Woodward, and David D. Van Tassel (Atlantic Highlands, N.J.: Humanities Press, 1978), p. 18.

be clear about the pattern of aging in contemporary society. Although it is good to explode the myths of aging, is exploding them enough to forestall continued social discrimination against the aging? Does ageism parallel in all significant formal respects the discrimination of sexism and racism?

THE CONCEPT OF AGEISM

Robert N. Butler, who coined the term, defined *ageism* as "a process of systematic stereotyping of and discrimination against people because they are old, just as racism and sexism accomplish this with skin color and gender. Old people are categorized as senile, rigid in thought and manner, old-fashioned in morality and skills. . . ."[2] In *Why Survive?*, Butler counters the social myths and stereotypes of aging. First among these is the myth of aging itself:

> The idea of chronological aging . . . is a kind of myth. It is clear that there are great differences in the rates of physiological, chronological, psychological and social aging within the person and from person to person. In fact physiological indicators show a greater range from the mean in old age than in any other age group, and this is true of personality as well. Older people actually become more diverse rather than more similar with advancing years. There are extraordinary "young" eighty-year-olds as well as "old" eighty-year-olds.[3]

Other myths Butler counters include the myth of unproductivity, the myth of disengagement, the myth of inflexibility, the myth of senility, and the myth of serenity. The elderly are capable of great feats of energetic output; the works of Artur Rubinstein, Golda Meir, and Pablo Picasso immediately come to mind. Anyone old enough to recall those sturdy individuals who came to the United States before the turn of the century from countries such as Italy, Poland, and Ireland and who worked in the railroad yards

2. Robert N. Butler, *Why Survive? Being Old in America* (New York: Harper & Row, 1975), p. 12.
3. Ibid., p. 7.

and foundries of the Northeast and Midwest can have no doubt that the hard brown bodies of those grandfathers were as strong at sixty and seventy as the bodies of most youths today are at twenty and thirty. Those men were not taught to grow old gracefully.

The elderly are also capable of a richly integrated social and personal engagement. Those immigrant grandfathers had wives who had produced a half dozen offspring or more and who remained central figures in their children's lives well after those children had left home to raise families of their own. The focus of the immigrants was the immediate and extended family—their children, their numerous cousins, and aunts and uncles. There was room aplenty here for engagement.

Inflexibility too is more a trait of personality and circumstance than of age. Butler argues that older people whose options may be narrowed by job discrimination and declining earning power may attempt to retaliate against the young by voting down expenditures for education and social programs. Their voting pattern demonstrates not that they have grown conservative with age but that they are trying to protect their own interests, confident that no one else will.

Senility, too, Butler argues, is a generalized term that in the popular imagination includes not only senile dementia and Alzheimer's disease but also anxiety, depression, paranoia, and forgetfulness. Often symptoms are caused by poor diet and substandard living conditions that in turn may be caused by a decline in social esteem or the loss of a loved one. In these cases, the apparent senility may be treatable and reversible. In other cases genetic malfunction or arteriosclerosis may irreversibly damage the brain, producing a severe impediment. But if such damage appears early in late life (at sixty to seventy years of age), it ought to be considered a condition of the sort that can occur at any stage of life; if it appears later (at eighty or ninety years), it may be regarded as a predictable, but not an inevitable, consequence of aging. In either case, the stereotype equating aging with senility is gratuitous.

The last of Butler's myths—the myth of serenity—is an idealization of late life as a period of carefree living, a time for adults to finally relax and indulge themselves in hobbies, travel, and homemaking. In reality, aging is more likely to bring with it anxiety, depression, and anger. What appears to be serenity in fact may be resignation, a sense of futility, and perhaps even a desire to keep the young in ignorance of what is to come.

To counter these myths, Butler suggests that national and local social policies be restructured to eliminate poverty, malnutrition, and discrimination in housing and work; and redirected to improve the standards of health care and nursing home care and to increase opportunities for continuing education and training. But he also suggests the need for pervasive changes in social life, without which the policy goals he envisions could not be realized:

> American society and institutions have grown fixed, inflexible and class oriented despite the continued existence of "social mobility," the social scientists' term for "getting ahead." There are now hard-core rich as well as hard-core poor; military, technological and social classes; public and private bureaucracies; tedious tenure in academia; seniority in unions and Congress. . . . The Protestant ethic, the dread of death, the worship of technology, efficiency and productivity—all for their own sake—contribute still further to the already-described compartmentalization of life's activities. America has arrived at middle-age, one might say.[4]

But we cannot decompartmentalize a society without affecting drastically the meaning it attaches to work. If that meaning is to be found in the product that results from work, then the age of the worker is unimportant and the symbolic dimension of the correlation between age and role diminishes. To concertgoers who love music, it does not matter whether the virtuoso is sixteen or eighty. Furthermore, a change in the meaning of work requires changes in the meaning of life. For those espousing the Protestant work

4. Ibid., pp. 389–90.

ethic, to live is to embrace the opportunity to work and to fail to do so is to fail as a person.

The question we must confront, then, is whether a comprehensive revolution in the meaning of life and work can be achieved. Revolutionaries have persistently erred in believing that changes in mental life could bring about changes in social life. It is difficult to hold the ongoing rhythms of social life in abeyance for more than a year or two, as was attempted after 1789 in France, as though the new mind need not go out into the old world before it first produces the new world. If structural change is slow, however, the new mind must eventually resist the inertia of the old system; and if it is too slow, the new mind may give up before any significant effect is achieved.

If traditional social systems balance continuity and efficiency, we must ask whether maintaining that balance morally justifies certain forms of ageism. Continuity requires that new arrivals be allowed freedom and spontaneity both to generate their enthusiasm and to give them a sense of commitment to the system. A society that emphasized efficiency alone would be like a vast medieval guild in which the new arrivals were apprentices looking forward to the day when they too would become old masters. Adolescents and young adults would have little status and would be rigidly controlled in breeding colonies to guarantee continuity. The emphasis on efficiency has been the hallmark of paternalistic utopian (often religious) societies that the aged have controlled. With the aged in control, the potential for abuse of the young increases as their rights appear to conflict with those of the old. Education becomes exclusively a functional endeavor, akin to learning the methods of agriculture. The final product of social effort in the efficient society is never in doubt. But would it be desirable to achieve such a formalized continuity?

Genuine substantive continuity requires that new arrivals be free individuals who desire both to preserve a great deal of their society and to leave their own mark on it for later generations. We cannot, in a single generation, change the human animal, who has spent the last ten thousand years as the producer of the complex cultural and economic system we know, into a mere inhabitant of a fixed milieu. In an ever-expanding economic universe, such questions of social integration may be put aside. But if expansion ceases, the entire array of questions must be considered at once: Should the established old prosper at the expense of the young? Should both old and young in a wealthy society prosper at the expense of both old and young in an underdeveloped society? Should today's old prosper at the expense of tomorrow's young? And what should our guidelines be as we answer these questions?

Let us begin with some pictures of social systems that we would probably agree are morally repugnant. The first, a Druidic utopia, is a static society, a gerontocracy that does little more than perpetuate by ritual and secrecy the power of an inner circle. This is the priest-ridden society attacked in the nineteenth century by Marx, Freud, and Nietzsche. At the opposite extreme is the world Anthony Burgess created in *A Clockwork Orange,* a world in shambles where youthful gangs terrorize elders who have been reduced to powerless fools, a world of pseudo-revolutionary rhetoric that lacks hope or even a desire to hope. This is the world Plato attacked centuries ago.

Other social systems, no less repugnant, are possible between these extremes. In societies marked by racism and sexism, some inhabitants are not real members or some members have restricted roles. Under slavery, apartheid, and colonialism generally, all strata of the official class benefit at the expense of the support class. Although these societies need not be gerontocracies, their official traditions usually include reverence of old habits and symbols. Sexism, like racism, restricts roles, but perhaps more benignly. Historically in the West it has meant the restriction of the female role to breeding and nurturing, again not necessarily in a paternalistic setting, though usually so.

Does ageism have the same morally repugnant status as sexism and racism? How should we measure the degree of irrationality of each? Before answering this question we must decide whether exploitation results from utterly irrational beliefs or from rationally perceived opportunities. A society that enslaves some of its members because they were born on the first of the month might have an ideology to justify its behavior, but we are more likely to look to the societal function of such a practice than to its ideological justification to explain its rationality. In the age of navigational exploration, exotic (irrational) hypotheses to justify racism resulted from the inevitable culture shock of the Europeans who confronted native populations, but the practical opportunity to exploit the natives eventually came to dominate European views. Originally alien to the society of the exploiters, the exploited subjects were introduced into the workings of that society but segregated from its power. In cases of sexism the sister of an exploiter may herself be exploited. Even though the practical, functional contribution to society may be decisive in cases of sexism, ideology and mythology may weigh more heavily in these cases than in those of racism. Unlike the slave, the victim of sexism may be fully respected as a person in some roles (mother, lover) but not in others (politician, worker).

Racism has a higher coefficient of irrationality than sexism because exploitation based on skin color is hardly germane to the function served by the exploitation (slave labor). The argument that only equatorial peoples could work in cotton fields because only they had skin protected from the sun would preclude the use of such slaves in other functions. But slavery pervaded the culture of the South, and eventually the ideology of racism allowed de facto slavery to spread far and wide. Arguments for sexism have a richer source of ideological imagery: women, after all, are the only members of the species capable of producing children. Any role sexism forces on a woman invariably includes that function. Only women are born potential reproducers, whereas all people, not only blacks, are born potential slaves. Thus, sexism is more rational to the extent that the sexist form of exploitation is superficially justifiable.

The more interesting question, however, is whether sexism is ever objectively justified. Let us imagine a variation of Aristophanes' *Lysistrata* in which women, instead of withholding their sexual favors to end a war, withhold them to end society itself. It might well be argued that these women are abusing their right to privacy and are obligated to use their bodies to propagate the species. However, this point does not include the nonideological factor that women traditionally have also had to raise the children they give birth to. Moreover, if women are obligated to use their bodies for propagation, men have an equally sexist role obligation to fertilize ova. So the sexism advocated in this extreme example is in fact speciesism. Objectively speaking, sexism is as groundless as racism.

What about ageism? To begin with, the natural boundary between victim and victimizer differs from that in the other two forms of exploitation. White people do not become black people, nor do men become women. If ageism is exploitation of the old by the young, the victimizer is destined to become a victim. If ageism is exploitation of the young by the old, then the victim who lives long enough becomes the victimizer. The more usual definition of ageism as the exploitation of the old by the young suggests yet another difference between it and racism and sexism. The social efficiency achieved by racism and sexism involves a compulsion to perform. At the extreme, slaves are beaten and tortured; women are raped by their husbands and imprisoned in the home. Exploitation involves positive tasks to be performed. With ageism, however, the failure to act makes one a victimizer; the absence of care, not the presence of abuse, in most cases, is at issue. This difference changes the nature of the victimization and consequently the degree of guilt of the victimizer. A person who declines to hire an older worker harms that person, but also gives a younger worker an opportunity; similarly, someone who refuses to hire a younger worker—who might be, for example, seeking a first job— gives the older worker an opportunity to continue. In the Old South, however, slavery did not deprive poor nonslaves of the opportunity to work because, had they traded places with the slaves under the existing socioeconomic system, they would have had to become slaves also.

The virulence of ageism, then, is its neglect, the failure of positive duties. It is less irrational than sexism, for people who someday will be old themselves can plausibly justify discriminatory conduct on grounds other than pure bigotry. Furthermore, moral and legal traditions in the West have long regarded the breach of negative duties (duties not to harm) more seriously than the breach of positive duties (duties to help). And finally, the racist is directly responsible for the very condition of slavery, having paid the ship captains to round up the slaves and enforcing imprisonment on the plantation. The sexist's responsibility is more covert, though perhaps more resourceful in "husbanding" a force already established in nature. The ageist, however, may be guilty of no positive intervention at all and might even prefer that all the aged disappear overnight. The moral repugnance of ageism is thus all the more difficult to establish.

Societies have manifested a combination of racist, sexist, and ageist tendencies, all of them irrational by the standards of social liberty and harmony enunciated since the Enlightenment. As noted, however, ageism is the least irrational inasmuch as it marks a mode of discrimination applicable sooner or later to all members of a society and gains plausibility from the point of view of both evolution and function (that is, efficiency). Discrimination based on skin color or ethnic origin is never justified if it is motivated by a desire to use one person as a means to another's end. If all slaves were immortally young and healthy and all masters forever old and feeble, there would be a natural basis for discrimination according to tasks. But racism would not be justified on any grounds unless only certain races or ethnic peoples were the immortals. Indeed, in such a situation, most probably the immortal races would rise up and be their own masters.

Similarly, as I have noted, sexism may be justified in the name of the supposedly higher value of speciesism. This sexism would take the form of narrowly defined procreative roles for men and women, but if propagation is the sole function concerned, such sexism would hardly be justified in other areas of social life. With ageism the questions of efficiency and function are central, so the standards for assessing discrimination become broader. Again, we must ask how much care a society should give to the elderly.

It has been suggested that a society that would refuse to construct a bridge that would last only a few years and carry only half of the predicted volume of traffic would probably invest in the young at the expense of the old.[5] The young will be around longer and their education and care will have a multiplier effect in returning benefits to society. The bases for such discrimination in favor of the young are (a) that a society should invest in its future because humankind should continue and should prevail, and (b) that whatever maximizes well-being and dignity in a society is desirable. Little attention has been given to argument (a) until recently, when it has figured in discussions of environmentalism and animal rights. To give priority to humanity is to espouse a form of speciesism that itself requires justification. Does humankind *deserve* to live on? Is human life the highest of all moral goods? We have no satisfactory answer to these questions. Those who assume that there will continue to be some form of social life speak of our obligation to future generations. But there is no indication that such an obligation is strongly felt today or will be felt in the near future. To complicate matters further, there is the question of our obligation to *past* generations, whose labors we now preserve as if the entire planet were a museum to past genius. Haven't we an obligation to pass on the music of Mozart to coming generations—as well as to pass on the poetry of Shakespeare, the works of Michelangelo, and the thinking of Aristotle? In short, the justification for argument (a), insofar as one can be clearly stated, is purely pragmatic: although we

5. Donald Marquis, "Ethics and the Elderly: Some Problems," in Spicker, Woodward, and Van Tassel, *Aging and the Elderly*, pp. 341–55.

may have grave doubts that the life of humankind in general is as worthwhile as it once was thought to be, we acknowledge that we might be mistaken.

If we substitute the word *flourish* for *prevail* in (a), we confront an even more difficult problem. To ensure that humankind flourishes, society must maintain a high standard of living. Ageism, it might be argued, is justified as the least repugnant option for meeting that condition. The old may be asked to make sacrifices on the grounds that they have had their share of the good life and should be ready to accept less. Lucretius advised the old in his poem *De rerum natura*:

> Why dost thou not give thanks as at a plenteous feast,
> Cramm'd to the throat with life, and rise and take thy rest?
> But if my blessings thou hast thrown away,
> If indigested joys pass'd thro', and would not stay,
> Why dost thou wish for more to squander still?[6]

But the old could not be asked to make too great a sacrifice. They could not, for example, be asked to die so that the young might flourish. In fact any society that demanded such a sacrifice from its elderly would not be a flourishing society; to flourish, civilization must offer its elderly a life of dignity and respect, if not one of great comfort and luxury.

If the well-being of society is the basis for discrimination, as in argument (b), the elderly may be asked to make sacrifices not only to ensure social continuity but also to obviate the need for even greater sacrifices by other members of the society. But circumstances must be considered before such sacrifices are required. The significant and rapid historical changes that have shaped contemporary societies might already have demanded great sacrifices of the generation now aging. Can this aging generation be asked to give up even more? Although sacrifices in late life might justifiably be asked of a generation that in earlier life had benefited from

6. *De rerum natura*, Book III, ll. 130–34, trans. John Dryden, in *World Masterpieces*, 3d ed., vol. 1, ed. Maynard Mack (New York: W.W. Norton, 1973).

similar sacrifices by others, often there are no such early sacrifices. To the extent that the present comfort of the young is
directly attributable to the previous efforts of the old, the
sacrifice of the old should be less and indeed the obligation of
the young greater.

Even argument (b) requires that we take a historical, not a
synchronic or static, view of society. Only if we take a historical view can we develop a balanced analysis of utilitarianism
as it applies to the aged. Those who value aid to the young
over aid to the old argue that being young is a more desirable
and potentially beneficial state to both the young and the old.
The young, in other words, are able both to experience happiness more intensely and to experience it for a longer period of
time. Utilitarianism, in this view, is oriented toward the future: the more limited the future (as with the old), the lower
the payoff of one's efforts and commitments.[7] But a utilitarianism oriented toward the future must also consider the intergenerational dynamics of a society, for any society that
places little value on its old seriously jeopardizes its ability to
maintain long-range stability; its young will consume whatever riches they can before reaching old age rather than re-
plenish them for the next generation, who, they have good
reason to believe, will victimize them in their old age also.

A utilitarian analysis, with its emphasis on positive duties,
is possible; it must consider the dynamics and interplay among
four or five generations so that it does not focus on each person
as a unit at a given moment but must take into account a
transgenerational view: the old were not always old and the
young will soon enough be old themselves. Only from a narrow, static position can one say, "Whatever the achievement
of some of the elderly, in general they are not capable of creating value to the extent that those in younger age groups are."[8]
Before requiring sacrifices of the elderly, it is important to
consider how much value they have already created.

If we justify argument (b) from a transgenerational per-

7. Marquis, "Ethics and the Elderly," p. 349.
8. Ibid., p. 347.

spective, we can formulate some policy guidelines for maximizing utility. These guidelines flow from the notion of a social contract between generations to protect the legacy of the past and to improve on it where possible. Thus a generation that has worked hard to improve the quality of social life should be rewarded, whereas one that has squandered its inheritance and now requires the new arrivals to pay the cost should not be. What might be ageism in the former case need not be in the latter. Each generation is responsible for maintaining the aggregate wealth of a society; this wealth is not created afresh with each new generation, for generations do not arrive all at once. The need to maintain wealth continuously perhaps explains the trend from private wealth to corporate wealth. Private wealth can benefit from the assets of corporate wealth, but the potential dissipation of the relatively small share of the corporation after the death of a corporate officer has far less effect than the once-common squandering of lifelong labors by a single son who took over the family business after his father's death.

The need to assess ageism in relation to the transmission of wealth suggests yet another link between the philosophy of aging and the political philosophy of socialism. Corporate wealth, in spite of all that has been said against it, is more like social, or publicly held, wealth than private wealth. In corporate capitalism the corporation is an ultimate economic reality that dispenses all benefits and preserves all sources of value (for example, patents, trade secrets, and so forth). Under socialism society at large is the ultimate economic reality. If, as I have argued, the aim of socialism is to construct a social reality for the full lifespan, then its preservation of societal wealth in the most continuous and homogeneous fashion serves as the basis for deciding how to allocate that wealth across generations. Capitalism proper has no philosophical basis, short of the standard appeal to Christian charity, for claiming that the old should be subsidized. The old, many of whom were once laborers who helped entrepreneurs toward their goal of acquiring riches, deserve some credit for remaining loyal to the capitalists' dreams and endeavors. But because they too *could* have become capitalists—so the standard dogma maintains—they now must be content with their precarious fate. Under socialism, the deception of this dogma is unmasked. Each person has the same *kind* of allegiance to the production of wealth. "Equal opportunity" does not mean equal opportunity to be opportunistic but equal opportunity to contribute and share. Socialism will never eliminate the inequality of lost opportunity, but at least it seeks to make the effects less permanent than does capitalism.

So far the justification of argument (b) has been somewhat formal in nature, with criteria suggested for establishing the relative degree of sacrifice. Yet should *any* sacrifice be made on behalf of the elderly? The answer to this question, as I noted, depends on one's sense of life's purpose. The capitalist believes that individuals should live for themselves and for their immediate progeny and counterpoises against this belief the pseudosocialistic doctrine that one should live for the state. Actually the counterpoise is more accurately construed as one between egoism and utilitarianism, between positive duties directed exclusively to the self and positive duties directed to others as well. In a socialist society, the social production of wealth is publicly recognized as a free enterprise involving many individuals and is characterized by public planning and consensus, as well as by a lack of secrets about why the production is needed and who benefits from it. Because the purpose of research and development and of production proper is always in clear view, the degree of an individual's contribution is not decided *ex post facto* but is itself always in view. As a result, the manner of establishing an entitlement in late life is straightforward. A just society requires a just dissemination of its wealth. This requirement by itself, however, does not justify sacrifice. Individual sacrifices can be justified only if one makes the further assumption that an individual ought to do whatever is possible to preserve a just society, including making sacrifices for it. The elderly would be willing to make sacrifices for a society worth preserving. These would not be sacrifices by the old for the young but by the old for present and future generations, in the name of past generations.

The justification of (b) is now complete. A just social system justifies necessary sacrifice on the grounds that such a society makes investing in the future a desirable and worthwhile choice. The young do not automatically benefit if well-being is maximized. The past history of a society, the past contribution of the elderly, and, most important, the degree to which justice prevails in the society all determine who benefits. Most of these conditions are already recognized as values by members of capitalist societies. Even the most hard-boiled entrepreneur would probably find it pointless for people to work a lifetime to amass a fortune so that their children could purchase cocaine or light cigars with hundred-dollar bills. Indignation about such a scenario would result in no small part from the belief that great imagination and effort are needed to produce a fortune. And although an entrepreneur would shy away from recognizing the role played by many others in the creation of a fortune, there would be no hesitation about recognizing either its great social value or the potential it represents for producing even greater social value.

PATERNALISM

So far I have argued that before we can decide how to treat the elderly, we must discover whether a given society holds and desires to hold its wealth in common. If it does, then entitlement is automatic at all stages of the life cycle and allocation depends on the degree of stability and continuity of the society. If it does not, then we have the present situation, in which entitlement is confused, responsibility diffused, and the elderly increasingly pressured to accept an earlier onset of sociological age even at a time when the onset of biological aging is being postponed. "Our existing policies on aging," Stephen Crystal has noted, "tend to isolate the aged from participating in the central institutions of our society, including the family and the workplace."[9] The reason for this isolation is clear: those who are not yet old tend to think of the elderly as obsolete citizens whose human dignity demands that they be cared for but who might make the world better by not staying on too long. This opinion, in turn, results from a blurred idea of entitlement.

The absurdity of trying to establish a clear line of entitlement can be seen in debates about Social Security. Many of the elderly feel entitled to their retirement benefits because they have paid into the fund that supplies them. In contrast, some say they are not so entitled because they receive more than they contributed. Neither side is correct. Social Security is not an actuarially sound insurance program; it rests on more pervasive notions of social entitlement. In this case entitlement is less than what some believe and more than what others believe. But more important, the program is grafted onto a social system that is not sure how to comprehend, let alone resolve, the basic social questions of property and the flow of wealth. Philosophically, Social Security is a house of cards built upon a house of cards.

Although it may seem pointless to advance a philosophy of aging that seems to require the complete revamping of an ongoing political economy, philosophers must consider all the ramifications of a system of closely related ideas and beliefs. Such a system may be thought of as interrelated in that modifying one part leads to stresses and strains on other parts. As the population ages, these strains become more apparent, but it is not fully clear what can be done to relieve them. It has been suggested by critics of Social Security that we must either increase public transfer payments or modify the private nuclear family to provide the social support of the traditional extended family. Both options are already quasi-socialistic, yet without a ponderous socialist ideology. An increase in payments is likely to result in a contest between young and old; a decrease in the social support

9. Stephen Crystal, *America's Old Age Crisis: Public Policy and the Two Worlds of Aging* (New York: Basic Books, 1982), p. 10.

system is likely to diminish the status of elderly citizenship. Both options raise the question of paternalism: is it desirable and, if not, is it avoidable?

Paternalists regard a person as needing continuous help because of some permanent failure of ability. One does not take a paternalistic attitude toward the drowning person one tries to save, because the need for help is immediate and the loss of ability temporary. Only the need for long-term care engenders paternalism. Often, too, paternalism is based on the view that care is a gratuity and not the result of an obligation. If someone has a true entitlement to care, it seems inappropriate to consider the person giving the care paternalistic. We cannot, for example, attribute a paternalistic attitude to the slaves who waited upon the aging plantation owner. Confused lines of entitlement lead us to regard the motivation for care as paternalistic. Under socialism, the grounds for a paternalistic approach, in theory at least, are much narrower than under capitalism, where wealth is unevenly distributed and the need for charity greater. Each person in a socialist society is fully entitled to the goods and services of that society. Socialism, however, is not entirely without paternalism. Indeed, some would say, socialism institutionalizes it.

Is paternalism ever desirable? One can argue against paternalism that individuals know their own interests better than some public officer in charge of seeing that those interests are met. Subjects of a paternalistic interest, in other words, become victims of mass-produced services that reduce all standards to the lowest common denominator. Such services are no more than placebos to quiet individuals and keep them off in a corner of society. The very presumption of paternalism is that its subjects no longer have autonomy and self-determination.

One can argue in favor of paternalism, as Thomas Halper has, that autonomy is meaningless without the goods and services necessary to realize it, that no inherent conflict need exist between private recipient and public official, that modern society renders everybody more or less incompetent with time, and that the motivation for paternalism is the desire to help.[10] Halper, however, does not take up the crucial issue of gratuity versus entitlement. Slaves cannot act paternalistically toward their aging master because his power and authority still determine their destiny. Similarly, retired workers, as long as they control sufficient wealth, remain as autonomous as the slave master and cannot be treated paternalistically. Once the question of controlling wealth is reformulated as a question of administering wealth, however, the opportunity for paternalism is greatly diminished, if never entirely eliminated. Then the preservation of the old by the young is not a direct act of gratuity, as if it were a transfer from haves to have-nots.

Is paternalism unavoidable? If the basis of support for the elderly is entitlement, not gratuity, should wealth be distributed equally regardless of age? I have already argued that some discrimination based on age would be justified in a more or less socialistic context. But does that justification mean that such discrimination in the usual sense is also entirely eliminated? Not necessarily. In the socialist context, the basis for entitlement is the elderly person's past history as a productive worker and contributor to the society. But many factors beyond productivity alone determine the production of wealth: disease, the effects of technological innovation, fashions, and all the scars of past history. Social justice itself is precarious, requiring constant vigilance to mitigate the disruptive effect of these factors. At times the unit of wealth produced per fixed unit of work may be less or more depending on such factors. Even socialism cannot and should not desire to control this variation of effort and result by establishing rigid standards of production and consumption. In times of less wealth, it must modify the standard of living for all citizens according to standards that recognize the contribution to efficiency and continuity each citizen makes.

10. Thomas Halper, "Paternalism and the Elderly," in Spicker, Woodward, and Van Tassel, *Aging and the Elderly,* pp. 321–39.

Even if we assume that the elderly still participate actively in such a society in a way perhaps unknown since earliest times, some—the very old or infirm—may receive less than is possible because their deaths are imminent. Such persons contribute little either to efficiency—in fact they diminish it—or to continuity by reminding newer arrivals of the continuous life of the community. Their entitlement derives almost exclusively from their past contributions. But if those contributions, because of illness or disaster, were small relative to the benefits received in late life, it would be hard to justify benefits on any but paternalistic grounds. The people in need can no longer care for themselves and only their having been born into the just society entitles them to enough of its benefits to preserve life with dignity. Yet such people receive benefits because the socially minded citizens and politicians are aware that society is not a machine—no invisible hand guides it—but a frail human creation that is continually re-created. This paternalism may be altogether irradicable, and for good reason.

SOME PHILOSOPHICAL REFORMS

I have already questioned the usefulness of an interpretation of the status of the elderly based on the achievement of a new social revolution. Philosophical clarity is not the only benefit of this rather utopian approach. The excursion into utopian fantasy also enables us to assess the increasing number of more practical proposals advanced to improve the quality of later life. We cannot significantly change the status of the elderly until we significantly change all other parts of society, particularly the control of wealth. This view is hardly novel. In *The Aging Enterprise,* Carroll L. Estes has criticized the public policy of the United States toward the aged, calling for "a new perception of old age and a clear understanding of the social, economic, political, and cultural factors that create the very problems now being assiduously discovered by social scientists and policy makers."[11] Estes's conception of social justice is that

> differences in life prospects are just if the greater expectations of the more advantaged improve the expectations of the least advantaged and that the basic structure of society is just throughout provided that the advantages of the more fortunate further the well-being of the least fortunate. Society's structure is perfectly just provided that the prospects of the least fortunate are as great as they can be.[12]

By Estes's standard, the present situation is not even partially just.

The present crisis, as Crystal argues, is that we must attempt to redistribute the wealth among all segments of society at a time when the older segment is growing but the amount of wealth is not. The basic structure of our society may not permit what might be termed "inadvertent justice." We cannot expect that the circumstances of those who are less well-off will inevitably improve relative to their expectations; at some point their expectations may be dashed. We might make a smooth transition to a just society if the clearly comprehended and formulated interests of all segments of society could be thoroughly debated. But such a debate is hardly possible in the current scene. The problem of a mechanical democracy where votes are frequently taken but the alternatives rigged is as important to us today as it was to those who hotly debated it in Hellenic times. Increasingly, the cultural imbalance between rich and poor warps the democratic process: the rich, knowing how the world works, unerringly perceive their interests and figure out how to preserve them; the poor base their views on the existing social reality, which they only murkily perceive. Since the fall of the eighteenth-century ancien régime, the techniques of control and manipulation have advanced far more for

11. Carroll L. Estes, *The Aging Enterprise* (San Francisco: Jossey-Bass, 1979), p. 227.
12. Ibid., p. 242.

those with economic power—who have usually originated the techniques—than for those without such power. Thus, Marx's desire to arm the poor with the tools of theoretical analysis has been thwarted most easily where those tools would have been most useful.

Nonetheless, we should not undervalue the philosophical insights and reforms that some reformers have proposed. Perhaps the ideological revolution precedes a more thoroughgoing economic revolution; indeed the proposed reforms would probably bring about an economic revolution if implemented for a longer period of time. Among such proposals are the following:[13]

1. *An end to social policies that segregate individuals according to age.* This reform would overturn legislative mandates that place individuals in fixed age groups and thereby perpetuate prevalent distinctions between social classes. It also is directed against social conventions that enforce conformity to a social clock. The purpose of this reform is to produce intergenerational cohesion and flexible role patterns at home and at work.

2. *A change in the meaning of work.* The work ethic that defines the value of persons by what they do intrinsically devalues the very young and the very old. To survive, a society must place a high value on work. Postindustrial society, however, while subscribing to the work ethic, persistently denigrates actual work. A janitor does much work, but that labor is not considered significant; if a machine could do the work more cheaply, the janitor would be replaced. By contrast, a trader on the stock market, who formulates sophisticated market strategies by 10:00 A.M. and makes a hundred times what the janitor makes by noon, is said to have done real work because no machine could do that job.

---

13. Ibid., pp. 227–47; Butler, *Why Survive?* chaps. 13–14; Gerald J. Gruman, "Cultural Origins of Present-Day 'Ageism': The Modernization of the Life Cycle," in Spicker, Woodward, and Van Tassel, *Aging and the Elderly,* pp. 359–87.

3. *A change in the meaning of life.* Because of the connections between the work ethic and our definition of the meaning of life, any change in one will affect the other. We know that meaningful work, intellectual stimulation, physical health, the happiness of fellowship, true love and robust passion, a sense of achievement, and a hope in the future all make life worth living. In defining the meaning of life, we must recognize more of these dimensions instead of focusing on regulated activity, the goals of which are primarily economic. Individuals must be able to express and enjoy themselves in public as well as in private life, and they must have opportunities to work hard in private life as in public life on significant tasks.

4. *A change in the meaning of death.* The ancient stigma of death and dying persists, along with the belief that the slow death of aging is a curse or punishment for sin. The more recently developed biological conception of death as nature's way of sacrificing the old for the young is hardly an improvement. A new perspective on death may be required, one that enables us to choose between living or dying. Whether immortality is possible—either theologically or technologically—as long as we have no choice in the matter, we are terrified and may even see life as an inherently tragic enterprise. But terror in the face of tragedy need not be the only response. Although the death of a child or accidental death is tragic, is the death of the long-suffering? And if we could achieve technical immortality, would any death be a tragic mistake, or could death still be chosen? What is important is that individuals formulate their own death scenarios and refine them as life goes on.

Such philosophical changes seem impossible in light of the hard reality of everyday life. Individuals cannot effect changes in themselves unless everyone changes collectively at once. Consequently, the philosophical proposals should be viewed in conjunction with the points I have made previously: (a) that a socialist economic system most justly realizes the need for social efficiency, continuity, and stability;

(b) that a socialist social system provides the most appropriate setting for life in all stages of the life cycle; (c) that analysis of the allocation of wealth should be based on the concept of entitlement; but (d) that in some circumstances the relative condition of the aged may justly, if temporarily, decline. The last point concedes that no social system may be entirely blind to age. Socialism represents a social contract between generations to preserve and, if possible, increase wealth, but at times that contract comes under strain and enthusiasm for it may need to be rekindled. However, the adjustments needed at such times would probably bring about a return to conditions far less severe than those of today. Some age discrimination is unavoidable. Because the social animal, like any individual organism, moves through space and time, it must continually confront imbalances and overcome difficulties.

In the process of comprehending the philosophical meaning of aging we have arrived at a less grandiose but hardly insignificant insight—that the traditional, ahistorical political ideologies, which have postulated their truths on an atemporal view of the nature of human life, may in fact be logical responses to a prescribed view of the proper composition of society. Such ideologies pretend to be indifferent to age. The capitalist imagines an ideology that works for young, eager entrepreneurs as well as for the comfortable burgomaster and banker. The socialist conceives an ideology that frees the young from class injustice and the old from social insecurity. But neither capitalist nor socialist directly and specifically links these precepts to a particular philosophy of the human life cycle. Historically each has emphasized specific values in the life cycle, remaining silent about the values of the other.

A new level of theoretical discussion is required to link traditional political systems of belief not only with the development of modern society but also with both the interactions of generations in a given society and a thoroughgoing search for the values that are to be preserved throughout the life cycle. No political philosophy should be embraced that nurtures only some stages of the life cycle, not only because each of us must take our turn in all stages but also because it is counterproductive to have a variety of political philosophies operating at once in a society but benefiting only some individuals.

Until now the socialist tradition has come the closest to providing a political philosophy for the full life cycle by revealing how belief and value systems derive from historical socioeconomic conditions of production and consumption. But even traditional socialism fails to think radically and historically about such systems in the generational context and instead postulates a single answer for all generations. Would socialism still be an appropriate political philosophy if everyone over thirty succumbed to a genetic or environmental catastrophe or if the birth rate mysteriously plunged? Where rapid societal growth is required, a philosophy that makes homeostasis its hallmark may not be the most useful in guiding social life.

We must investigate, without recourse to political dogma, the conditions for realizing social justice.[14] Capitalism must give up its view of human motivation as acquisition and competition, and socialism must give up its view of capitalism as a form of false consciousness. As I have mentioned, socialist critique includes an analysis of some factors that generate the capitalist ideology but usually excludes others—the changing determinants of the biological life cycle, the effects of social ecology on lifespan, and the relation between political philosophy and increasingly successful efforts to prolong life.

It is not enough, of course, to say that we must base our choice of political philosophy on lifespan and demographics.

14. Components of this effort to look at social justice in a broad political context can be found, for example, in discussions of priorities for allocating resources and health care in situations of dire scarcity and emergency (e.g., Gerald R. Winslow, *Triage and Justice* [Berkeley and Los Angeles: University of California Press, 1982]) or discussions of the ideological influences on medical practice in the United States (e.g., Vincente Navarro, *Medicine Under Capitalism* [New York: Prodist, 1976]). Navarro is led to conclude that "we cannot have a progressive health movement in the absence of a progressive political movement" (p. 96).

Ultimately, the clash of ideologies may derive from a fundamental clash of values, the resolution of which must be
achieved before the more contextual, nondogmatic view of
political philosophy suggested here may be adopted. In the
analysis of the four proposals noted above, I have contrasted
two views of the meaning of the life cycle. The view associated with capitalism sees human life volcanically—that is,
as a seemingly isolated driving process of self-expression, a
struggle of the self against the world that reaches a climax
and then ends in retirement and extinction; the other, associated with socialism, sees human life as a river, connected
to other rivers, bound with the totality of forces, progressing
slowly in a more or less fixed course whose value lies not in
the power to deviate sharply but in the continuity of communal consciousness.

As our population ages and the globe becomes more
crowded with human life, the values and reforms described
above are the ones we should embrace. The adventurist who
once dreamed of finding in a faraway place a spice that all
civilized persons would want on their tables has turned to
outer space where these values still apply. But those of us
who remain behind in the generations to come must confront
squarely the choice between homeostasis and planned destruction and insecurity.[15] And in so doing we must become
self-conscious about our deepest values; we must think carefully about the proper metaphors for the entire living process
and discover ways to communicate these to all age cohorts. In
this case, a process of averaging might have to occur. Age
and youth would be attributes not tied exclusively to stages of
chronological aging. The new young would be less young
than their predecessors because youth would no longer be
perceived as a time of free enjoyment; the new old would be
less old because they could express a wider range of desires
to the society at large without looking foolish.

15. See Joseph Esposito, *The Transcendence of History* (Athens, Ohio:
Ohio University Press, 1984), chap. 7.

5

The Law of the Elderly

So far I have examined the concept of aging in the natural and social sciences and have investigated the relation between ageism and the requirements of a just society. This chapter enters the confounding realm of legal reasoning to assess the current status of ageism in the legislative and judicial framework. Perhaps because legal discourse as manifested in the opinions of the higher courts is often a mask for the true operating premises of court decisions, the analysis of legal reasoning is rarely gratifying to those who seek consistency and thoroughness. Justices do not like to reveal the many factual claims on which they construct an argument. If they clearly assert their position, critics can argue more effectively against it. So they erect numerous procedural, stylistic, and metalegal barriers to keep the secrets of the court. They rely on the doctrines of separation of powers and judicial restraint on judicial activism to justify apparent impartiality, even though such justification really derives from the courts' acceptance of the status quo. The courts' analysis of discrimination based on age is a good example of this purposeful obfuscation.

AGE DISCRIMINATION

In 1967 Congress passed the Age Discrimination in Employment Act (ADEA). The purpose of the act was "to promote employment of older persons based on their ability rather than age . . . [and] to help employers and workers find ways of meeting problems arising from the impact of age on employment."[1] The act also specified that age discrimination

1. *United States Code Annotated*, vol. 29, sec. 621–34, p. 534.

would be lawful "where age is a bona fide occupational qualification reasonably necessary to the normal operation of the particular business, or where the differentiation is based on reasonable factors other than age."[2] Strictly speaking, there is no logical connection between chronological age and the occupational qualifications of adult workers. If we could slow down the aging process, it might be possible for an individual with a chronological age of eighty to have a biological age of twenty. Chronological age, in other words, serves as a proxy for other qualities a person is thought to possess.[3]

Age discrimination is the product of a complex intellectual activity involving inductive, deductive, and hypothetical inferences. These inferences are partly empirical and partly conventional (that is, social). Inferences in personal affairs tend to be predominantly empirical, but in organized business affairs they tend to be more closely tied to fixed social norms. We may recognize a great range of abilities and attitudes among individuals of the same age in our own experience. But these discriminations disappear when we are asked to help formulate personnel policy for a business with a high social visibility. Then we reject the case-by-case method of forming inferences and use a deductive model based on marketing research and generalizations passed down by policy makers.

Soon after the age discrimination law was passed, the courts were asked to define more precisely a bona fide occupational qualification with respect to age. Precedent deci-

2. Ibid., p. 537. In October 1986, Congress passed an amendment to ADEA making it illegal for employers of more than twenty workers to require retirement at any specified age and ordering continued health coverage for older workers. The fact that the bill exempted tenured university professors and public safety officers for a seven-year transition period suggests an increasing burden on future courts to settle disputes between employers and employees who feel they are being asked to retire too early. However, the amendment may go a long way toward replacing age with more personalized criteria in determining when retirement is proper.

3. See Bernice L. Neugarten, "Age Distinctions and Their Sound Functions," *Chicago Kent Law Review* 57 (1981): 823.

sions were emerging in the area of sex discrimination. For example, traditional association of either men or women with occupational roles did not constitute a legitimate occupational qualification. In *Weeks v. Southern Bell Telephone and Telegraph*, the Fifth Circuit Court ruled that although the "strenuousness" of a job might be a bona fide occupational qualification, "traditional roles" could not.[4] Furthermore, the court held that the employer needed to substantiate the claim that all or nearly all women could not do the traditionally male job in question. In *Diaz v. Pan Am*, the same court held that a company could not justify hiring only women as flight attendants with the claim that women better fulfilled the role of comforter to passengers.[5] Comfort, the court held, was not the essence of the airline business.

These two cases made clear, as the wording of the ADEA did not, that a bona fide occupational qualification could be defined only in relation to the germane nature and function of the task for which a person was hired. The wording of the act referred to qualifications "reasonably necessary to the normal operation of the particular business." Plainly it was not the intent of Congress to allow an employer to justify sex or age qualifications based on the argument that such qualifications had previously been normal or the claim that they were "reasonably necessary" for continuing normal operations. Here the court applied the criterion of normalcy to the task involved: whether it was carried out in the specified manner, whether the desired product or service was attained, and so forth. *Diaz* provided a criterion—a "business necessity" test—that helped distinguish legitimate occupational qualifications from unlawful discrimination.

The courts were asked to settle a number of age discrimination cases that were specifically related to the age issue and to ADEA, cases in which a prospective employee was denied employment because he or she had reached retirement age or in which an employee, having retired at a speci-

4. 408 F.2d 228 (1969).
5. 442 F.2d 385 (1971).

fied age, brought suit against the employer on the grounds that he or she was still fit enough to work and perform well. In the first decision, *Weiss v. Walsh*, the court ruled that Fordham University had to withdraw its offer of the Albert Schweitzer Chair in Humanities from Paul Weiss because Weiss had passed sixty-five years of age: "Being a classification that cuts fully across racial, religious, and economic lines, and one that generally bears some relation to mental and physical capacity, age is less likely to be an invidious distinction" than are racial and sexual distinctions. Furthermore, the court held, "notwithstanding great advances in gerontology, the era when advanced age ceases to bear some reasonable statistical relationship to diminished capacity or longevity is still future."[6] Clearly, the court was in no mood to treat Weiss's circumstances as unusual. It did not regard Fordham's willingness to hire Weiss as an indication of either Weiss's present ability or the likelihood of his future productivity. Instead, it required that someone from the class of persons below age sixty-five be chosen to fill the position based on a statistical generalization about age and ability.

This statistical generalization, coupled with the criterion of normalcy, would become the primary justification for age as a bona fide occupational qualification. This generalization, for example, was used to justify a maximum hiring age of thirty-five for bus drivers. In *Hodgson v. Greyhound*, the court noted that although bus drivers between ages fifty and fifty-five had safer driving records than younger drivers, this may have been in part because of the seniority system that allowed older drivers to choose safer, less strenuous routes.[7] Old applicants without seniority would have been subjected to the strenuous routes. That the "essence" of Greyhound's business was safe transportation justified age as a qualification for employment. In a similar case, the Fifth Circuit Court reasoned that "available [medical] tests cannot distin-

6. 324 F. Supp. 75 (1971).
7. 499 F.2d 244 (1976).

guish those drivers not yet affected by the more crucial age-related accident-causing impairments like loss of stamina, etc."[8] Therefore, all an employer had to do to justify an age qualification was to show that a greater risk of injury or death might reasonably be assumed in the absence of such a qualification.

In 1976, in *Murgia v. Commonwealth of Massachusetts Board of Retirement*, the United States Supreme Court rejected the ruling of a district court that a law requiring a state police officer to retire at fifty "bore no fair and substantial relation to [the] object of the legislation and was unconstitutional and void."[9] The Supreme Court ruled that

> since physical ability generally declines with age, mandatory retirement at fifty serves to remove from police service those whose fitness for uniformed work presumptively has diminished with age. This clearly is rationally related to the State's objective. There is no indication that [the state statute] has the effect of excluding from service so few officers who were in fact unqualified as to render age fifty a criterion wholly unrelated to the objective of the statute.[10]

Although there was no question that officer Murgia was physically qualified to remain at his job—he had passed physical exams throughout the decade prior to his fiftieth birthday—the justices did not think this consideration was relevant. Instead, they employed the so-called rational basis test for equal protection under the law. That test requires that if a statute (a) does not violate a fundamental right, (b) can reasonably be seen to advance some proper governmental purpose, and (c) treats all persons in the class to which it refers equally, then the statute is constitutional. The Supreme Court's decision followed from the belief that Murgia did not have a fundamental right to work (the courts do not recognize such a right), that it was reasonable to assume

8. 531 F.2d 224 (1976).
9. 376 F. Supp. 753 (1974).
10. 427 U.S. 307 (1976).

that ability declines with age, and that the state has an interest in public safety, and thus in the requirement that all
officers over fifty retire.

On the face of it, the Supreme Court presented a passive
rebuttal to Murgia's claim. The justices seemed to say that
the burden of proof was his to show that the state's policy of
retirement at fifty was unreasonable and discriminatory. The
rational basis test is satisfied if there is *any* reasonable basis
for claiming that the practice under question furthers a legitimate purpose. But in fact the court took a substantive
position on the issue—that physical ability declines with
age—as indicated in the quote above. Had the justices not
done so, they would have had to face squarely the problem
of deciding where to begin applying the rational basis test.
They assumed that Murgia was not the victim of unconstitutional discrimination in belonging to the class of persons
over fifty, as they believed that persons over fifty were less
able to carry out the duties of a uniformed officer. Had they
placed Murgia in the class of fit persons, they might have
reached a somewhat different conclusion. In that case, the
burden would have been on the state to prove that criteria
more refined than age could be established for assessing
fitness. But the court held that there was no need to establish such criteria because the rational basis test did not require it.

To follow the court's reasoning, we must return to the
claim that classification by age does not violate the constitutional requirement of equal protection. To violate equal protection, a classification must delineate a "suspect class" and
must employ "suspect criteria." The court, although it has
not defined a suspect class, has traditionally regarded it as a
"discrete and insular" class, based on characteristics that are
accidents of birth, or as a class subjected to a history of intentionally unequal treatment before the law. Race, religion, and
national origin are said to be suspect classes. Yet gender
classes are not deemed suspect as long as their unequal treatment is required by significant governmental objectives. These
objectives outweigh the requirement of minimum rationality.

In other words, discrimination against men or women is allowed only if there is a good reason to allow it; it is not allowable merely because it is somehow rational. Thus pregnancy need not be covered by state disability insurance because that could threaten the financial soundness of the insurance program. The court, moreover, found constitutional a law that gives tax exemptions to widows but not widowers on the grounds that widows needed more financial assistance when a spouse dies. The basis for such special treatment by the court may be that although sex is an accident of birth, it is a pervasive one that cuts across all cultures and races. Age, like sex, is pervasive, but it is not an accident of a single event (birth) as much as it is, so to speak, an accident of a continued series of events (living).

It may appear that the courts have used these distinctions to demarcate constitutional behavior, but in fact they have used them only *ex post facto* to justify their conclusions. Although to reconstruct the thinking that led to such conclusions is at best to speculate, such a reconstruction sheds light on the underlying assumptions of the justices. I have already noted that they assume ability declines with age. They probably also assume that general utilitarian considerations should determine the choice of class to be protected by law. Classes are never natural but are always constructions of one sort or another. The classes of men or women, for example, are practically circumscribable but the classes of men's and women's roles are not. Race and age are other characteristics that either legitimately or illegitimately define a class. If the class of Africans is a subclass of persons, the treatment of Africans but not other persons as slaves is arbitrary and unconstitutional. Yet if the class of Africans is a unique class of primitive persons, as the ideology of the white supremacist has maintained, then both the arbitrariness and the inequality of the slaves' treatment disappear, and they may be regarded as children slowly being socialized in the ways of the white civilization. The initial choice of protected class also affects the outcome in abortion cases. The Supreme Court has justified abortion on the grounds that a woman's right to privacy is a fundamental right. The relevant class is that of women rather than that of pregnant women as mothers. If the court had chosen the latter class as relevant, then it would have deemed that a mother who sought to separate herself from her unborn child is responsible for her decision to abandon her social and personal commitment. The court, however, regards the act of abortion as the private act of a *person*, a mother-to-be who wishes not to be a mother.

There is no systematic treatment of the construction of classes included in the courts' thinking because, as in much of legal reasoning, the talisman of justice is always an answer to the question of the possible effect on the status quo of the decisions at issue. If we abandon the crude dichotomy between natural and suspect classes, however, and focus on those characteristics for which the class names serve as proxies, we can distinguish the following four classes: permanent-pervasive, temporary-pervasive, permanent-insular, and temporary-insular. The status quo is a mixture of the four, and when it changes, so might membership in the various classes. For example, when the Industrial Revolution began, slavery moved from permanent-pervasive to permanent-insular.

In analyzing the constitutionality of a practice, the courts hypothesize about the impact of possible reclassifications on the status quo, bringing fundamental political philosophy to bear on the empirical question at issue. The justices may reason, for example, that it is not good social policy to keep the older members of a society employed for too long at the expense of younger members. Furthermore, the courts may have been unwilling to mandate more refined criteria of fitness in the Murgia case and in others based on the belief that a person progressing in a career should be subject to fewer and fewer tests of capability as an employee. Such tests, the justices may feel, are fine for the competitive young but not for the security-seeking elderly. Finally, to mandate practices of accountability in the relation between employee and employer enlarges the burden of both, for as employee responsibility increases, employer autonomy might decrease.

The courts have sought most strongly to protect classes that are permanent and insular in cases of race and national origin and classes that are temporary and insular in cases of religion. Court decisions have given less support to classes that are permanent and pervasive in the cases of sex, and justices have been reluctant to regard people of a given age with no claim to unequal treatment as belonging to a temporary and pervasive class. Traditionally, insular minorities have needed the protection of the courts, but the protection of minorities is not a court's goal per se in its espousals of equal protection. The more fundamental issues are social justice and equal protection under the law in general. The rights of minorities to both equal protection and social justice are easier to violate because as a practical matter minorities often have less power. Their insularity, however, is neither a necessary nor a sufficient condition for considering them a suspect class. A class is suspect if its permanent characteristics have traditionally been signals for unequal treatment, the assumption being that people ought not to be penalized for characteristics they cannot change, particularly if the characteristics are unrelated to the nature of the unequal treatment. Although generally there is no transition from one of the four classes to another, it may be possible to discover that a class hitherto considered temporary is in fact permanent. The courts have never addressed the question of whether poverty might constitute a suspect class because they assume that poverty is a temporary condition even though it is often lifelong and pervasive. If it could be argued from a statistical point of view, however, that for the vast majority poverty is a permanent characteristic, the courts would have to revise or reverse their rulings.[11]

One might argue quite plausibly that the aging belong to a permanent and pervasive class and consequently that a higher standard of rationality ought to be used to test the constitutionality of laws that discriminate against them. The aged do not and will not become young again. Furthermore,

11. See *San Antonio School Dist. v. Rodriguez*, 411 U.S. 1 (1973).

one may also argue that despite their numbers the elderly still suffer from a functional insularity in modern industrial society; they are a permanent part of the population but not a permanent part of the work force, especially in positions of responsibility. Their situation thus resembles that of native populations in traditional colonial societies. And finally, one may argue that discrimination against the aging population has been a prominent part of the relatively brief history of industrial societies. In other words, age discrimination in certain contexts does "command extraordinary protection from the majoritarian political process."[12]

In *Vance v. Bradley*, the Supreme Court seemed to relax further the interpretation of age as a bona fide occupational qualification. Bradley, a member of the Foreign Service, was forced to retire at age sixty as mandated by the Foreign Service retirement system, even though had he belonged to the civil service, he would have been able to work until age sixty-five. The Department of State argued that it could discriminate on the basis of age because foreign service is hazardous and wearing. The court accepted this view, adding that "at age sixty or before many persons begin something of a decline in mental and physical reliability."[13] The unwillingness of these elderly jurists—Justice Marshall dissenting—to consider the nature of the occupation or the options the Department of State might provide to senior officers indicated that the court is disinclined to take seriously the injustice that age discrimination can represent.

Not all cases have gone this way, however. In *Houghton v. McDonnell Douglas* the Eighth Circuit Court ruled that age was not a bona fide occupational qualification for test pilots. Thus Houghton could not be forced by his employer to stop testing airplanes because he was fifty-two. A doctor testified that Houghton was 99.9 percent certain not to suffer a heart attack or stroke while in flight. The court also accepted statistical evidence that the aging process "occurs more slowly

12. *USCA* Const. Amend. 14.
13. 440 U.S. 93 (1979).

and to a lesser degree among professional pilots."[14] Similarly, in *Gault v. Garrison* the Seventh Circuit Court rejected a local school board policy requiring teachers to retire at age sixty-five.[15] The court found no reason to believe that age sixty-five marked a point beyond which teachers were unfit to teach.

These cases differ from *Murgia* in having no public safety issue. In *Houghton*, as in *Murgia*, there was no doubt that the plaintiff was fit. The underlying reasoning might have been that Houghton assumed the sole and entire risk of continuing to work and that no third party would bear the consequences of his taking that risk; in *Gault* there was no public safety issue at all. But this difference is not the point. I have already suggested that there are sufficient grounds for rejecting the rational basis test. In most age discrimination cases, the substantive question of whether the person involved still possessed the ability to carry out the tasks of employment was considered by the courts. And it ought to have been—that is, the general presumption that ability declines with age ought to be refined for each circumstance. Individuals should be given an opportunity to show their ability, and distinctions of ability should be established in and among occupational classifications. Ultimately, such distinctions involve inevitable tensions between labor and management: as the criteria of performance become refined and open, the employer retains less discretionary power and autonomy. This loss, however, must be weighed against the retiree's loss of autonomy. In the district court's decision in favor of Murgia, the justices noted that "the attractiveness of quick promotion must be weighed against the unattractiveness of early retirement."[16] Clearly we cannot resolve these conflicts except in relation to generally accepted beliefs about both the purpose of social labor and the individual

14. 553 F.2d 561 (1977).
15. 523 F.2d 205 (1977). With respect to college professors see *Nelson v. Mirva* 546 P.2d 1005 (1976).
16. 376 F. Supp. 754 (1974).

laborer's value in relation to that of aggregate social labor. Issues of value and purpose, however, involve not only age discrimination but also other considerations, including the impact of automation and the uses of education.

As the original legal requirement for bona fide occupational qualifications was modified, "the exception swallowed the rule."[17] To remedy this situation, the Equal Employment Opportunity Commission in late 1981 reconstrued the qualification narrowly, requiring the employer to prove that

> (1) the age limit is reasonably necessary to the essence of the business, and either (2) that all or substantially all individuals excluded from the job involved are in fact disqualified, or (3) that some individuals so excluded possess a disqualifying trait that cannot be ascertained except by reference to age. If the employer's objective in asserting a bona fide occupational qualification is the goal of public safety, the employer must prove that the challenged practice does indeed effectuate that goal and that there is no acceptable alternative which would better advance it or equally advance it with less discriminatory impact.[18]

Less discrimination based on age entails more discrimination based on ability. A reasonable retirement age is desirable so that individuals can rely on common practices, but that age should be readily set aside for persons willing and able to continue working. In this case, age is an administrative category, not a basis for coercion.

Howard Eglit has proposed five components of a "refined ageism": (1) that age should never be used as a measure of ability, (2) that the burden of proof justifying discrimination falls to the state and/or employer, (3) that the invidiousness of ageism differs with the context, (4) that age cannot be invoked to deny a constitutional right, and (5) that ageism against the old is more invidious than that against the young

17. Melodie A. Virtue, "A New Interpretation of the BFOQ Exception Under ADEA: A Remedy for the Exception That Swallowed the Rule," *American University Law Review* 31 (1982): 391–430.
    18. *Code of Federal Regulations*, 29, par. 1625.6.

because the old remain old the rest of their lives.[19] These points incorporate the distinction between age as an administrative category and as a basis for coercion. The courts do not err in asserting a correlation between age and ability; they err in granting more authority to act on such a generalization than the situations brought before them warrant. The anti-ageist must admit that in the eighth and ninth decade, few persons have the ensemble of abilities available to persons four or more decades younger. The pro-ageist must admit, however, that one's memory or reflexes are slower not because one is eighty but because chronological age may serve as a rough index of biological age. The measure of deterioration is entirely a medical question, and the relevance of that measure must be related to the essence of the business activity. The Equal Employment Opportunity Commission's requirement implies that businesses are merely functional and utilitarian entities whose purpose is to manufacture goods or supply services. The secondary, nonutilitarian, feature of modern complex corporate life—that it is conducted in an overall pleasing environment with young, attractive, cheerful workers—could never support a defense of bona fide occupational qualifications, even though it undoubtedly remains a considerable behind-the-scenes influence in arguments justifying age discrimination.

AUTONOMY AND MENTAL CAPACITY

Although in theory persons are the holders of entitlements and rights, in practice persons are emerging and evolving beings, and of course they are creatures who die by natural causes. Yet the process of becoming an adult is more organized and predictable than the devolution into the state of old age. Thus, the law pertaining to the early stages of life, prior to legal autonomy, is far less controversial than the law relat-

19. Howard Eglit, "Old Age in the Constitution," *Chicago Kent Law Review* 57 (1981): 904–8.

ing to the problems of advancing age, when loss of autonomy may become an issue. Whatever people believe about the rights of children and the unborn, they seldom demand that individuals prior to adolescence be treated in all respects as adults. Such condescension seems perfectly reasonable. Indeed a person who treats a child as an adult might conceivably be charged with abusing that child in certain circumstances. It is not unreasonable, for example, to describe events inaccurately to a child in order to make them more understandable. Education artfully combines information and misinformation to achieve the desired goal of producing autonomous adults. The presumption is that the blossoming autonomy of the child should be cultivated. After all, birth and growth normally constitute a process whereby autonomy continually increases. Consequently, enlightened paternalism toward children is justified because the natural course of events eventually undermines that very paternalism.

In later life, however, the situation is reversed, for autonomy fully exists and the risk is that it will be lost as health gives way to increasingly serious illness. The law has dealt with problems of a decrease in or loss of autonomy through guardianship or conservatorship proceedings, whereby all or a portion of the normal decisions of living are taken over by others on behalf of the person alleged to be incompetent. In guardianship, the loss of autonomy is complete—with the legal standing of a child, the incompetent can no longer buy or sell property, make contracts or gifts, vote, marry, consent to or refuse medical treatment, or choose a place of residence—whereas in conservatorship, the finances but not the daily life of the incompetent are managed by the conservator.

The legal justification for such proceedings is the paternal power—in contrast to the police power—of the state. This power, known as *parens patriae*, originally gave to the king the right to serve as a guardian of a person judged by a jury of twelve citizens to be either congenitally incompetent (an "idiot") or incompetent by circumstance (a "lunatic"), as specified in *De Praerogative Regis* of 1324. In modern times the state has to meet specified conditions before a person can be declared incompetent, but these conditions have not been as stringent as those governing the police power of the state to incarcerate a convicted criminal. Because the conditions are not stringent, there is great potential for abuse. In *The Right to Be Different* Nicholas Kittrie observed,

> In criminal law, we deal with the offender after the overt act; the *parens patriae* sanctions are often concerned with the prevention of criminal acts by dealing with those showing a proclivity toward anti-social conduct. Consequently, the *parens patriae* approach is likely to present an ever-expanding territory as our society continues to shift further from crime repression and management to crime prevention.[20]

Abuses are possible when the wrong indicator of the conduct to be prevented is chosen. The presumed proclivity of the elderly is not toward antisocial conduct but toward less competence. Signs of eccentricity or indifference could easily be taken as indications of advancing senility.

Generally, the legal justification for sanctions on conduct is that imposing them achieves a greater good than not imposing them or avoids a greater harm. Jurists argue furthermore that the sanctions must be measured not only by the good or harm involved but also by the potential for abuse of the sanctions themselves. Thus the greater the sanction, the more rigorous the procedures protecting it from abuse. Because traditionally in guardianship procedures the incompetent is assumed to benefit from guardianship and because the deprivation of liberty is less than in criminal proceedings, the court procedures used to empower guardians have been paternalistic in the worst sense. In many cases the person alleged to be incompetent does not benefit from guardianship but is victimized by relatives and third parties, often put away in a mental hospital or nursing home to wait for death. A study of such cases found that

20. Nicholas N. Kittrie, *The Right to Be Different: Deviance and Enforced Therapy* (Baltimore: Johns Hopkins University Press, 1971), p. 8.

> when a person was declared incompetent and was compelled
> to deliver his [or her] property to the management of others,
> no matter how benevolent was the intention of those who
> administered the property, the debilitated person lost a fairly
> basic attribute of citizenship. Indeed, . . . some other person
> or agency with an interest in the estate received more benefit
> or protection.[21]

The courts, however, have not regarded this loss of status
and well-being as serious enough to require more stringent
procedures for both ascertaining incompetence and assessing
motivations. According to the Fourteenth Amendment of the
Constitution, "no state shall . . . deprive any person of life,
liberty, or property, without due process of law." The United
States Supreme Court has clarified the relation between the
requirement for due process and "the extent to which an
individual will be condemned to suffer grievous loss."[22] The
more grievous the potential loss, the more stringent the
procedure. The court has also held that "the fundamental
requirement of due process is the opportunity to be heard 'at
a meaningful time and in a meaningful manner.' "[23] This requirement is particularly difficult to meet in guardianship
proceedings; the elderly person either may not know what is
at stake or, if he or she does know, may have no inclination
for self-defense in a proceeding overtly factual but actually
highly adversarial. Historically, when alleged incompetents
make no attempt to defend themselves before the court, it is
more likely that the court will appoint a guardian, usually the
person who has initiated the guardianship proceedings.

The Uniform Probate Code defines as incapacitated "any
person who is impaired by reason of mental illness, mental
deficiency, physical illness or disability, advanced age, chronic
use of drugs, chronic intoxication, or other cause (except minority) to the extent that he lacks sufficient understanding or
capacity to make or communicate responsible decisions con-

21. George J. Alexander and Travis H. D. Lewin, *The Aged and the Need
for Surrogate Management* (N. p., 1972).
22. *Morrissey v. Brewer*, 480 U.S. 471 (1971).
23. *Mathews v. Eldridge*, 424 U.S. 319 (1976).

cerning his person."[24] Such a definition sets a high standard for determining capacity. Impairment may result from both specified and unspecified causes, and indeed from noncauses ("advanced age"), and the requirement for capacity is satisfied only if a person makes "responsible" decisions. By these standards many persons are de facto incapacitated at periods of their lives when through frustration or anger or ignorance they lack "sufficient understanding or capacity to make . . . responsible decisions." A less psychological definition of incompetence is found in the New York Mental Hygiene Law, which defines as incompetent a person "who by reason of advanced age, illness, infirmity, mental weakness, intemperance, addiction to drugs, or other cause, has suffered substantial impairment of his ability to care for his property or has become unable to provide for himself or others dependent upon him for support."[25]

After a petition is filed in the appropriate state court claiming that the alleged incompetent cannot care for himself or herself and after that person has been notified of the filing, physical and psychiatric examinations follow. Alexander and Lewin, who studied reports of such examinations, note that although the law requires that a *causal* connection be established between physical condition and behavior, in fact such reports offer at best a precise medical diagnosis coupled with anecdotal remarks. Doctors writing the reports use terms and expressions such as *chronic brain syndrome, stroke, arteriosclerosis, senility,* and *senile psychosis* to describe the physical condition of the people they examined and terms such as *rambling, abusive, showing disorientation,* and *refusing to eat* to describe behavior. "Not one transcript examined," Alexander and Lewin report, "nor medical report studied revealed any attempt by the physician to detail the manner in which the patient's capacity to manage his estate has been affected by the underlying condition."[26] From both judicial and medical

24. Uniform Probate Code (ULA), sec. 5–101 (1983).
25. *New York Mental Hygiene Law* Part 1 (1973), sec. 77.01.
26. Alexander and Lewin, *The Aged and Surrogate Management,* p. 24.

perspectives, this fact-finding procedure has increasingly been criticized.[27] The courts are required to determine competency in an environment in which opposing interests are at stake. The reaction of a person under scrutiny in such a highly charged, threatening situation vindicates the position of the petitioner.

In *Rud v. Dahl*, an eighty-one-year-old resident of a nursing home, George Rud, challenged the constitutionality of the Illinois guardianship statutes.[28] Rud did not attend the hearing petitioned for by his brother, nor did the court appoint a legal counsel to represent his interests. After he was judged incompetent, he challenged the decision in the U.S. Court of Appeals. That court held that the general notice of a hearing met the informal requirement for due process in a civil (noncriminal) proceeding and that neither Rud's presence at the hearing nor that of counsel or a representative was required. In all likelihood, Rud's failure to make a timely defense was looked on by the court as a sign of his acquiescence. Rud, the court noted, could have asked for a postponement, and he could have afforded to hire an attorney to represent him. The court held that "the nature of the intrusion on liberty interests resulting from an adjudication of incompetency is far less severe than the intrusion resulting from other types of proceedings in which the presence of counsel has been mandated." It also ruled that "the technical skills of an attorney are less important, as the procedural and evidentiary rules of incompetency proceedings are considerably less strict than those applicable in other types of civil and criminal proceedings."

The case of George Rud and the opinion of the court

27. Annina M. Mitchell, "The Objects of Our Wisdom and Our Coercion: Involuntary Guardianship for Incompetents," *Southern California Law Review* 52 (1979): 1405–49; Thomas S. Szasz, *Law, Liberty, and Psychiatry* (New York: Macmillan, 1965); John J. Regan, "Protective Services for the Elderly: Commitment, Guardianship, and Alternatives," *William and Mary Law Review* 13 (1972): 564–622; Peter M. Hortsman, "Protective Services for the Elderly: The Limits of Parens Patriae," *Missouri Law Review* 40 (1975): 215–78.

28. 578 F.2d 674 (1978).

illustrate a serious problem with guardianship proceedings. Rud was diagnosed as having suffered congestive heart failure and pulmonary fibrosis, as well as cerebral dementia. There is little doubt that he was incapable of managing his affairs as a normal healthy person would have. But his competence to defend himself at such a hearing and his ability to respond successfully to the implications of the medical testimony are irrelevant to the constitutional question whether due process was followed. A sick person, indeed a very sick person, has liberty to lose even if its loss has few of the ramifications it has for a healthy person. The very informality of the proceedings to deprive a person of that liberty makes it difficult to isolate and rebut the presumptions of the court. In effect, the court may have assumed, Rud's plea was already moot because of his physical condition and advanced age.

The ruling in *Rud v. Dahl* may not indicate the current trend in such cases. In the past the courts have tended to place the burden on the alleged incompetents, giving much weight to the articulation of their responses to claims made about their capacities. Increasingly, the burden of proof is shifting to the petitioners, who now have to provide "clear and convincing" evidence, not merely a relatively stronger case than the person under judgment. In 1938 the California Supreme Court terminated the guardianship of Fannie Waite because she had not been given an opportunity to testify at her hearing, rejecting the claim that guardianship was needed because she had married a man thirty years her junior and because she had exercised poor business judgment in the purchase of property.[29] Similarly, the Iowa Supreme Court in 1951 reversed the guardianship of Martin Olson on the grounds that he had not behaved irresponsibly in keeping his money locked in a safe instead of in a bank, or in going to town for a beer after his wife's death, or in failing to attend church services regularly. The court said of Olson's three children who petitioned the court to be appointed guardians: "None of them apparently desires to give him a home now. Their only interest, so they

29. *In re Waite's Guardianship*, 97 P.2d 238 (1938).

say, is to preserve his property for him, and to do so they have been actively willing to besmirch, and to take from him, his good name."[30]

The recent trend in thinking about the limits of guardianship is indicated even more clearly in the ruling in *Lake v. Cameron.*[31] In September 1962 Catherine Lake, aged sixty, was found wandering around by a police officer and was taken to District of Columbia General Hospital. She was judged "of unsound mind" and the court transferred her to a psychiatric hospital. Two psychiatrists testified that she was suffering from "chronic brain syndrome" and had frequent lapses of memory. Mrs. Lake asked the district court to release her, and during the hearing a psychiatrist testified that although she suffered debilitation from arteriosclerosis and brain disease, she was harmless to others and would not intentionally harm herself. Her court-appointed counsel suggested that even though she was asking for full release, "her real complaint is total confinement in a mental institution."

The Court of Appeals ruled that the lower court had erred in committing Mrs. Lake to a psychiatric hospital when a less restrictive alternative would have been sufficient. Had Mrs. Lake had sufficient funds, the court noted, she would not have been committed. Consequently, the court placed the burden of exploring other alternatives on the lower court. The dissenting justices criticized this five-to-four decision on the grounds that Mrs. Lake herself had the burden of proving that her present confinement was illegal and overly restrictive. They also believed that Mrs. Lake's placement in a mental hospital was no more restrictive than placement in a rest home. Ultimately the justices disagreed in this case over the judicial system's support of the "accused." Should the system make incompetence harder to prove and should it require and specify the conditions of guardianship? Or should it regard the proceedings as a sci-

30. *Olson v. Olson*, 46 N.W.2d 1 (1951).
31. 364 F.2d 657 (1966).

entific investigation, conducted by fully autonomous persons, whose only motive is to find the truth?

The groundwork in *Lake* was expanded in a decision on a case heard in 1980. In *Meyer v. Sanderson*,[32] Mary Sanderson, aged seventy-six, who had been made a ward of her daughter, asked that a stronger burden of proof be used in guardianship proceedings. Her doctor of twenty years testified that she was a strong-willed, stubborn, tough person who was not competent to manage her financial affairs and who thought that her daughter wanted to take all her money. The court ruled that because Mrs. Sanderson had been placed in a rest home against her will by her daughter and had been removed from the town where her friends were, she was entitled to a hearing in which the evidence against her competence had to be "clear and convincing." "To allow many of the rights and privileges of everyday life to be stripped from an individual 'under the same standard of proof applicable to run-of-the-mill automobile negligence actions' cannot be tolerated."

According to the standards for guardianship and conservatorship proceedings set out in the Uniform Probate Code, priority to serve as guardian is given to a spouse, adult child, parent, or any relative who has resided with the incapacitated person for more than six months prior to filing the petition. The guardian "has the same powers, rights and duties respecting his ward that a parent has respecting his unemancipated minor children." When people are incapable of protecting their financial assets, the courts may appoint conservators for the estates. Here the courts give priority to individuals suggested by the incapacitated person (if that person has sufficient mental capacity to make a suggestion) and then to a spouse, adult child, parent, or relative. Conservators have complete control over estates and are entitled to reasonable compensation for managing them. Conservators must administer the estates as would a prudent person,

32. 165 Cal. Rptr. 217 (1980).

and if they have special skills, they have a duty to use them. Conservators are also allowed to benefit from using the funds of an estate. Nothing prohibits them from purchasing with those funds property they themselves intend to purchase later from the estate. Nothing prohibits them from using estate funds either to make gifts to charity or to purchase the services of friends who are attorneys, auditors, or financial advisors to help administer the estate. If the estate consists of stocks, the conservators may vote as they see fit, and in their own interests, at stockholders' meetings. And the conservators are able to use estate funds as collateral for loans to be repaid from the assets of the estate.

The reasoning of the code is that by giving conservators maximum leeway to administer estates and financial interests in the growth of the estates' assets, the wards will benefit as well. However, when an estate is unusually large, it is possible for the court to revoke some decisions of the conservator. In the case of *Salz v. Salz*,[33] the New York Supreme Court required that Mrs. Salz, conservator of her husband's six-million-dollar estate, sell the family business, which involved the purchase and sale of Postimpressionist art. Such a business was "too volatile," the court ruled, and could not be carried on prudently by someone not an expert in the field.

Because the transition from autonomy to incompetence is usually gradual, a major complaint about surrogate management of persons and property is its all-or-nothing character.[34] Although the courts hold individuals accountable for their actions as guardians and conservators, in practice the ward loses autonomy as the guardian gains power. The asymmetry between guardianship and conservatorship proceedings is curious and revealing. When a person's well-being is ostensibly to be protected, often state social service agencies are assigned the burden of care and the guardian merely makes the decisions that ensure this care. However,

33. 436 N.Y.S.2d 713 (1981).
34. Regan, "Protective Services for the Elderly," p. 608.

when a person's wealth is at stake, the conservator takes a direct interest in providing "care." One suspects that a primary concern in such proceedings is the orderly preservation of wealth for those likely to inherit it.

The Model Guardianship and Conservatorship Act proposed by the American Bar Association's Commission on the Mentally Disabled attempts to overcome this all-or-nothing problem. The act proposes that procedures be established to give as much decision-making power to the putatively disabled person as possible. It distinguishes partially disabled from fully disabled persons and establishes an oversight commission as well as "disabilities resource officers" in each state. The oversight commission would establish multidisciplinary evaluation teams to assess a person's mental capacity, and the resource officers would collect and disseminate information to the parties involved in the hearing. The proceedings themselves would be governed by the standard of evidence established in *Lake* and *Sanderson*—that is, the petitioner must explain "why the requested protection and assistance is the least restrictive dispositional alternative which will meet the needs of the respondent."[35] The report of the evaluation team must include a description of both the respondent's mental and physical condition and "adaptive behavior and social skills."

The court, in turn, is advised to outline specific alternatives best suited to the care and well-being of the disabled person. Then, if a "limited personal guardian" or "personal guardian" is appointed, that guardian is required to submit a plan of care, developed with the resource officer, describing the services necessary and the means of obtaining them. A guardian may not place a ward in an institution without a formal commitment hearing in which the ward has separate counsel or defense. Similarly, a conservator must submit to the court financial plans for the management of the estate. Limited conservators will have limited and specific duties; unlimited conservators will have the freedom the Uniform

35. *Mental Disability Law Reporter* 3 (1979): 270.

Probate Code specifies, though with more explicit requirements regarding the title to and sale of property.

The proposed act represents a shift from familial to state
involvement in protective services. It makes more distinctions regarding capacity and includes more steps in the
hearing and review process. It represents a compromise position in the absence of any consensus in our society about
the ultimate responsibility for the care of the sick, the incapacitated, and those with what the act calls "developmental
disabilities." It does not, however, define the proper use of
the estate of a person judged to be incapacitated. This definition requires consideration of a different set of values.

The court appoints as guardians those who are most
willing to place the interests of the ward on a par with their
own. But this congruence of interests may be impossible
when, as is usually the case, the younger generation must
care for the older. Either the guardian directly cares for the
ward or, more realistically, pays for such care. Although the
guardian involved in direct care may make a great personal
sacrifice and may appreciably improve the comfort of the
ward, more likely, however, such improvement seldom occurs. If the ward is difficult to manage, the guardian soon
becomes exhausted and either turns against the ward or
pays for a substitute caretaker, whose care may be more
than minimum but seldom achieves the maximum possible
through loving dedication. The quality of the care provided
by the substitute depends on the amount of money available
to pay for it. Wealthy individuals may have personal ser-
vants and doctors; poorer individuals must rely on care that
is mass-produced.

As the courts have increasingly come to recognize, the
yielding of autonomy is not by itself the answer, for the
autonomy of the guardian and the interests of the ward do
not always coincide. Indeed the yielding of autonomy may
easily be against the ward's interests. The problem of guardianship is to establish a procedure that best reflects the
disabled person's own interests. Here natural familial devo-
tion, assumed in the priority established for selecting a guar-

dian, must be weighed against the difficulty of the guardian's duties. Even the most loving son or daughter will grow weary from the rigors of caring for a frail parent year after year. On balance, it may be more in the ward's interest and in the interest of family members as well if another individual becomes guardian. But who? The motivation of individuals with only a financial interest in the care of the elderly would be highly suspect. There is an ample supply of old people and more than enough individuals guilty of failing to care personally for their elderly relatives to make competition among entrepreneurs in the marketplace an insufficient guarantee of good care. Should the young be asked to care for the old? To answer the question, we must measure the sacrifice made against the results achieved. Most people would find odious a situation in which the young members of society devoted themselves to caring for individuals with increasing disabilities. Only in a time when persons could dedicate such work to a higher spiritual authority could such a system be sustained.

Perhaps a better alternative to ensure care and preserve dignity would (1) establish guardianship as a social relation between an individual and a group, (2) define the activity of the group as primarily social rather than economic, and (3) compose the group from among the nonworking young and the healthy old. Such a group, which might be called a guardian society, would operate a moderate-sized physical facility, whose building and maintenance costs would be borne by the taxpayers. The staff of the facility would include some health care professionals but would be made up predominantly of young and old volunteers. Each facility would serve a geographical area and would be subject to the usual regulatory procedures applied to similar establishments.

The structure of a guardian society, in short, would be similar to that of a public school district. Each child knows which school to attend because school assignments depend on one's place of residence. Similarly, elderly persons would know where they could go when no longer able to care for themselves or be cared for at home. Indeed, such persons might well have worked for a number of years after retirement at such a facility along with their neighbors, both young and old. Appropriately, the healthy old should play a major role in the care of the infirm, for they share life experiences and history. But they must play that role as active members of society at large. Thus both segments of the older population can benefit. And the young too should help, with early exposure, public yet intimate, to life beyond the isolation of their cohort. As they help, they will begin to get a sense of the broader contour of the life cycle.

If we can thus easily sketch a plan to care humanely for the aged infirm, the care of their estates remains a thorny, complex issue. The law of wills gives individuals broad testamentary power to dispose of their estates as they see fit. If people choose to disinherit their families, they may do so provided they are not subject to "undue influence." The wisdom of the allocation of money is seldom questioned by the courts even though there is ample precedent for questioning it. In *Eyerman v. Mercantile Trust Company* the Missouri Court of Appeals ruled that because a person who directs that his house be destroyed at his death affects the property values of the adjoining homes, he is denied this course on grounds of "public policy":

> Although public policy may evade precise, objective definition, it is evident from the authorities cited that this senseless destruction serving no apparent good purpose is to be held in disfavor. A well-ordered society cannot tolerate the waste and destruction of resources when such acts directly affect important interests of other members of that society.[36]

Similarly, the courts have voided a testator's request that his money be physically destroyed.

Although mental capacity is the salient factor in determining whether persons shall have control over their estates, it is not usually relevant in determining how a person's estate should be disposed of after death:

36. 524 S.W.2d 210 (1975).

The fact that there exists a generally deteriorating mental condition or that old age is accompanied by mental slowness, poor memory, childishness, eccentricities, and physical infirmities does not show lack of testamentary capacity. . . . Mental derangement sufficient to invalidate a will must be insanity so broad as to produce general mental incompetence or insanity which causes hallucinations or delusions.[37]

Yet on far shakier grounds individuals have been made conservatees! How can we account for this discrepancy? One can argue that *entitlement* and the *use* of assets are separate matters. Conservatees are denied the use of their assets but they remain entitled to them. The central focus in drawing up a will is the individual's right to dispose of assets as he or she sees fit. It is assumed that whoever receives the assets after the death of the testator will use them in a way not at odds with public policy. But it could also be argued that the choice of the person to be given such assets does indeed affect public policy. At some point, the right to dispose of assets as one sees fit must be balanced against the right of society to use those assets in a socially beneficial way. Without such a perspective, no taxation whatsoever could be justified. Thus, the court will allow a father to specify that his son receive part of his estate on the condition that the son marry but not on the condition that the son remain celibate, for "a condition calculated to induce a beneficiary to marry, even in a manner desired by the testator, is not against public policy. A condition calculated to induce a beneficiary to live in celibacy or adultery is against public policy."[38]

We should now ask whether conservatorship as currently practiced satisfies the standard of public policy. The conservator is charged with conserving the estate and should not risk its dissolution, as the *Salz* decision indicates. But the conservatee's inability to manage the estate is no ground for losing its maximum benefit. Indeed, in compensation for the

37. *Evans v. Liston*, 116 Ariz. 218 (1977).
38. *Matter of Liberman*, 18 N.E.2d 658 (1939).

loss of control, the conservatee should be given not just an adequate benefit or the "accustomed" benefit of the estate but maximum benefit. Perhaps such a proviso would decrease the number of petitions for full conservatorships.

A broader question, however, concerns the most socially just use of estate assets. In the law of wills, the spouse, offspring, and family are the favored beneficiaries because both the existence of families and their work as motivated and efficient quasi-economic units are in society's interest. On these public policy grounds, the conservator of an estate should be a family member who employs directly the financial assistants other conservators use. But if no family members are available or if those available are themselves incapable of managing funds efficiently, are the only alternatives then the legal and banking community or the bureaucracy?

In most cases, an elderly person who requires full conservatorship also needs limited guardianship. If so, the guardian society itself would have a presumptively beneficial interest in the conservatee's estate. If the funds of the estate are not to go to family members who can make good use of them, they could best be used to endow services for the elderly. Such funds could be invested like pension funds and the dividends could be used to support both the guardian society and the conservatee. This public policy use of funds differs somewhat from those uses justified by bankers and lawyers, but it is a bona fide public policy use worthy of consideration nonetheless.

6

Dying in a Technological World

Throughout the history of the human species old age has signaled approaching death. Although aging is generally thought to be not a disease but a natural condition, it is still true that aging is regarded as a power that causes death. People who are aging are slowly dying, at least in the sense that the direct causes of nonaccidental death are themselves often caused by the decay of aging.

In the first chapter I analyzed biological aging and determined that from a theoretical standpoint aging implies either consent or powerlessness: either it is allowed to take place or else it cannot be resisted. From a practical standpoint, however, we cannot make such a choice because we have not yet found a way to reset the biological clock. It appears that someday we may have to decide whether to *allow* individuals to age biologically. The possibility of technologies to extend life raises new questions about the meaning and value of human life. This chapter will consider some of these new questions and some older ones as well.

LIFE EXPECTANCY AND LIFESPAN

Life expectancy, the average number of years an individual can expect to live, has been greatly increased in recent decades, at least in the developed countries. Half of all ancient Romans are thought to have died before their twenty-third birthdays. During the next nineteen centuries life expectancy increased by twenty to thirty years, and in the last century alone has again increased by that amount.[1] More

1. Vladimir V. Frolkis, *Aging and Life-Prolonging Processes*, trans. Nicholas Bobrov (New York: Springer, 1982), p. 306.

and more people are dying close to the outer limits of the human lifespan, which is thought to be between 110 and 120 years. If progress in medicine continues, if cancer and cardiovascular disease become curable, then it is possible that all who do not die by accident or suicide will live the maximum lifespan. This possibility may have a profound effect on our idea of the timeliness or untimeliness of death, and perhaps on the meaning of life itself. Unless birth rates decrease, there will be more elderly persons in society enjoying relative good health until the very end. It is also conceivable that mortality might decline gradually (because of accidental death) with no maximum lifespan at all. If it becomes possible to replace all the corruptible organs of a body with artificial organs, lifespan could be increased much beyond 110 years. But in that case we would have to ask *what* is being preserved, what is allowed to live longer, and whether such preservation is desirable. I will turn to these questions shortly.

LIFE EXTENSION AND NATURAL DEATH

Technologies to extend life have consisted of biochemical treatments of one or more of the putative aging processes, designed to nullify these processes and correct, if possible, the damage they have done. These treatments include modification of diet (for example, decreasing caloric intake to increase life expectancy); nucleic acid therapy, including immunotherapy to nullify self-attack; the use of inhibitors such as procaine hydrochloride (gerovital), the corticosteroids, and the antioxidants; and the use of activators such as L-dopa and the thyroid hormones. Besides the biochemical techniques there are the treatments in which machines administer the operations of biological processes. Such machines include external life-support systems for the various vital organs and the circulatory system.

It becomes increasingly difficult to define a *natural* death for those who accept all the medical treatment available in a modern hospital. Although individuals can die a purely natural death, they cannot do so casually, for they must have some idea when dying is about to take place before they can decide to let it happen "naturally."

Let us consider three possible ways of dying. In the first a person rejects all medical treatment for any illness or trauma. Although even a simple cut can lead to infection, blood poisoning, and death, this person accepts the risk in a desire for a natural death. Such a person would have to answer the objection that it is unreasonable to accept death when a cure might easily be achieved with little intervention in the natural processes of the body. Historically, most church authorities and religious individuals have not objected to medical treatment once its effectiveness became clear. Nonetheless, purists remain who insist that treatment contravenes divine destiny. They appear in courts of law, insisting that they can distinguish the artificial and the natural in a clear, unambiguous way and affronting the general populace, who accepts medical treatment. The purists must somehow support their normal life processes in an entirely natural way and must decide whether it is natural to wear glasses or to live in heated shelters. Eventually the naturalist position of a modern person in modern circumstances would have to be defended and elaborated in a highly theoretical fashion, almost to the point of absurdity.

In the second possibility, a person accepts some medical assistance but desires a natural death as well. This person must decide when treatment should cease and death should be allowed to occur. But how can a person make a meaningful decision? If the person accepts considerable medical treatment for a disease, then death can never be the natural death that would have occurred, for by allowing the treatment the person has postponed death by days or years. The more frequently medical intervention is chosen, the more difficult it becomes to decline further intervention. Increasingly a natural death becomes a fiction of mind. Only when all hope of regaining health is lost does the person choose to die "naturally."

Perhaps one way to avoid this slippery-slope problem is to specify in advance the circumstances in which a natural death can be allowed to take place. A person may decide that all medical treatment of major illnesses should cease after, say, age fifty-five. But this person may be in uncommonly good health at that age. What happens then if a sudden illness strikes? Even now, we must concede that the good health this person enjoys at, say, age forty would have been unnatural in Roman times; medical advances may soon make the expectation of good health as natural at seventy as it is today at forty. Thus the slippery slope reemerges. The only way to get around it is to decide to hold to a specified demarcation point no matter what. Because death must come eventually, the acceptance of that point is reasonable—even if the conditions later change.

In the third possibility, a person rejects the very notion of a natural death either in the future or the present. Such a person is willing to do whatever is necessary to stay alive and regain health. But this person must still decide what it means to live a human life. If all death is artificial in the sense that it occurs because of a technological problem that could be solved with the appropriate biochemistry—death is an accident of ignorance, so to speak—then at what point does a hitherto human life cease to be human when it avails itself of all technological means in order to survive? What is the cost of survival? Consider the brain-in-the-bottle case. The brain of a diseased person might be removed to a nutrient solution and attached to a computer with appropriate sensory and display equipment. That person might be given artificial legs and arms and a mobile robotic body. If the apparatus differs from the body the person knew, however, he or she may have an identity problem, particularly if companions remain in their natural condition. But if the apparatus looks exactly like the person's own body, such problems might not occur. This person's view and experience directly oppose those of the believer in natural life and natural death. This person's life is, and has always been, an artificial condition, so the electronic body is no more artificial than the body that is flesh and blood. No death is natural, and life need not be natural either.

The three possibilities I have described suggest why one cannot take for granted the notion of a natural death. In our technological world we must decide how to live in the light of our own ethical and historical norms. The naturalist tends to judge the future by the past, whereas the artificialist tends to judge the past by the future. Each employs a specific set of values about the meaning of human existence, as does the person who employs both perspectives but at different times.

Daniel Callahan has suggested specific criteria for ascertaining when a death is natural: (1) when one's lifework has been acomplished, (2) when one's moral obligations have been discharged, (3) when the death would not offend the sensibility of others or lead them to despair about the human condition, and (4) when the process of dying is not marked by unbearable pain.[2] This definition is less radical than the one I outlined in discussing possible attitudes toward death. It applies more clearly to some conditions, moreover, than to others. The death of a youth by accident is unnatural if that youth would have lived for many more years; and such a death offends the sensibility of the youth's parents and loved ones. My interest, however, is death in the last decades of the life cycle. In this case, the problem of defining lifework become crucial.

Callahan relates lifework to vocational and professional goals, but he also notes that only professionals have professional goals. A laborer is presumably content to work well in a healthy condition and generally regards work as a means to the overall goal of living well. But then such a worker's death cannot be natural because it frustrates the goal of simply living, just as aging increasingly frustrates the goal of living well. Furthermore, if we accept aging as natural, then we must also accept changing goals as natural, for aging

2. Daniel Callahan, "Natural Death and Public Policy," in *Life Span: Values and Life-Extending Technologies,* ed. Robert M. Veatch (New York: Harper & Row, 1979), p. 164. See the criticisms of James F. Childress in the same volume, pp. 176–83.

means continually compensating for the loss of some capacities and developing new goals based on the attainment of others. It is not a matter of having a particular set of goals at the outset of maturity and continually working to achieve them. If, indeed, a person continues to develop capacities, then earlier goals will most likely become unimportant even before they are realized. Few among the aging would be accountable for the goals they developed at twenty-five.

Callahan's second and third criteria for natural death depend in part on the reactions of others. When he writes of discharging moral obligations, he means primarily those of parents to their children. These become less weighty as parents age and children grow to maturity. But if offspring continually make demands—though those demands may change as the years go by—it is conceivable that parental obligations may continue well into old age. There is no unqualified sense of obligation at work here. Parents at eighty may feel obligated to assist their children of sixty simply because they remain children to them, creatures whose very existence derived from parental acts.

Callahan's third criterion relates even more pointedly to the reaction of others:

> The death of an elderly person who has lived a rich and full life is apparently not, in any society, counted as an evil, symptomatic of a deranged and cruel universe. It may well be that mankind has simply rationalized that kind of death; since it cannot be helped, it might as well be accepted. Nor is there any way to determine whether, as many (though not all) elderly testify, their proclaimed readiness to die is a rationalization. One can only point out the brute fact that in the eyes of neither themselves nor others is death an evil.[3]

But to say that such a death is not an evil is not the same as saying that it does not affect one's sense of hope in human existence. The cause of despair is not death itself— even the violent accidental death of a youth is not an evil in the sense that an evil power has caused it—but the in-

---

3. Callahan, "Natural Death and Public Policy," p. 167.

evitability of dying and of aging generally. Why should the beauty of the beloved be taken away without complaint? Incapacitation by natural aging offends sensibility. Without such offense it is doubtful that the world's religions would have developed their elaborate rituals and myths to justify belief in life everlasting.

Callahan is reluctant to translate his four criteria into public policy. Just as there seem to be no philosophical standards for the achievement of natural death, there are no objective practical standards either. Among individuals at a given time, and even for a given individual at different times, the meaning of death is too varied to allow for a uniform description on which might be based a policy to permit or resist death on the grounds of its naturalness. The achievement of one person's goals is but a stepping stone to another person's. Philosophically sensitive progeny may deem the death of parents tragic, whereas more worldly offspring may find the same death timely, perhaps even overdue.

Prior to the fifteenth century death was thought to result from some divine command. In the *Iliad* when Hector and Achilles are poised to strike each other beneath the walls of Troy, the poet pauses to describe the father of the gods as he weighs on a balance the fate of each fighter. The balance tips in favor of Achilles; Hector dies. Death for the Greeks resulted from a moment of decision, although the process of deliberation itself might have been obscure. Later, in the Christian Middle Ages, death was an accumulated effect, the result of divine satisfaction or disgust. When the belief in supernatural explanation declined after the fifteenth century, death became plausible as a worldly effect of natural forces. But because, as I have noted, it is not possible to pinpoint precisely how a death can be said to be natural, it has been proposed that there are really other issues behind the natural death debate, issues in which life and death have positive valuations in their own right.[4]

---

4. Robert M. Veatch, *Death, Dying, and the Biological Revolution* (New Haven, Conn.: Yale University Press, 1976), pp. 293–305.

Death is often valued because it marks the end of suffering or a relief from boredom; or because it gives human life its particularly humane quality; or because it serves as the goad for progress. But valuing death for such reasons is really valuing life. When the quality of life is threatened, we value death as a mostly negative good: death is to be preferred to living with disease. Even the belief that the living desire to control the conditions of life because they will die implicitly accepts the superiority of life over death. As Robert Veatch argues, "Prolonging life and combating 'natural' death are goods that are part of man's responsibility in building human community."[5] Yet he also admits that if we cannot cure painful disease, there is little value in prolonging painful life. Until we can cure or prevent disease and aging generally, those who die are victims of our ignorance even if their deaths seem natural to us.

IS AGING A DISEASE?

In the first chapter I argued that nothing we know about biological systems suggests that local irreversibility of aging is possible even in principle. If aging results from biological living, from the mere functioning of organisms in an environment, then the factors that produce aging are linked in physical relations, each of which could be reversed so that the part of the organism affected by aging would retain its integrity. Only if aging were caused by psychic, or mind-on-body, influences could it be said to be irreversible—as long as psychic development itself could be established as irreversible. Mental vitality, however, seems to retard aging—or at least its usual manifestations—rather than advancing it.

H. Tristram Engelhardt, Jr., has noted that to call something a disease is to place it in a certain social context. "We will not discover if aging is a disease," he writes, "in the same way we might discover if the world is round or if an

5. Ibid., p. 302.

infectious agent is responsible for a type of cancer."[6] Rather, we might decide to call aging a disease if we adopted certain attitudes about the *status* of the aging person. For example, the aging person might be like the sick person, Engelhardt argues, in the following ways: (1) the aged are exempted from many social responsibilities; (2) the aged are not responsible for their state but rather suffer from a natural incapacity; (3) society considers aging, like sickness, to be something to postpone or eliminate; and (4) the aged require and should seek the help of the health care establishment. The first inroads we make in retarding or reversing the aging process will signal a change in nomenclature from *aging* to *disease*.

Even if aging is eventually regarded as a disease, it will be considered a disease endemic to the life process—just as we may discover someday that cancer is endemic to the life process in a regular, inexorable way. Everyone would contract the disease of aging, unlike hepatitis, for example, which is contracted under conditions more specific than merely being a genetically governed living organism. It is doubtful that aging will ever be a disease that selects its individual victims. If it did, it would have to be considered a high-level systemic disease of complex living organisms, not a disease of individuals per se.

PAIN AND EUTHANASIA

Where does the problem of pain fit into the view that aging is a disease and that no death is natural? Eliminating aging is a problem both of relieving pain and of establishing well-being and satisfaction with life. But pain is a notoriously elusive and ambiguous notion. If aging can be eliminated after age fifty, will it become painful not to have the physical powers of a twenty-year-old? Indeed, does the elimination of all painful disease signal the elimination of pain itself as well? Or is it

6. H. Tristram Engelhardt, Jr., "Is Aging a Disease?" in Veatch, *Life Span*, p. 189.

possible that a new set of pains will be introduced—like the adolescent's pains of frustrated expectation?

It is possible to distinguish psychically charged suffering from suffering that is not psychically charged. One's state of mind directly influences the impact of a psychically charged insult, whereas state of mind has little or no influence on insults that are not so charged. We can also distinguish pains that are, so to speak, "chosen" from those that occur without warning or effort. The pains that result from muscular exertion differ in a basic way from the pains of muscular fatigue in illness or old age. The pain of consummation differs essentially from the consummation of pain, even when the former results from an uncontrollable, thoughtless, willful activity. Enduring pain that is a by-product of exertion is a badge of courage; one may, under the right conditions, endure even acute pain and consider it "friendly." But the unfriendly pains of illness or old age are plainly evil, perhaps because they signify a loss of control, particularly future control. This loss of control leads to a loss of autonomy.[7]

Experience, of course, does not neatly divide suffering into friendly and unfriendly pains. The presumption that most pains lead eventually to a loss of autonomy led Seneca to conclude that pain has no place in life as it is meant to be lived:

> For living is not a good, but living well. Accordingly, the wise man will live as long as he ought, not as long as he can. . . . He always reflects concerning the quality, and not the quantity, of his life. . . . It is not a question of dying earlier or later, but of dying well or ill. And dying well means escape from the danger of living ill.[8]

It is doubtful that Seneca would have advised suicide after the slightest prick of disappointment in life, and he would doubtless have counseled optimism and broad judgment for

7. Laurence B. McCullough, "Pain, Suffering, and Life-Extending Technologies," in Veatch, *Life Span*, pp. 118–41.
8. Quoted in McCullough, "Pain, Suffering, and Life-Extending Technologies," pp. 118–19, from Seneca's "On Suicide."

adolescents. Only if pain threatened to proliferate like aging itself would his advice concerning suicide apply.

Seneca's advice presumes a fixed lifespan. If life extension is possible, however, one cannot so easily identify the last stages of life as just additional time to exist. The open-ended extension of life would make all of us adolescents, and our pains only temporary misfortunes. If Seneca endorsed living well, he could not have failed to endorse living well and long without seeming to advise a pursuit of momentary experience alone. Some pains may be justified because they make possible the long life that is a necessary, though not a sufficient, condition for living well.

Whenever painful medical treatment is employed, we measure both the potential benefit itself and the likelihood of attaining it against the known and unknown costs in pain. Where the efficacy of the treatment is unknown, we cannot make such an assessment easily. If our pain continues despite treatment, if the treatment itself produces new pain, or if we die soon after treatment, then we have suffered in vain. When such outcomes are likely, the possibility of euthanasia must be considered.

Although the term *euthanasia* means "good death," it is usually discussed in contexts where only a choice among various bad deaths is possible. The euthanasia issue today involves the person afflicted, competent helpers, friends and family, and the precedent-fearing public. The afflicted cannot give permission to terminate life without good grounds established in long medical experience. But when a person is powerless to effect his or her own death, there should be a strong presumption that the person's wishes will be seriously considered. The policy of the American Medical Association has been to resist patients' requests to have their lives terminated by active intervention (for example, by lethal injections) because doctors do not wish to think of themselves as involved in ending lives as well as in saving them. Only when great effort has been made to save a patient and the cause is hopeless is that patient allowed to die. The argument for this passive approach is presumably that until all effort has been made to save the patient, no one can be sure recovery will not take place, with the patient grateful afterward that a despairing wish to die was not granted. Moreover, in some illnesses the diagnosis can be fundamentally wrong. The practice of passive euthanasia in such illnesses would probably not result in patients' deaths, but active euthanasia most definitely would. In most illnesses, however, particularly severe burns, crippling injuries, blindness, and the like, where diagnosis is relatively certain, such a concern is unwarranted.

If objective criteria justify one person's killing another in a hospital setting, according to one argument against active euthanasia, those criteria take on a life of their own and imply that other persons outside the hospital who meet the criteria should also be killed. If the criteria for active euthanasia are utterly subjective, death can be thought of as a result of the whims and idiosyncrasies of the parties involved. There is, however, a third approach—one that depends on personal criteria but avoids reliance on whim.

In this approach, the individual patient and doctor discuss the issue of euthanasia. When a serious condition is diagnosed, the doctor's duty is first and foremost to cure the patient, perhaps with cool competence in doing so. The patient's duty is first and foremost to desire and will a return to better health. As treatment progresses, the doctor and the patient convey to each other any experience of disappointment in the hoped-for result. At that point, between them, they begin to discuss the possible worst-case scenarios, with the physician informing the patient of the likelihood of success and the risks to be taken. The patient shows good faith by taking these risks. If the results are positive, then the doctor can once again adopt a manner of cool competence toward the patient. If the patient's condition degenerates, the two discuss the question of euthanasia.

Because of the essential asymmetry of the relation—the doctor is well, the patient ill—the doctor must listen intently to the patient's pleas for relief from suffering, wondering inside how one would tolerate such pain and whether, in the patient's position, one would want to go on living. If there are grounds for genuine hope—not the abstract, a priori hope of the medical profession generally—the doctor must articulate that hope to the patient. But if the hope is only abstract, the possibility of active euthanasia must be considered. If the patient first brings up this possibility with the doctor in an adversary role, the doctor may seek outside consultation (which has probably been sought already) on the patient's condition. Once hope ceases to be personal and genuine, the patient may be granted the wish to die.

With this approach, any doctor who does not wish to engage in this adversarial tug-of-war should not be entrusted with curing either. Today doctors evade the question of euthanasia, hiding behind a manner of extreme bustle and business and at times transferring patients to other colleagues like so many pieces of furniture sent out for repair. Many doctors (allergists, for example) avoid this adversarial interaction with patients. Many others (geriatricians, oncologists, cardiologists) for whom the adversarial interaction seems unavoidable want no part of a life-or-death decision and hide behind the mechanistic model of treating illnesses or pathologies as the whole story of their occupation role.

The approach I suggest here narrowly construes the issue of euthanasia as one that involves neither friends and family nor the state and civil society. More traditional approaches emphasize the adverse effect of euthanasia on loved ones and on the professionalism of the medical community—as if euthanasia polluted all who came in contact with it. It is suggested that euthanasia might cause a depression among the bereaved so severe as to threaten their lives or that it might entice doctors and politicians to kill off the old and the deviant.[9]

Opponents of euthanasia fear not only these consequences but also the very attitude toward life that for them constitutes the particular immorality of euthanasia:

9. Arthur J. Dyck, "An Alternative to the Ethic of Euthanasia," in *Ethical Issues in Death and Dying,* ed. Robert F. Weir (New York: Columbia University Press, 1977), p. 291.

Those who decide for euthanasia seem to accept an ethic which ultimately privatizes and subjectivizes the injunction not to kill. Those who oppose euthanasia see the decision not to kill as one that is in harmony with what is good for everyone, and indeed is an expression of what is required of everyone if goodness is to be pervasive and powerful on earth.[10]

Here is the traditional view that individuals cannot make life-or-death decisions—presumably only God can do this—although those who espouse this view, as I noted earlier, have found it easy enough to support and even instigate wars and executions for their own purposes. Underlying this view is the fundamental conviction that one can avoid the anguish of choice through belief in a divinely ordained set of priorities. But before one can act on such a conviction, one must form it either by postulating divine reality in a hypothetical inference or by making a blind leap of faith. The first method is coolly scientific and encompasses the considerations taken up in the patient-doctor tug-of-war just described. The second method is fiercely private and subjective and as a source of legitimation is no different from the final period of decision making in the patient-doctor approach when hope is clung to or lost. No way has yet been found to make decisions except through the anguish of individual minds. Those who espouse the traditional view of euthanasia seldom concede this point, for they are uncomfortable with the inextinguishable subtleties around which every conviction revolves.

THE MATTER OF SUICIDE

Euthanasia, in the most sympathetic sense, is a form of suicide. The afflicted person requests death at the hands of another because that person is either physically or psychologically unable to bring about his or her own death. A person may desire death but fear that the attempt to die will not succeed and will perhaps only worsen the physical condition. At the heart of all fear of suicide is the fear of a

10. Ibid., p. 295.

failure that makes another attempt impossible. Not only death, in other words, but also the certainty of death is desired.

How far should suicide be considered a private right of the autonomous individual? While the doctor-patient partnership grants legitimacy to euthanasia, on whom can the isolated individual rely in the struggle with suicide? In the case of euthanasia the issue is medical. As a society we rule out euthanasia on nonmedical grounds or, if the medical question is central, where patients are not in a position to speak competently themselves. In the case of suicide the issue is psychological or, more properly, philosophical. Unless the potential suicide is severely paranoid or deluded, he or she will consider life and its value. But someone considering suicide is hardly in a condition to assess this value coolly. Potential suicides first contemplate the act for specific reasons; but once the idea of killing one's self arises, continued reflection on the original problem becomes clouded. The demeanor of such a person reflects this difficulty: in this sense the potential suicide can be said to cry for help.

Traditionally, suicide has been regarded as a sin and as an anti-human act of despair. Intervention in the name of God or the state has been justified to prevent it on the grounds that the suicidal state of mind, being psychological, is only transient (whereas death is permanent); that all life is good; that the effects of suicide on others are destructive; and that the 10 to 12 percent success rate for suicide attempts constitutes a prima facie case for the ambiguous intent of all suicides.[11] Such intervention contains elements of bad faith and manipulation. We cannot undermine the status of a belief by saying that it may pass away. *All* beliefs may pass away, including the one that opposes suicide. Nor can we argue against acting on a belief because it is transient. The Christian martyrs chose death in the name of their beliefs

11. William F. May, "The Right to Die and the Obligation to Care: Allowing to Die, Killing for Mercy, and Suicide," in *Death and Decision*, ed. Ernan McMullin (Boulder, Colo.: Westview Press, 1978), p. 127.

and did not postpone dying because they thought they might change their minds at a later time. Postponement would have been an act of intellectual cowardice. Common to martyrdom and suicide are strong convictions and the desire to act on them.

Moreover, to prevent suicide because of its consequences for others does not follow. First suicide is made out to be a terrible thing, and then it is condemned for producing terrible effects. The way around this logical bind is to lift the invariable stigma of suicide and let each case stand or fall on its merits, producing sometimes good effects, sometimes bad ones. We may see all suicides as ambiguous cries for help in part because of our inability to investigate fairly the position of the potential self-killer. A fair investigation could take the form of an extended dialogue between the would-be suicide and a philosophical practitioner of some sort—someone who is neither a close friend, nor a lover with a great emotional stake in the issue, nor a psychologist with a detached, analytic view. The philosophical practitioner would employ the Socratic method and, unlike the psychologist, would *demand* that the potential suicide, now an adversary, present a consistent and plausible defense of the desire for death. Such a process would either rationalize an act of legitimate suicide or reveal a confused and vindictive suicide for what it is—death by mental accident and mistake. Of course a stubborn but unreasonable defense of suicide is always possible. But once suicide is given credence, once it ceases to be an outlaw act, the proclivity toward silence about it will be overcome, and the would-be suicide's reasons for desiring it will be revealed in such an encounter.

Would suicide be justified on grounds of old age alone? Perhaps in some circumstances. For the sake of argument we might imagine an extreme situation. A person lives so long, say 150 years, perhaps because of some genetic variation, and as a result is so lonely and enfeebled that he or she cannot bear to live on purposelessly for even another day. Although not ill, strictly speaking, this person endures, like all persons no longer young, the chronic annoyances of aging. The senses are dimmed; contemporaries have died. Yet the mind is remarkably nimble and experience can still be quite vivid. This person complains (most likely to no one in particular) of being tired of observing the human comedy. Wisdom came long ago, and the joy of enlightenment soon wore thin. Three or four generations have come along, each with its own sense of self-importance, each making the same foolish mistakes, each creating the same misery. Like the preacher of the Old Testament, this old person is tired of life and is convinced that there is nothing new under the sun and that the time has come to die. And suicide is the manner. None of the consequentialist arguments against it apply: nobody is left to cry; the aged person, to most people, is a curiosity only.

I have designed this case to explicate by contrast the situation we face. Seldom if ever do people live so long as to be entirely isolated from their original cohort, yet in a remarkable number of local situations individuals may feel isolated and left behind by friends and relatives. Surely it is possible for someone aged seventy to feel that human life is an idiot's tale that signifies nothing. Can someone that age justify suicide on such grounds? What about someone fifty or even forty? Age is a factor, but in a paradoxical way. Young would-be suicides, no matter how literate and sophisticated, cannot argue convincingly that life is meaningless because they have not lived long enough to see it from a wide perspective. Age, however, is a less central issue than the quality of experience. We are less likely to believe the claims about life in general of a person who has lived an isolated life. How could this person know? What has he or she done? In short, although age is a sufficient reason for preventing suicide in the young, it is not by itself sufficient to justify such prevention among the old. The old must be taken seriously when they complain that life is too long, but their complaint must not go unchallenged. They must reveal that they have reflected a goodly while on the question, and in depth.

But suppose a person cannot present a coherent defense of suicide. This person may have the presence of mind to realize that life has been limited and parochial and may believe that it is now too late to do anything to change it. Here the response is that it is never too late to grow mentally. The mind formulating the argument that age justifies a despairing suicide has the very dexterity needed for the enlargement of experience.

Finally, some individuals may contemplate suicide because their memories are too painful to recollect. It is conceivable that no therapy or philosophy could dispel the pain. New intellectual facts cannot offer relief, for the past is recalcitrant to the method of encounter and enlightenment. Age in such cases could justify suicide, for the longer people have lived with pain, the more they earn the right to free themselves from it.

PERSONHOOD AND THE VALUE OF LIFE

If my heart can pump blood in your body, in what sense is my heart *mine?* Why spend a thousand dollars to keep a dying kidney patient alive for one day when that same money could be used to inoculate a thousand poor children against smallpox? These questions can be raised today because of advances in the technology of medical treatment. Scientific innovations have always challenged entrenched commonsense moral convictions, but never have they raised challenges as pervasive as today's. Consider the technological advances in life support and extension that make possible the transplanting of vital organs from one organism to another. Such a possibility destroys once and for all the notion of organic necessity. An organism no longer has an interior; everything is external. Some parts are more essential to life than others, but no single part is indispensable by virtue of its uniqueness. Real hearts now can be replaced by artificial hearts.

We are fascinated by such a situation, treating a person with an artificial heart as a creature detached from natural life as we know it. And perhaps because of our detachment, we have not fully digested the implications of such a situation. We have seen how such implications affect our notion of a natural death. On a deeper level they also affect the very concept of personhood. For example, if my brain can be transplanted into your body, is the new entity fully me, or is it now partly you because I have inherited your immune and endocrine systems, which may have functioned differently from mine? Conventional techniques for identifying persons offer little help in answering such questions.

One answer is that conventional beliefs gradually change to accommodate choices made piecemeal over a long period of time. First a person chooses an artificial heart; later that person's grandchild chooses to have its brain attached to a computer. And just as people of the old frontier could not think of working in a factory or dying in a hospital, so we cannot think of a life without arms and legs. But such attitudes can change as conditions change.

There is another, more troubling answer, though. Although the technological revolution of the past thousand years has produced great changes in life as it begins, progresses, and ends, these changes have not cast doubt on the fundamental integrity of the individual person. Scientific endeavor, it was generally believed, would continually enhance the innate dimensions of natural personhood. Only with Rousseau, Marx, and later Nietzsche was that belief questioned. But even these writers conceived the conflict between science and the individual as largely political. Now with organ transplants and the possible externalization of intelligent activity in the form of computers, the specific ontogenetic and phylogenetic life history of the individual no longer defines the individual's personality and humanity. Rather, personality is a matter of patterned information exchanges. At birth, then, a human signal receiver and sender is produced; maturity is its state of maximal exchange; and in the period of aging and dying signal transmission declines, leading to the final shutdown of the system through death. In other words, we may have reached the point in technological development when the natural flow of incremental decisions about life and personhood may no longer

be the desired approach. Instead we may have to make pervasive policy decisions that affect our concept of a person in
some undesired, if not yet entirely clear, fashion. We can no
longer be sure, as prophets of progress have been, that what
the future brings will be both destined and desired. Hitherto
we have believed that history should not be tampered
with—that the decisions and effects would never add up to
circumstances both unanticipated and undesired—because
we believed that history was locked into the world of nature
where man and woman find their natural places.

So it may be that we must decide the conditions of personhood now and plan the course of future research accordingly.
We have been reluctant to limit scientific research because we
assumed that scientific knowledge and ambition could not
threaten what we cherish most. Hindsight, however, does
not support such optimism, and in the area of conceptual
change we cannot retrace our steps because change tends to
take place over many generations.

There is little basis for assuming either that history is
always greater than the individual or that the individuals of
each age are perfectly suited to live in that age. The idea that
the course of history is inexorable is a remnant of a theological way of thought no longer in keeping with the approach
of modern science. Such a belief couples the old eschatology
with the confidence that modern science can always react
swiftly enough to the unanticipated consequences of earlier
scientific work. Also implicit here is the faith that one generation can always remedy the ills bequeathed to it by
another. Only blind faith allows history to become whatever
it will, as if it has a destiny all its own. Such beliefs must
now be rejected because they stand in the way of achieving
a humane science.

The view that each person fits well into a particular time—
so that reclassifying persons, for example, as automata for
processing information will injure no person's sensibility—
overlooks the problem of transitions between generations.
Generations overlap and the old live simultaneously with the
young. Even when changes take place slowly, some individu-

als are caught between standards of appropriateness and morality that conflict. This problem specifically and chronically affects the old, particularly as life expectancy increases. Strategies are needed for coping with these conflicts. At the turn of this century at least a few Victorian gentlemen must have found unthinkable the idea of driving a horseless carriage, with its noise and odors and convulsions. Few people today would consent to a brain transplant, and many would not accept an artificial heart. Although it is not always the case that the values of older people are more entrenched than the values of the young, people seldom discard old values for new just because they are new.

Even if we allow a belief in autonomy and tolerance to guide us in defining personhood, we cannot avoid the conflicts that arise on an institutional or structural level. Along with a change in the concept of personhood may come a change in the value of individual life. How do we assess the worth of a single life? In most cost-benefit analyses age is a weighty factor in deciding the value of a life because the older the person, the smaller the stream of benefits produced. Similarly, when a life is valued according to the energy and skills required to produce its current condition and the expected value to be derived from the continuation of that condition,[12] the lives of the old—but also those of the immature—are devalued. Even aside from the undesirable consequences of such a view, one can argue that the very notion of a life having a single value that can be socially measured and compared with the value of other lives is fundamentally incoherent.[13]

The mode, the risks, and the consequences of an individual's death determine whether society paid a high or low price for any given person's death. The death of a doctor in a nuclear war is a lesser loss—in human capital—than that of a doctor in

12. For an analysis of various life-valuation methods, see Gavin H. Mooney, *The Valuation of Life* (London: Macmillan, 1977).

13. Nicholas Rescher, *Risk: A Philosophical Introduction to the Theory of Risk Evaluation and Management* (Washington, D.C.: University Press of America, 1983), chap. 14.

a conventional war because after a nuclear war a doctor has fewer opportunities to produce social benefit than after a conventional war. Similarly, after comparing the expense of caring for senile patients with the cost of eradicating communicable diseases among infants, we might decide to focus on the latter. But when the cost-benefit analysis ranges freely over the *entire* spectrum of social investments, we get a different picture: old age need not be pitted against infancy and youth but can be weighed against unproductive investment, new but obsolete military hardware, pork barrel and boondoggle civic projects, and a whole range of policies.

It may be argued that before we can assess the value of a person, we must determine the macroallocation of social wealth that is most just.[14] The American medical system has emphasized acute care and frontier exploration over preventive and long-term care, perhaps on the assumption that solving the most difficult research problems will in due course solve the more mundane policy problems as well. But in the meantime the cost of routine hospitalization has risen so high that people fear illness less as a cause of physical helplessness than as a cause of impoverishment. Two mechanisms for allocating care—the ability to pay and the demand for care (first come, first served)—keep the problem of macroallocation at bay. Behind them is an intuition that persons should be rewarded for their own efforts and a belief that luck in being at the right place at the right time is unquestionably fair. We choose these mechanisms, however, only because we fear the difficulty of choosing others.

We need not face a terra incognita of new priorities to address the problem of justly allocating wealth, however. Everyone knows the answer here: in modern economic society even private funds are often so poorly invested that they produce neither a useful or desired commodity nor long-term employment. Many projects are poorly researched and

14. Frank Harron, John Burnside, and Tom Beauchamp, *Health and Human Values: A Guide to Making Your Own Decisions* (New Haven, Conn.: Yale University Press, 1983), chap. 7.

planned and indeed may even have been conceived with failure as a perfectly acceptable outcome. Even the entrepreneurial psychology of a free market economy does not justify this waste of resources, for it fosters laziness and a decidedly uncapitalist carelessness about the consequences of one's decisions.

That such an aberrational economy exists is proof that too much capital is available for poorly conceived adventures. When capital is not dear enough, its power to produce benefits declines in a free economy, and much of it ends up in the wrong hands. Thus macroallocation is not only a theoretical requirement for justice but also an economic possibility even in today's economy. In practice this means that by reallocating wealth we can support a much higher level of health care than hitherto, leaving the basic economy intact and postponing the consideration of more fundamental issues of life and death until a later day.

7

The Obsolete Self

Will old age forever be a stigma? Even if in the future we regard it as a disease, we will make little progress in erasing the stigma until we eliminate aging itself. In fact, we may take a step backward if we label aging as a disease but fail to provide a cure for it. We remain in that situation with respect to cancer and can hardly say that a person with cancer is regarded as less victimized than a person with old age. It does not matter that everybody gets old, for if aging is a disease, its ubiquity makes it a plague or epidemic. As I noted earlier, to call old age a disease is to label the aged person unfortunate and to imagine an undiseased state as the desired alternative.

But calling old age a natural condition may not be acceptable either. Perhaps *ideal* old age is a natural condition that can be applauded as an accomplishment. But this condition is rarely found except in fiction. There are what psychologists like to call elite agers—individuals who stay active and healthy well into their seventh and eighth decades—but in today's world these individuals are miracles of nature, not norms to follow.

Most of the afflictions of aging result from specific life circumstances—the lives individuals have led, their psychic temperament, their working conditions, their use of leisure time, their interpersonal relations, and so forth. Life is a process that progressively differentiates individuals. By age sixty, people may have nearly completed the psychophysical sculpting of their appearance and personality. No one can stop the aging process, but no one ages outside the context of concrete living either. It is a fact of life that stress causes aging, as does backbreaking labor. A thirty-five-year-old

Gatsby is younger, slimmer, and more alert than the thirty-five-year-old mechanic who works in a petroleum stench from morning to night servicing Gatsby's limousine. So old age is natural in only a general sense, and to accept too readily the belief that it is natural is to fail to see the ways we may change its course. Aging, even from a strictly biological point of view, does not happen automatically or inevitably but relates to the way organisms live from moment to moment.

We know that very rapid biological aging is more than a theoretical possibility if aging is a genetically programmed event. The rate of aging may also be governed by psychic factors—which have not yet been isolated. Aging takes place in time and is never, strictly speaking, a cause of our bodily condition. Our senses wear away because we use them, and their loss of function, like that of any frequently used tool, results from use and not, properly speaking, from the wear itself. However, the functional theory of aging suggests that wear is a function of *proper* use. A hammer lasts longer if its handle is used as a grip rather than as a chisel.

Rather than regarding aging as either a natural condition or a disease, perhaps we should regard it as a dynamic, holistic variable on the physical level, the way attitude and mood are dynamic variables on the psychic level. If it is a dynamic variable, there are no "hard facts" of aging; no biological clock or other quasi-theological supernatural entity serves as a prime mover, impervious to feedback and recalibration. Theoretically this possibility means that species-specific lifespan is also a part of biological theology, a concept functioning in contemporary theoretical biology the way the notion of heavenly bodies as divine creatures functioned in sixteenth-century astronomy—as a barrier to scientific knowledge and manipulation.

If the simpleminded notion of biological aging might become obsolete, could we change our notions of psychological and sociological aging to render the prevalent views on which these notions are based obsolete as well? The stereotypes of psychological aging include the widely held belief that old age is that last stage of the life cycle, a period of looking back and recollection, a time when tomorrow means just the day after today. It is also a time of renewed childishness, or foolish narcissism, of frail thought and shaky emotions. But most of all old age is a time when the self experiences a loss of center. The aged self is obsolete from a psychological perspective because it is like a cage without a bird or like the image in Michelangelo's poem quoted in the introduction to this work: a wasp in a leathery bag. The wasp is the soul or self, now only a tiny presence unable to fill out the bodily frame with its vital energy.

The stereotypes of sociological aging are similar. Aging individuals are persons with declining abilities and obsolete knowledge. The shorter the social lifespan of whatever is modern and up-to-date, the more quickly social obsolescence occurs. Rapid technological advance greatly intensifies the process. New technological breakthroughs in a highly competitive economic environment mean that only the most recently trained initiates possess the information that is in greatest demand. Other individuals must move into the managerial class—where they help guide the corporate entity away from possible extinction—a move that guarantees they will not be able to keep abreast of the latest theoretical developments. Only a few individuals—almost all of them men— stay on the cutting edge of business and industry because they hold positions of great power. They are not obsolete, but only because in an economic system that places great value on rank, no one outranks them. If the workplace were more democratically structured, obsolescence would fall equally on all.

It is significant that primarily the young are given access to the latest information through the educational system; young people are thought to be in the best position to use the information, whereas it is assumed that older individuals are either incapable of relearning a subject or have no time to do so. It is considered inefficient to move individuals back into learning when they are useful as well-seasoned workers and managers. Implicit in this view is the belief that the individual has a limited useful life as a worker, which only becomes less valuable if the worker takes time off for relearning. One can hold such a belief only if one fails to consider the full life of seven or more decades. In the full lifespan, individuals have plenty of time to upgrade skills several times.

Cultural stereotyping also has a powerful influence in a society conscious of modernity. Not only the skills but also the values of aging individuals are thought to be obsolete. It is generally assumed by young and old alike that to age is to grow more conservative and more fearful of risks and novelties. Such an assumption, however, requires a more concerted defense than is usually made. True enough, the aging individual is familiar with the events and times of a world gone by, but past events are always fully modern in their own time; to have been part of them is to have been part of a modern era, with all of the excitement and danger that implies. Even if everything is old-fashioned from some later perspective—including specifically modernist movements—everything is not obsolete as well. The failure to make this distinction is at the heart of cultural stereotyping. When the architects of the Italian Renaissance turned to the structural forms of Greco-Roman antiquity, they were turning to the distant past, but they perceived its vitality. Such a past was not obsolete to them but rather more fully modern than the forms of the Gothic world around them. Sometimes the present is feeble and enfeebles the imaginations of those shaped by it, while the past is vigorous and progressive—and so too those shaped by it.

Specific socioeconomic conditions are likely to determine whether a person becomes more conservative or more radical in old age. The conservatism of youth is well known, as is the radicalism of many an aging revolutionary. Appreciating the consequences of actions and decisions with the experience of years can make one either more conservative or more radical. Youth is often blind to consequences and the conditions that bring them about. The older person knows more clearly how the world works and is thus more likely to understand the roots of conflict and injustice. Yet many an older person nostalgically embraces the earlier days simply because they are old-fashioned.

I discussed in an earlier chapter how cohort and familial allegiance create in the aging person both the desire to stay young and keep abreast and the sense that the present constitutes a betrayal of things and persons past. In response to these conflicting feelings, the aging person may withdraw into a shrinking world, and that person's life may become more internalized and retrospective, less firmly planted in the present. As the latest generation creates new fashions, earlier generations risk looking foolish if they embrace them, perhaps because they assume that they have had their chance and should not meddle in the fashions of the present day. Any cohort, however, can, without asking the permission of another generation, express itself in modern terms. Fashions may change for all generations, guided by the same social and ideological influences that give a look of modernity to the work of the latest generation. Too often the aging are willing to rest content with their past achievements, thinking these must remain untouched, ready for the museums of folk art of the future.

Cultural stereotyping leaves the aging person feeling cut off and even rancorous. Popular cartoons play on this idea. In a cartoon that appeared in *The New Yorker*, a couple in late middle age are seated in their living room, each holding a martini. The man is saying, "A young man seated beside me at the lunch counter borrowed my pen to write down the telephone number of a young woman seated beside him. How was your day?"[1] More damaging than the sense of alienation and stagnation this cartoon suggests is the feeling of rancor captured in a cartoon by Jules Feiffer. Here a grim elderly face is caught thinking out loud:

> You're born and you know you're the center of the universe . . . and childhood is the process of learning you're not the center of the universe . . . and adolescence is the process of coming to terms with not being the center of the uni-

1. *The New Yorker*, November 14, 1983.

verse . . . and maturity is the process of forgetting you ever
thought you were the center of the universe . . . and old age
is watching others become the center of the universe . . . and
hating them.[2]

Feiffer suggests that egocentricity is never overcome. The
old are jealous of the young—not this or that young person,
who is destined to become old soon enough, but the perpetual stream of new persons brought into being by our mating
urges and the mysteries of nature. Perhaps the most difficult
question confronting philosophers of aging is whether such
rancor can be overcome without fostering a resignation that
waits only for death.

BEYOND OBSOLESCENCE

Because the problem of the philosophical meaning of aging is
in fact a complex cluster of biological, psychological, and sociohistorical problems, any philosophical solution must tease out
the various subsidiary problems involved. Primary among
them is the biological status of aging, considered at several
points in this work. If aging is a temporary medical pathology
of our species, then we need not be concerned about any
psychosocial issues. But I have noted the danger of this notion that aging is a disease with specific, correctable causes.
As long as it is inevitable—a destiny for all—aging is not a
condition to pity; if it is a disease, it may become just that.
Furthermore, if aging has specific external causes like the
slow-acting viruses or proto-viruses now suspected of causing Alzheimer's disease, it becomes possible to think of remaining immune from aging or, worse, of contracting the
disease from others.

The most difficult period, especially for the aging, would
be that time before scientists find a cure but after they have
become convinced that the disease model is the correct one.
In the absence of a fountain of youth, aging seems part of the

2. *The Village Voice*, June 13, 1982.

natural, uncontrollable landscape; if such a fountain is suddenly discovered, aging will at once disappear from the landscape because all will desire to drink from it. In the real world of biochemistry, however, a sudden disappearance is unlikely because there is probably no single biological pathway to the heart of the regenerative vital processes. Complex organisms are hierarchies of hierarchies, shaped by the circuitous effects of nearly countless evolutionary trials and errors. To reassemble and rationalize such creatures without destroying their integrity may well be beyond the capacity of natural and artificial intelligence.

If and when aging is vanquished, will the idea of social obsolescence disappear? Not necessarily. In a world conscious of modernity it matters little that a person may be made to look young. It is the *mind* that is said to be obsolete. So if bodily aging is overcome, efforts must be made to overcome the stigma of being old-fashioned as well. This is a chore for psychologists and philosophers and would most likely involve a complete revamping of the prevalent views of human social life—a task I have only touched on here. Even if we do not end aging itself, however, we can still take steps to overcome the stigma of being old. As noted, we can point out the illusion of thinking about the past as if it were *always* in the past, just as we can point out to the young that the old were not always as they appear now. Although both tactics are obvious, their implications are seldom driven home because older generations do not try to vividly recreate their past for the young. So it is not surprising that the young see the past as dead and abstract—a mere world of dates and facts and figures with no real events or actors.

Much else can be done in a world with aging bodies. As I have suggested already, we can change our thinking about the relation of individuals to society. Many centuries ago Thomas Hobbes called the aggregate of persons—that is, society—a great Leviathan, an immense imperturbable being that moves forward with resolute determination, allowing nothing to deflect its progress. That image has changed little since Hobbes's time. The conflict between the individual and the group may well be irreconcilable. Perhaps modern civilization cannot get along without a proliferation of formalized roles that individuals enact in structured settings when they have little or no time for personal acquaintance or sympathetic understanding. How, then, can we change even one dimension of that mass activity, in this case the relation of young to old and the patterns of age-grading?

One way to humanize the Leviathan might be to reject it as a model of lifelike activity. In fact we do not think of society as a living organism at all. In Hobbes's time the mighty whale perhaps approximated what Hobbes really had in mind—a juggernaut, a vast working robot. To say that society is impersonal or that market forces operate at its heart is to concede that nothing truly human governs it. Its action, however complex and sophisticated, is beyond the reach of human reason and feeling. Macroeconomists and political strategists only dimly understand it. We have come to think of productive industrial and postindustrial civilization as a large machine: we feed young workers into it and it spews out both productive goods and services and its waste products, the aging individuals it has used up and the projects at which it has failed.

A truly organic model would regard society as alive and integrated at every moment and its members as living individuals fully engaged in it. This model suggests that the useful life of the individual can be much longer because his or her importance is derived not from economic value at a given moment but from the belief that to be fully human is to be engaged in useful work. Even in an aging organism a vast number of cells and most organs continue to function well beyond their prime; if they did not, the organism would abruptly perish. Because humans can procreate, we can easily think of society as an organism able to replace vital organs and structures whenever it desires. Yet only if society is a machine can it readily incorporate external materials. If some parts and functions of an organism are devoted to replenishment, that organism cannot replace its parts with external transplants. Its revitalization must, instead, be gradual and highly organized. It achieves organic integrity through the aggregate working of all its roles and functions.

From this organic perspective, the symbolic importance of an individual's aging per se is diminished. To be young or old does not signal a peculiar social status. Although aging still signals the approach of death and departure, it does not signal a person's obsolescence as much as the coming need to replace that person in the ongoing social enterprise.

Social obsolescence is tied to the notion that some activities and products are obsolete; this notion itself results from measuring value not by a society's ability to keep people stimulated and content, but by its increasing production of novel products. To the extent that both traditional socialism and capitalism embrace the cults of modernity and progress that shape these values, they cannot solve the problem of social obsolescence. Only if we cease to regard individuals as means of production and the present society as a tool for constructing future society will we see the futility of stigmatizing aging in economic and cultural life. If we do not believe in a grand destiny that we as a species must fulfill, then we will be less inclined to rush initiates into the system and to expel older members from it prematurely. The humane society, its eye on both the value of what it produces and the means and manner of production, is most clearly at odds with the worldview of the entrepreneurs who regard material and human energy as theirs to tame and shape into their own personal dreams of social and personal value.

A recent report on aging for the United Nations concluded that "matters will tend to worsen for the elderly unless new perspectives about them . . . are examined."[3] The United Nations World Health Organization proposes that governments recognize the desirability of implementing policies that reflect the following principles: the elderly must be recognized as beneficiaries of societal development and must be seen as a

3. Philip Selby and Mal Schechter, *Aging 2000: A Challenge for Society* (Cambridge: MIT Press, 1982), p. 19.

heterogeneous social group; old age must not be an "age of no consent," but rather the elderly must have opportunities for independence through access to health care, adequate housing, and transportation; and the elderly should be given opportunities to remain socially and economically engaged and cohesively bound with the younger generations on personal and social levels.[4] None of these principles is realizable or perhaps even desirable unless we rethink completely the meaning and purposes of social life. But we cannot change society overnight. We need a blueprint that tells us how to proceed at each step. There are many places to begin, perhaps none better than the crucial junctures of early education and late retirement. Education must not cease after the first two decades, nor should work begin only then. Similarly, retirement should not begin after six or seven decades, but extended periods of recreational activity should be possible throughout the lifespan; nor should work end finally and in some ritualized fashion, except *ex post facto*, when illness leads to death.

Perhaps the elephant is more apt than the Leviathan as a social symbol, for it is a creature of great longevity and memory, with a long period of gestation, and a disposition that is patient unless it is provoked. A society with these qualities would suit the entire lifespan and would be congenial to all generations. Such a society might overcome the idea of psychological obsolescence that stigmatizes the elderly as hollow beings. Individuals who remain active and productive lessen the risk of loss of center, the diminution of psychic energy or drive. Instead their various social roles continue to validate them as persons of standing. Their confidence promises even greater confidence so that as aging individuals they will feel at home in society at large, not simply in the extreme environments of the boardroom or retirement community. They will show affection without fearing to seem foolish, and they will pursue recreation intensely without fearing to seem irresponsible. It is up to the elderly to educate both themselves

4. Ibid., pp. 187–91.

and the younger generations. They must educate themselves about the possibilities for aesthetic experience and
sexual activity. And they must shape the thinking of the
young about their elders, giving the young a rich developmental picture of life and encouraging the young to place
their elders in a broad generational context and to see them
as evolving beings, continually differentiating even though
they are creatures of a particular historical period.

Aging individuals, moreover, need to make greater demands on themselves, taking risks and refusing to make the
reluctant compromises that eventually burn rancor into the
soul. Accustomed to an age-calibrated social clock, we easily
accept the view that certain experiences can be had or sought
only at certain times of life, regardless of our physical or
psychological condition. Sexual excitement, for example, is
generally thought to be the property of those under age forty.
In fact, much of that youthful excitement comes from the
novelty and mysterious adventure sexuality represents. We
must wonder whether the young would be as interested in
sex if they had to experience it as an utterly predictable ven-
ture. Not sexual response but sexual circumstance may
change over the years.

There is no good reason for an adult to act like a teenager.
Most likely having known love, an adult individual no longer
wishes to be in love only with love itself. And having known
physical intimacy, the individual need not seek it out except
among persons able to share a wide range of intimacies. Sexual excitement in the human species may have been triggered
since prehistoric times by its presence elsewhere in the larger
cohabiting group or clan; once that clan became fragmented
into isolated breeding units, the more rarefied excitement of
fantasy increasingly had to be substituted for vicarious excitement. If so, such excitement is less a function of age than of
imagination. B. F. Skinner and M. E. Vaughan suggest that
some pornography is useful in creating excitement:

> When life is no longer very exciting, we read exciting books
> and watch exciting movies and plays, and when life is no

longer very amusing, we read funny books and watch funny movies and plays. When our life is no longer very erotic, should we not read erotic books and watch erotic movies and plays? We not only identify with people we read about or watch, we respond in our own way to what they respond to. We are excited because others are excited and because of what they are excited about.[5]

An adult should not be like a teenager in another respect: the teenager wants to experience the unconditioned loyalty of true love for the first time; the adult knows what that loyalty is like, and, having found it, stops seeking it. Sexual excitement is not incompatible with such loyalty; that one can remain sexually attracted to the same person for decades is borne out by the studies of sexologists. Whether one experiences such excitement over a long period is determined by individual circumstances and decisions, however. Although our mating urges appear to be well formed, sexual energy is harnessed to a poorly conceived social mechanism. Our rituals of courtship are too simple to meet our real needs. As civilized, psychologically complex individuals we require more information about ourselves and our partners. Because the full consequences of our decisions bloom only in later years, we can easily associate these consequences with the ancillary condition of our aging.

Sexual liberation across the lifespan, like courting, is an issue that cannot be dealt with on a completely personal level. Sexual stereotyping is a social phenomenon with an important social function. Sexual taboos, as noted earlier, help regulate the orderly working of the social clock by setting the time for such socially significant events as marriage and parenthood. But sexuality for *individuals* is more than the vehicle it represents to social theorists or sociobiologists. A happy accommodation is possible between individual freedom and social stability. Traditional societies have been unduly cautious and conservative, attempting to control behav-

5. B. F. Skinner and M. E. Vaughan, *Enjoy Old Age: A Program of Self Management* (New York: Norton, 1983), p. 122.

ior and attitudes more than necessary in the belief that extra control is a harmless way to guarantee the degree of control the society desires. However, as we understand these mechanisms for efficiency and homeostasis, we may see more clearly what control is necessary and what is overkill.

Most of the theoretical and ideological reforms I have considered require either specific structural changes in the workings of everyday economic life or changes in widely held values and attitudes about the social significance of aging. But there is also a rich inner world of attitudes that are often externally shaped but have no clear social manifestation or function. I noted earlier, for example, that aging in a psychological sense means that one possesses a biography of one's self, still unfolding, to be sure, but already formed in its broad contours. Perhaps, then, the very burden of self-consciousness can prompt a desire for a Buddhist release from the world and the discovery, in Malcolm Cowley's words, of "the nirvana of dozing in the sun." Cowley describes the pleasure of such a release:

> Those pleasures [of old age] include some that younger people find hard to appreciate. One of them is simply sitting still, like a snake on a sun-warmed stone, with a delicious feeling of indolence that was seldom attained in earlier years. A leaf flutters down; a cloud moves by inches across the horizon. At such moments the older person, completely relaxed, has become a part of nature—and a living part, with blood coursing through his veins. The future does not exist for him. He thinks, if he thinks at all, that life for younger persons is still a battle royal of each against each, but that now he has nothing more to win or lose. He is not so much above as outside the battle, as if he has assumed the uniform of some small neutral country, perhaps Liechtenstein or Andorra.[6]

This psychological aging does not in fact require biological aging. Even computers might conceivably experience it some day.

6. Malcolm Cowley, *The View From Eighty* (New York: Viking Press, 1980), pp. 12–13.

The heart of the issue of psychological aging is the problem of maintaining novelty in experience. The functional view of biological aging hypothesizes that if novelty can be maintained, self-repairing systems could go on forever processing information, changing states, and repairing themselves. Individuals, however, have great difficulty keeping experiences fresh and new. They cannot be repeated exactly, and somehow what turns experiences into "experience" does not compensate the individual for the loss of freshness, surprise, and newness. The progressive decline of novelties is a fundamental asymmetry in life.

A capacity for long-range memory is partly responsible for the rising specter of boredom in later life. But this is only a partial explanation. We must not only have memories but also evaluate them. And to do this we must have a view of what it means to live a full life. Having the same experience many times over can lead to boredom and lack of interest, but perhaps we are too quick to judge or categorize an experience as boring or predictable when we recognize a few familiar traits in it. And perhaps we judge and categorize because we believe that life itself is a boring enterprise, a hopeless journey toward boredom.

It is hard to imagine a different view of life, however, unless we also imagine the restructuring of human consciousness. As John Dewey pointed out years ago, our consciousness requires a blend of novelty and predictable uniformity, desiring neither one nor the other in pure and consistent doses.[7] Too much novelty leads to confusion and fear; too much uniformity of experience leads to boredom and extinction. Individuals must seek new sources of excitement as other sources—simple sensory experiences and new places, tasks, and people—become elusive.

But there is a wide range of novelties that are complex and intellectual, not simple and sensory. Any individual who becomes absorbed in a specific subject notices that

7. John Dewey, *Art as Experience* (New York: Capricorn Books, 1934), chap. 3.

greater involvement widens one's horizons in that area and that the distinctions needed to remain absorbed become richer, the higher the standards of performance become. Any person who works at a given task long enough is bound to feel a sense of growth and increasing capacity. We do not feel this way about living in general because we cannot experience that sense of growth in the practical, utilitarian activities of the socioeconomic arena, which invariably represents a narrowing horizon for us, and because we identify life itself with that arena. We must give more effort to developing outside interests, but not in predictable ways or by using standardized products and procedures. We can make such an effort well into late life, at which time a good doze in the sun is altogether appropriate.

ENLIGHTENED AGING

An enlightened view of aging rejects the belief in obsolescence. Growing old is no less difficult than growing up once we cease deluding ourselves about its ultimate meaning. Overcoming the feeling that one is obsolete does not, however, mean the end of aging itself. Biological, psychological, and sociological aging together form a web of influences whose strands we cannot break. If some influences decline, others probably will take their place. Even with an end to biological aging, there would remain grading by chronological or psychological age as the social Leviathan sees fit. The conventional standards, stigmas, and taboos now imposed on the inherited natural world would be imposed on a world created by human choice.

I have sought to guard against the cult of youth in my thinking about the elderly, with its distinction between the old old and the young old. Attacking ageism by claiming that age discrimination is never justified and that a society in which age is irrelevant is possible invites a backlash that is as unfounded as ageism itself. In Victorian times it was thought that one aged according to the spiritual and social integrity of one's soul. Decrepit old age bespoke a life of little discipline and courage; healthy old age was a reward for a life of successful risk taking and pursuit. Now the anti-ageists offer a similar interpretation: the old old have somehow failed to come up to standard.[8] The great proliferation of how-to books about aging in recent years, often full of self-congratulation and even smugness, may only produce among the aging violent swings between the opposing poles of exhilaration and alienating depression. Neither aging nor the prospect of aging should become another ideological weapon in a ceaseless war of generations.

8. See Thomas R. Cole, "The 'Enlightened' View of Aging: Victorian Morality in a New Key," *The Hastings Center Report* 13 (1983): 34–40.

Selected Bibliography

CHAPTER 1

Adelman, Richard C., and George S. Roth, eds. *Altered Proteins and Aging*. Boca Raton, Fla.: CRC Press, 1983.

Behnke, J. A., C. E. Finch, and G. B. Moment, eds. *The Biology of Aging*. New York: Plenum Press, 1978.

Burnet, Frank M. *Immunology, Aging, and Cancer: Medical Aspects of Mutation and Selection*. San Francisco: W. H. Freeman, 1976.

Calow, Peter. *Life Cycles: An Evolutionary Approach to the Physiology of Reproduction, Development, and Ageing*. London: Chapman and Hall, 1978.

Caplan, Arthur L. "The 'Unnaturalness' of Aging—A Sickness Unto Death?" In *Concepts of Health and Disease: Interdisciplinary Perspectives*, edited by Arthur L. Caplan and H. Tristram Engelhardt, Jr. Reading, Mass.: Addison-Wesley, 1981.

Comfort, Alexander. *The Biology of Senescence*. New York: Elsevier, 1979.

Coni, Nicholas. *Ageing: The Facts*. New York: Oxford University Press, 1984.

Danon, D., N. W. Shock, and M. Marois, eds. *Aging: A Challenge to Science and Society*. Vol. 1, *Biology*. Oxford: Oxford University Press, 1981.

Davies, I. *Ageing*. London: E. Arnold, 1983.

Dawkins, Richard. *The Selfish Gene*. Oxford: Oxford University Press, 1976.

Esposito, Joseph L. "Conceptual Problems in Theoretical Gerontology." *Perspectives in Biology and Medicine* 26 (1983): 522–46.

Finch, Caleb E., and Leonard Hayflick, eds. *Handbook of the Biology of Aging*. New York: Van Nostrand Reinhold, 1977.

Fries, James F., and Lawrence M. Crapo. *Vitality and Aging*. San Francisco: W. H. Freeman, 1981.

Frolkis, Vladimir V. *Aging and Life-Prolonging Processes*. Translated by Nicholas Bobrov. New York: Springer, 1982.

Georgakas, Dan. *The Methuselah Factors: Strategies for a Long and Vigorous Life*. New York: Simon and Schuster, 1980.

Harsany, Zsolt, and Richard Hutton. *Genetic Prophecy: Beyond the Double Helix.* New York: Rawson, Wade, 1981.

Hayflick, Leonard. "The Strategy of Senescence." *Gerontologist* 14 (1974): 37–45.

Hershey, Daniel, and Hsuan-Hsien Wang. *A New Age-Scale for Humans.* Lexington, Mass.: Lexington Books, 1980.

Johnson, John E., Jr., ed. *Aging and Cell Function.* New York: Plenum Press, 1984.

Kohn, Robert R. *Principles of Mammalian Aging.* 2d ed. Englewood Cliffs, N.J.: Prentice-Hall, 1978.

Langone, John. *Long Life: What We Know and Are Learning About the Aging Process.* Boston: Little, Brown, 1978.

Makrides, Savvas C. "Protein Synthesis and Degradation During Ageing and Senescence." *Biological Reviews* 58 (1983): 343–422.

Medawar, Peter B. *An Unsolved Problem in Biology.* London: Lewis, 1952.

Miller, A. P. "A Computer Model of the Evolution of Specific Maximum Lifespan." *Mechanisms of Ageing and Development* 16 (1981): 37–54.

Minot, Charles S. *The Problem of Age, Growth, and Death.* New York: G. P. Putnam, 1908.

Mori, M., et al. "Codon Recognition Fidelity of Ribosomes at the First and Second Positions Does Not Decrease During Aging." *Mechanisms of Ageing and Development* 22 (1983): 1–10.

Pelletier, Kenneth R. *Longevity: Fulfilling Our Biological Potential.* New York: Delacorte Press, 1981.

Richardson, I. W. "The Metrical Structure of Aging (Dissipative) Systems." *Journal of Theoretical Biology* 85 (1980): 745–56.

Rockstein, Morris, and Marvin Sussman. *Biology of Aging.* Belmont, Calif.: Wadsworth, 1979.

Rosenfeld, Albert. *Prolongevity: A Report on the Revolutionary Scientific Discoveries Now Being Made About Aging and Dying, and Their Promise of an Extended Lifespan Without Old Age.* New York: Knopf, 1976.

Roy, A. K., and B. Chatterjee. *Molecular Basis of Aging.* Orlando, Fla.: Academic Press, 1984.

Samis, Harvey V., Jr., and Salvatore Capobianco, eds. *Aging and Biological Rhythms.* New York: Plenum Press, 1978.

Segre, Diego, and Lester Smith, eds. *Immunological Aspects of Aging.* New York: Marcel Dekker, 1981.

Strehler, Bernard L. *Time, Cells, and Aging.* New York: Academic Press, 1962.

Walford, Ray L. *The Immunologic Theory of Aging.* Baltimore: Williams and Wilkins, 1969.

———. *Maximum Lifespan.* New York: Norton, 1983.

Wantz, Molly, and John E. Gay. *The Aging Process: A Health Perspective*. Cambridge, Mass.: Winthrop, 1981.

Warthin, Aldred Scott. *Old Age: The Major Involution*. New York: Paul B. Hoeker, 1929.

CHAPTER 2

Abraham, G., P. Kocher, and G. Goda. "Psychoanalysis and Aging." *International Review of Psychoanalysis* 7 (1980): 147–55.

Anderson, J. E., ed. *Psychological Aspects of Aging*. Washington, D.C.: American Psychological Association, 1956.

Birren, James E., et al., eds. *Aging: A Challenge to Science and Society*. Vol. 3, *Behavioural Sciences*. Oxford: Oxford University Press, 1983.

Birren, James E. *The Psychology of Aging*. Englewood Cliffs, N.J.: Prentice-Hall, 1964.

Botwinick, Jack. *Aging and Behavior*. New York: Springer, 1973.

Bromley, Dennis B. *The Psychology of Human Ageing*. 2d ed. Baltimore: Penguin, 1974.

Datan, N., and H. W. Reese, eds. *Life-Span Developmental Psychology*. New York: Academic Press, 1977.

De Beauvoir, Simone. *The Coming of Age*. Translated by P. O'Brian. New York: G. P. Putnam, 1972.

Erikson, Erik H. *Identity and the Life Cycle*. New York: Norton, 1980.

———. *Insight and Responsibility*. London: Faber and Faber, 1964.

———. *Life History and the Historical Moment*. New York: Norton, 1975.

———. "Reflections on Dr. Borg's Life Cycle." In *Aging, Death, and the Completion of Being*, edited by David D. Van Tassel. Philadelphia: University of Pennsylvania Press, 1979.

———, ed. *Adulthood*. New York: Norton, 1978.

Evans, Richard I. *Dialogue with Erik Erikson*. New York: Harper & Row, 1967.

Feibleman, James K. *The Stages of Human Life: A Biography of Entire Man*. The Hague: Martinus Nijhoff, 1975.

Fisher, Seymour, and Roger P. Greenberg. *The Scientific Credibility of Freud's Theories and Therapy*. New York: Basic Books, 1977.

Freud, Sigmund. *The Standard Edition of the Complete Psychological Works of Sigmund Freud*. 23 vols. Translated by J. Strachey. London: Hogarth Press, 1953–1974.

Gedo, John E., and Arnold Goldberg. *Models of the Mind: A Psychoanalytic Theory*. Chicago: University of Chicago Press, 1973.

Gorman, B., and A. E. Wessman, eds. *The Personal Experience of Time*. New York: Plenum Press, 1977.

Hall, G. Stanley. *Senescence: The Last Half of Life*. New York: Appleton, 1923.

Hazan, H. *The Limbo People: A Study of the Constitution of the Time Universe Among the Aged.* London: Routledge and Kegan Paul, 1980.

Hultsch, David F., and Francine Deutsch. *Adult Development and Aging: A Life-Span Perspective.* New York: McGraw-Hill, 1981.

Jonas, Hans. *The Phenomenon of Life: Towards a Philosophical Biology.* New York: Dell, 1966.

Jung, Carl G. *The Collected Works of C. G. Jung.* Translated by R. F. C. Hall. Vol. 8, *The Structure and Dynamics of the Psyche.* Princeton, N.J.: Princeton University Press, 1978.

Kastenbaum, Robert. "Cognitive and Personal Futurity in Later Life." *Journal of Individual Psychology* 19 (1963): 216–22.

———. "On the Meaning of Time in Later Life." *Journal of Genetic Psychology* 109 (1966): 9–25.

Kaufman, I., and N. E. Zinberg, eds. *Normal Psychology of the Aging Process.* New York: International Universities Press, 1978.

Kegan, Robert. *The Evolving Self: Problem and Process in Human Development.* Cambridge: Harvard University Press, 1982.

Kimmel, Douglas C. *Adulthood and Aging: An Interdisciplinary Developmental View.* New York: Wiley, 1979.

Lerner, R. M., and N. A. Busch-Rossnagel, eds. *Individuals as Producers of Their Development: A Life-Span Perspective.* New York: Academic Press, 1981.

Piaget, Jean. *Adaptation and Intelligence.* Translated by S. Eames. Chicago: University of Chicago Press, 1980.

Revere, V., and S. Tobin. "Myth and Reality: The Older Person's Relationship to His Past." *International Journal of Aging and Human Development* 12 (1980–81): 15–26.

Riegel, Klaus F. "Toward a Dialectical Theory of Development." *Human Development* 18 (1975): 50–64.

Seidenberg, Robert, and Hortence S. Cochrane. *Mind and Destiny: A Social Approach to Psychoanalytic Theory.* Syracuse, N.Y.: Syracuse University Press, 1964.

Sill, J. "Disengagement Reconsidered: Awareness of Finitude." *Gerontologist* 20 (1980): 457–62.

Sulloway, Frank J. *Freud: Biologist of the Mind.* New York: Basic Books, 1979.

Weiss, Paul. *You, I, and the Others.* Carbondale, Ill.: Southern Illinois University Press, 1980.

Zaner, Richard M. *The Context of Self.* Athens, Ohio: Ohio University Press, 1981.

Zimbardo, P. G., G. Marshall, and C. Maslach. "Liberating Behavior from Time-Bound Control: Expanding the Present Through Hypnosis." *Journal of Applied Social Psychology* 1 (1971): 305–23.

CHAPTER 3

Achenbaum, W. Andrew. *Old Age in the New Land*. Baltimore: Johns Hopkins University Press, 1978.
Amoss, Pamela T., and Stevan Harrell, eds. *Other Ways of Growing Old*. Stanford, Calif.: Stanford University Press, 1981.
Bengston, V., M. Furlong, and R. Laufer. "Time, Aging, and the Continuity of Social Structure: Themes and Issues in Generational Analysis." *Journal of Social Issues* 30 (1974): 1–30.
Breasley, C. Paul. *Social Work, Ageing and Society*. London: Routledge and Kegan Paul, 1975.
Buss, A. R. "Generational Analysis: Description, Explanation, and Theory." *Journal of Social Issues* 30 (1974): 55–71.
Clark, Robert J., and Joseph J. Spengler. *The Economics of Individual and Population Aging*. Cambridge: Cambridge University Press, 1980.
Cumming, Elaine, and William E. Henry. *Growing Old: The Process of Disengagement*. New York: Basic Books, 1961.
Derenski, Arlene, and Sally B. Landsberg. *The Age Taboo: Older Women–Younger Men Relationships*. Boston: Little, Brown, 1981.
Fischer, David H. *Growing Old in America*. New York: Oxford University Press, 1977.
Fortaine, J. S., ed. *Sex and Age as Principles of Social Differentiation*. London: Academic Press, 1978.
Gilmore, A. J. J., A. Svanborg, and M. Marois, eds. *Aging: A Challenge to Science and Society*. Vol. 2, Part 1, "Medicine," and Part 2, "Social Sciences and Social Policy." Oxford: Oxford University Press, 1981.
Gore, Irene. *The Generation Jigsaw*. London: Allen and Unwin, 1976.
Gubrium, J. T., ed. *Time, Roles, and Self in Old Age*. New York: Human Sciences Press, 1976.
Hendricks, Jon. *Aging in Mass Society: Myths and Realities*. 2d ed. Cambridge, Mass.: Winthrop, 1981.
Hess, Beth B. *Aging and Old Age: An Introduction to Social Gerontology*. New York: Macmillan, 1980.
Johnson, Elizabeth S., and John B. Williamson. *Growing Old: The Social Problems of Aging*. New York: Holt, 1980.
Kalish, Richard. *Late Adulthood: Perspectives on Human Development*. 2d ed. Monterey, Calif.: Brooks Cole, 1982.
McPherson, Barry D. *Aging as a Social Process: An Introduction to Individual and Population Aging*. Toronto: Butterworths, 1983.
Melamed, Elissa. *Mirror, Mirror: The Terror of Not Being Young*. New York: Linden Press, 1983.
Monk, Abraham, ed. *The Age of Aging: A Reader in Social Gerontology*. Buffalo, N.Y.: Prometheus, 1979.

Myerhoff, Barbara G., and Andrei Simic. *Life's Career—Aging: Cultural Variations on Growing Old.* Beverly Hills, Calif.: Sage, 1978.

Quadagno, Jill S. *Aging in Early Industrial Society.* New York: Academic Press, 1982.

Spicker, Stuart F., Kathleen M. Woodward, and David D. Van Tassel, eds. *Aging and the Elderly: Humanistic Perspectives in Gerontology.* Atlantic Highlands, N.J.: Humanities Press, 1978.

Stearns, Peter N., ed. *Old Age in Preindustrial Society.* New York: Holmes and Meier, 1982.

CHAPTER 4

Barrow, Georgia, and Patricia Smith. *Aging, Ageism, and Society.* St. Paul, Minn.: West, 1979.

Bondeson, William B., et al., eds. *New Knowledge in the Biomedical Sciences.* Dordrecht, Netherlands: D. Reidel, 1982.

Butler, Robert N. *Why Survive? Being Old in America.* New York: Harper & Row, 1975.

Crystal, Stephen. *America's Old Age Crisis: Public Policy and the Two Worlds of Aging.* New York: Basic Books, 1982.

Estes, Carroll L. *The Aging Enterprise.* San Francisco: Jossey-Bass, 1979.

Kastenbaum, Robert, ed. *Old Age on the New Scene.* New York: Springer, 1981.

Levin, Jack, and William C. Levin. *Ageism, Prejudice, and Discrimination Against the Elderly.* Belmont, Calif.: Wadsworth, 1980.

Navarro, Vincente. *Medicine Under Capitalism.* New York: Prodist, 1976.

Olson, Laura K. *The Political Economy of Aging: The State, Private Power, and Social Welfare.* New York: Columbia University Press, 1982.

Winslow, Gerald R. *Triage and Justice.* Berkeley and Los Angeles: University of California Press, 1982.

CHAPTER 5

Alexander, George J., and Travis H. D. Lewin. *The Aged and the Need for Surrogate Management.* N. p., 1972.

Deford, Gill, et al. "Developments in the Law of the Elderly Poor." *Clearinghouse Review* 17 (1984): 958–65.

Eglit, Howard. "Old Age in the Constitution." *Chicago Kent Law Review* 57 (1981): 904–8.

Gelfant, Barbara B. "Reality Orientation: A Clinical Approach to Senility." *Medical Trial Technique Quarterly* 31 (1985): 369–81.

Horstman, Peter M. "Protective Services for the Elderly: The Limits of Parens Patriae." *Missouri Law Review* 40 (1975): 215–78.

James, Lavinia. "Damages in Age Discrimination Cases—The Need for a Closer Look." *University of Richmond Law Review* 17 (1983): 573–88.

Kittrie, Nicholas N. *The Right to Be Different: Deviance and Enforced Therapy.* Baltimore: Johns Hopkins University Press, 1971.

Mitchell, Annina M. "The Objects of Our Wisdom and Our Coercion: Involuntary Guardianship for Incompetents." *Southern California Law Review* 52 (1979): 1405–49.

Neugarten, Bernice L. "Age Distinctions and Their Sound Functions." *Chicago Kent Law Review* 57 (1981): 809–25.

Nolan, Bobbe S. "Functional Evaluation of the Elderly in Guardianship Proceedings." *Law, Medicine, and Health Care* 12 (1984): 210–18.

Quade, Vicki. "Elderly Victims: Assets Taken by Relatives." *ABA Journal* 71 (June 1985): 20–21.

Regan, John J. "Protective Services for the Elderly: Commitment, Guardianship, and Alternatives." *William and Mary Law Review* 13 (1972): 564–622.

Szasz, Thomas S. *Law, Liberty, and Psychiatry.* New York: Macmillan, 1965.

Virtue, Melodie A. "A New Interpretation of the BFOQ Exception Under ADEA: A Remedy for the Exception That Swallowed the Rule." *American University Law Review* 31 (1982): 391–430.

Whitman, Gloria, Roger Vaughan, and Arthur Boyd. "Creating Opportunity: Strategies for Increasing Economic Self-Sufficiency of Older Americans." *Public Administration Review* 44 (1984): 439–43.

CHAPTER 6

Barber, Bernard. *Informed Consent in Medical Therapy and Research.* New Brunswick, N.J.: Rutgers University Press, 1980.

Beauchamp, Tom L., and James F. Childress. *Principles of Biomedical Ethics.* 2d ed. Oxford: Oxford University Press, 1983.

Brody, Howard. *Ethical Decisions in Medicine.* 2d ed. Boston: Little, Brown, 1981.

Childress, James F. *Who Should Decide? Paternalism in Health Care.* New York: Oxford University Press, 1982.

Frolkis, Vladimir V. *Aging and Life-Prolonging Processes.* Translated by Nicholas Bobrov. New York: Springer, 1982.

Gordon, Theodore J., ed. *Life-Extending Technologies: A Technology Assessment.* New York: Pergamon, 1979.

Harron, Frank, John Burnside, and Tom Beauchamp. *Health and Human Values: A Guide to Making Your Own Decisions.* New Haven, Conn.: Yale University Press, 1983.

Kurtzman, Joel. *No More Dying: The Concept of Aging and the Extension of Human Life.* Los Angeles: J. P. Tarcher, 1976.

McMullin, Ernan, ed. *Death and Decision.* Boulder, Colo.: Westview Press, 1978.

Marshall, Victor W. *Last Chapters: A Sociology of Aging and Dying.* Monterey, Calif.: Brooks Cole, 1980.

Mooney, Gavin H. *The Valuation of Life.* London: Macmillan, 1977.

Pellegrino, Edmund D., and David C. Thomasma. *A Philosophical Basis of Medical Practice: Toward a Philosophy and Ethic of the Healing Professions.* New York: Oxford University Press, 1981.

Ramsey, Paul. *Ethics at the Edge of Life.* New Haven, Conn.: Yale University Press, 1978.

Rescher, Nicholas. *Risk: A Philosophical Introduction to the Theory of Risk Evaluation and Management.* Washington, D.C.: University Press of America, 1983.

Veatch, Robert M. *Death, Dying, and the Biological Revolution.* New Haven, Conn.: Yale University Press, 1976.

———, ed. *Life Span: Values and Life-Extending Technologies.* New York: Harper & Row, 1979.

Weir, Robert F., ed. *Ethical Issues in Death and Dying.* New York: Columbia University Press, 1977.

CHAPTER 7

Abbo, Fred E. *Steps to a Longer Life.* Mountain View, Calif.: World Publishers, 1979.

Bortz, Edward. *Creative Aging.* New York: Macmillan, 1963.

Cole, Thomas R. "The 'Enlightened' View of Aging: Victorian Morality in a New Key." *The Hastings Center Report* 13 (1983): 34–40.

Comfort, Alexander. *A Good Age.* New York: Crown, 1976.

Cowley, Malcolm. *The View from Eighty.* New York: Viking Press, 1980.

Neuhaus, Ruby, and Robert H. Neuhaus. *Successful Aging.* New York: Wiley, 1982.

Selby, Philip, and Mal Schechter. *Aging 2000: A Challenge for Society.* Cambridge: MIT Press, 1982.

Skinner, B. F., and M. E. Vaughan. *Enjoy Old Age: A Program of Self Management.* New York: Norton, 1983.

Thomae, Hans, and George L. Maddox. *New Perspectives on Old Age: A Message to Decision Makers.* New York: Springer, 1982.

Index

Abortion, 110, 171–72
Achenbaum, W. Andrew, 114n.3
ADEA (Age Discrimination in Employment Act), 165–66, 167
Age discrimination, 132, 147–54, 162, 165–77
Age grading, 131–33, 160
Ageism, 141–54, 176–77, 230
Aging: biological conception of, 8–27; clock, 35, 76; concept of, 2, 11, 24, 27, 53, 110; functional theory of, 44; as irreversible, 14–16, 38; language of, 23, 66; new attitude toward, 5–6, 48, 155–64, 216–31; normal, 12–13, 20, 106; paradigm of, 43–44; programmed, 35–36; psychological, 2, 53–57, 80–99, 137–38; rate of, 16–17; social, 121; sociological theory of, 2–3, 108–17, 138–39; and species, 28, 217; study of, 25–27; theories of, 13, 27–45; unit of, 33, 38, 46
Aldehydes, 32
Alexander, George J., 180n.21, 181n.26
Alienation, 113, 119
Almagor, Uri, 129nn.13, 15
Aluminum, 32
Alzheimer's disease, 142, 221
Amoss, Pamela T., 113n.2, 116n.5
Animal rights, 149
Annelids, 31
Anthropoids, 31
Antibodies, 37
Apartheid, 145
Aristophanes, 147
Aristotle, 22, 55, 139, 149
Arteriosclerosis, 44, 181

Artifacts, 56
Autoimmune system, 36–37

Bacon, Francis, 4
Baez, Joan, 6
Baruch, Bernard, 7
Baxter, P.T.W., 129n.15
Beatles, 121
Beauchamp, Tom, 214n.14
Beauty, 4, 56, 130
Beauvoir, Simone de, 1, 5, 65, 79, 114
Biesele, Megan, 113n.2
Birds, 31
Body, human, 9, 46, 137, 196; aging, 57–63; image of, 59–61
Boredom, 44, 45, 199, 229
Brier, Judith, 133n.17
Brim, Orville G., Jr., 124n.10
Bühler, Karl, 82
Burgess, Anthony, 145
Burnside, John, 214n.14
Butler, Robert N., 141–44, 160n.13

Callahan, Daniel, 197–99
Camus, Albert, 4
Cancer, 26, 45–49, 60, 194, 201
Capitalism, 116, 134–36, 152–56, 163
Catalytic agent, 19
Cells, 33–34, 35, 88–89; normal, 46–49
Childress, James F., 197n.2
Chromosomes, 27
Cicero, 4
Clark, Robert J., 126n.12
Cochrane, Hortence S., 94n.28
Coelenterates, 31
Cole, Thomas R., 231n.8

241